"…and if

Duffy should

appear…"

"…and if Duffy should appear …"

Stephen Francis

To order additional copies of this book, contact:
Xlibris Corporation
1-888-795-4274
www.Xlibris.com
Orders@Xlibris.com
37929

Contents

ACKNOWLEDGMENTS

Special thanks to my editor, Rick Kruse, for the time and effort spent on this book. Also, thanks to Billy McPhie for his historical help, Kevin Flaherty for his humor and friendship, Bill Reagan for loyalty and memories, and Frank Coughlin for his continued guidance and a critical mind. Thanks Mackie, Conor, Will and Fran.

I never could have completed this work without the help of my wife Jane. Thanks for your continued support and encouragement.

I would be remiss if I didn't acknowledge the work of the nuns, priests, teachers, and coaches at St. Mary's and Lorain Catholic. Your influence affected my life greatly, and, despite the stories reflected here, or perhaps because of them, you have my everlasting gratitude. Your dedication is amazing and we are all better for having served under you. Special thanks to Jim Lawhead and Tim Rose for the valued influence you had on my life.

More than anything, though, this book is dedicated to my late father, William T. Burke, who challenged me when I was fourteen years old to get a job at The Lorain Journal and become a writer.

This is for you, Dad, and thanks.

WE WILL REMEMBER

"We will remember . . . . all our lives. And even if we are occupied with important things, even if we attain honor or fall into misfortune—still let us remember how good it once was here, when we were all together, united by a good and kind feeling which made us, for the time . . . . perhaps better than we are. "You must know that there is nothing higher and stronger and more wholesome and good for life in the future than some good memory. People talk to you a great deal about your education, but some good, sacred memory . . . . is perhaps the best education. If a man carries many such memories with him into life, he is safe to the end of his days."

Fyodor Dostoyevsky
"The Brothers Karamazov"

". . . . and if Duffy should appear . . . ."

Give a cheer, give a cheer
For the boys who drink the beer
In the cellars of St. Mary's High.

They are brave, they are bold
For the whiskey that they hold
In the cellars of St. Mary's High.

For it's guzzle, guzzle, guzzle
As it dribbles down their muzzle
Shout out your orders loud and clear . . . .
"More beer!"

And if Duffy should appear
We'll say "Duffy have a beer!"
In the cellars of St. Mary's High.

(added years later)
And if Biggy should come in
We'll say, "Biggy have a gin!"
In the cellars of St. Mary's High.

(added a few years later)
And if Neumann should stop by
We'll say, "Neumann have a rye!"
In the cellars of St. Mary's High.

Lyricist unknown

1

St. Mary's Academy and
The Story of Monsignor James J. Duffy

I think the smell is the first thing that I remember about Monsignor Duffy.

A near-lethal combination of stale cigar smoke, brandy, beer, whisky and sacramental wine was enough to scare just about anyone, much less a timid fifth-grader who had just moved to a new school. I caught my first whiff of Father Duffy when he entered our classroom to hand out the report cards in March of 1962. He strode to the front of the room with a sort of regal waddle.

He called my name and I went to the front of the room and stood next to him as he sat behind the teacher's desk. He opened my report card and grunted and nodded and eventually pointed to the "C" in handwriting. He grunted again, a little louder than the first time, and I knew what he meant.

"Yes, Father," I mumbled. "I, I, I, promise I'll work harder to improve that grade."

He grunted again and handed me my report card. As I returned to my seat I heard sort of a strange guttural sound coming from deep within his throat. By the time I returned to my seat he was coughing up some of the most vile, disgusting goo any of us had ever seen. He reached into his pocket and pulled out a crusty, yellowed handkerchief and wiped the goo from his mouth. He looked at it for a second before he folded up the handkerchief and put it back into his pocket. If it was possible, he now smelled even worse. We were disgusted and frightened at the same time. I know I will never forget the first time I ever got close enough to smell Monsignor Duffy.

When Monsignor Duffy was the Celebrant at a Mass we were serving as altar boys, it was time to be on your best behavior! Sometimes we had to fake it and act like we really knew the Latin responses! I can tell you that sniffing the cork on the wine bottle in the sacristy made those Masses easier to live through.

The Right Reverend Monsignor James J. Duffy was actually a well-respected man in Lorain, Ohio. He was recognized as a religious and civic leader. He was a classic Irish priest, gruff in his ways and tough and mean in some dealings with people, but wise and wonderful and gentle when called for. I don't recall many people I know seeing the gentle side of Father Duffy, but they tell me that it did, indeed, exist.

St. Mary's Academy was first built in 1885, and graduated its first class in 1910. In the summer and fall of 1888 a two-story brick building was erected under the guidance of Father Joseph Eyler, Pastor. The 50 X 74 foot building, with foundations, cost $10,000. Only one teacher served the school in 1885, with a second teacher joining the school in 1886. At that time there were 127 students. With only two teachers! Nuns were part of the school from the very beginning, as the school was serviced by Sisters of the Sacred Heart of Mary, the Sisters of St. Mary's, and, finally, the Sisters Servants of the Immaculate Heart of Mary (IHM), who arrived in 1905. The first Principal was Sister Brigette, and fifteen other IHM nuns served as Principal, including Mother Mary Donald. The athletic department at St. Mary's was organized in 1924. The first sport sponsored by St. Mary's was basketball, with football being offered from the first season in 1928. In 1923, under the guidance of Father J. Johnston, the present building was built and dedicated and the previous school dismantled. The building was dedicated on February 20, 1924. The building combines Greek, Roman, and Gothic architecture, and occupies about half of the block between 7th and 8th Streets on Reid Avenue in downtown Lorain. In 1957 Monsignor Duffy expanded the building, adding a library, gym, cafeteria, band room, and home economics department. The addition was named Johnston Hall, and was dedicated by Monsignor Duffy and others on October 22, 1958.

2

My First Day At St. Mary's Academy

Every person with any connection to the Midwest or northern part of the United States has heard a version of this story, usually told by grandpas . . . . "Why, when I was your age I had to walk to school. Three miles. Uphill both ways. Through three feet of snow. With no boots on!" Well, that's a good place to start.

In December of 1962 my family moved from just outside of Elyria, Ohio to 2021 West Erie Avenue in Lorain. My mother still lives there. There is an absolutely fabulous view of Lake Erie from the front porch of my mother's house. My oldest brother, Bobby, was already a freshman at St. Mary's Academy. He had to ride a city bus with a couple of different transfers in order to get to St. Mary's Academy every day for the first semester. My father, who graduated from St. Mary's in 1937, wanted all of his kids to experience the wonder that was St. Mary's.

Jack, my second oldest brother, was in seventh grade, my older sister, Veronica, was in sixth grade, I was in fifth grade, and my younger sister, Julia, was four years old. The four oldest kids would enroll at St. Mary's, since it housed grades 1-12 in one three-story brick building in downtown Lorain. The church and the school basically take up one block in Lorain, from 7th Street to 8th Street on Reid Avenue. There was a play—ground at the dead end of 7th Street, but that was it as far as a 'campus' was concerned, unless you want to include the rectory where the priests lived and the convent where the nuns lived, which stood next to the church and next to the school, respectively.

So, we moved to Lorain during the Christmas break of 1962. On January 4, I was to enter the fifth grade at St. Mary's. We all got up that day, got dressed (shirt, tie, dress pants for the boys, uniform for my sister) and got ready to leave. We had one car then, and it wouldn't start. My father said a few strong words, went in the house, called St. Mary's, and told them that we would be late. We walked, as a family, the two miles to St. Mary's. When I have grandkids I will be able to honestly say, "Why, when I was Your age I walked to school, two miles, through a foot of snow, with boots on that didn't fit," and I will be telling the truth!

I've never really been a shy person, and I wasn't that day, either. I walked in about 45 minutes late, and Mrs. Placencia, our teacher, introduced me to the class. The very first thing anyone said to me was spoken by Gar Yunker, who asked me as I went to my seat, "Do you like football?" I stopped, looked at him, and said, "I love it!" I thought I might have found a friend right off the bat. I had the distinct opportunity to actually have played a year of football at St. John's School in south Lorain. Even though we had gone to St. Vincent de Paul School, my brothers had the chance to play football for St. John's which was the closest school that had a football team. Both of my brothers were good football players, especially as they went through high school.

I don't really remember much about fifth grade, except that my brother Jack always seemed to be getting in to trouble with the 7th grade teacher, Sister Mary Elna. I do remember that my fifth grade class was very large. There were 53 students in one classroom at St. Mary's Academy. I can't even imagine a classroom today with 53 students, but back then it was almost normal.

If I don't remember much about fifth grade, I do remember something very important that happened in sixth grade. Something happened that changed all of our lives and our entire country.

The big event that occurred during 6th grade happened on November 22, 1963, when President John F. Kennedy was killed. Because he was the first Catholic President, he was obviously an absolute hero to nuns, priests, and really all Catholics.

On that Friday afternoon, school stopped and a radio was turned on over the loudspeakers in the school. Lots and lots of people were crying, especially adults, but most of us 6th graders couldn't really fathom the importance of the event.

I remember going to early Mass the next Sunday, and, after our usual delicious brunch, my brothers and my father and I were over at Lakeview Park running pass patterns when a girl came running out onto her front porch and screamed, "Somebody just killed the guy who shot the President!" Millions of people saw that live, but we were over at the park playing football when it happened.

3

The Frightful Hurricane Elna

I was a well-behaved, hard-working student in grade school, so I really don't think I deserved what happened on the first day of school my 7th grade year. Sister Mary Elna (everyone called her "Hurricane Elna" because every once in awhile she absolutely lost it, going crazy! We figured she may have gotten bitten by a mad dog once and never took shots for it, and every once in awhile . . . . well, you'll see). She sort of reminded me of the second Nanny in the original movie "The Omen."

As I just mentioned, at this point in my life I was sort of a "goody-two-shoes," a kid who rarely did anything wrong. At least I rarely got caught doing anything wrong, which is a big difference, I suppose. Well, on the very first day of 7th grade Sister Mary Elna is calling the roll. She gets down to me and says, "Stephen Francis." I raised my hand and said with a smile, "That's me, Sister." She glared at me and asked, "Are you related to Bob and Jack Francis?" "Why, yes Sister," I answered, "Those are my brothers." She pointed a crooked finger at me and snarled, "I'll be watching you this year." What a way to start a school year! A teacher who already hated you because your older brothers were in trouble sometimes. In reality, only my brother Jack got into trouble in school. My oldest brother, Bob, was really a good student and never really did much wrong, but, I guess he had his days too.

During 7th grade I played CYO football on the St. Mary's 7th-8th grade team. We didn't have enough kids go out for the team to make two teams, so we all played on one team. There were two leagues, a "Lightweight" league and a "Heavyweight" league. The weight limits were 145 pounds for heavyweight and 115 pounds for lightweight. We had two guys on the team who weighed over 115 pounds, so we had to play in the heavyweight division. We got killed! We played seven games, and, in those seven games, we didn't score a single point. We got shut out all seven games. We got beat 66-0, 52-0, 44-0, etc.

I do need to jump ahead a bit and explain that the next year, my 8th grade year, we only had one kid go out for the team who weighed over 115 pounds, so they decided to have us play in the lightweight division. Mackie MacGregor, the one big kid, didn't get to play that year, but he still went on to a good high school and college career, so he got to play enough football.

Perhaps you can imagine what a team that had gotten crushed the year before playing heavyweight would do with most of the same players the next year playing lightweight. That's right, we crushed everybody. We had the three biggest kids in the league on our team . . . . me, Santo Atkinson, and Patsy Conrad. Patsy was the center, I was the quarterback, and Santo was the running back. We had a great coach, Mr. Dan Petticord, and we could have destroyed teams even worse than we did. Santo, who was a great high school player and earned a scholarship to the University of Cincinnati, is a member of the Lorain Sports Hall of Fame. He rarely got to carry the ball in the second half of games that year. We were so far ahead that the coach didn't want to run the score up that badly. We went from not scoring a point in 7th grade to not giving up a point in 8th grade. That's right, we shut out every team we played that year. The coach at least let us play defense in the second half of games.

Back to the Hurricane Elna incident . . . . shortly after the school year started, I was sitting in class and there was a bee in the room flying around. We get lots and lots of bees in Ohio in August and September. They love to fly into open pop cans—what a surprise you get when you go to take your next drink! Anyway, this bee was flying around. I reached up to swat it with my hand, as I had seen my brother do on numerous occasions. The girl sitting across the aisle from me, Jacqueline Plato, also reached up to swat it. As we swung our arms, they hit each other, making a clapping sound. Hurricane Elna turned around and glared at me. "Stephen Francis, what do you think you're doing?" she snarled.

I tried to explain, "Well, Sister, there was this bee flying around and I went to swing at it . . . ."

"I don't want to hear anything from you!"

"Then why'd you ask me to explain myself?" I responded. Oops! Big mistake talking back to her. It only took her a second, but she lost it. This was one of her classic explosions. She sort of screamed and grabbed a yardstick. Not one of those flimsy things they make now, but this was a triple-thick sucker, at least a half inch thick. She came down the aisle at me with the yardstick. It's important to note that we had 42 kids in our class in 7th grade, meaning that the desks were extremely close together. I don't know what got in to me, but I wasn't going to sit there and let this nun beat me with a yardstick, especially since I really hadn't done anything wrong. I got out of my desk, put my hands up to sort of defend myself, and started moving away from her, all the while trying to explain myself. She was having none of it. Remember, she was out of control. She started swinging this yardstick at me as I ran away from her. With the rows being very close together, she was hitting everyone BUT me. I stayed far enough away from her that I eventually tired her out and she simply screamed for me to go to the office, where I was going to have my very first encounter with Mother Mary Donald, or Biggy Rat, as everyone called her.

Mother Mary Donald (Biggy Rat) was the Principal of St. Mary's Academy. She was a big, nasty, mean-spirited, wicked woman. She was an imposing woman, about six-feet tall and about 190 pounds, with one eyebrow all the way across her face. She also had a bit of a moustache. In many ways she was scarier than Monsignor Duffy. Hell, I think he might have been afraid of her! I know that most of the teachers were afraid of her, as well as most of the students. Fear is, indeed, a motivating force, and she motivated the hell out of most of the people she met!

Fortunately for me, she wasn't in the office when I reported there, but her secretary, Mrs. Obridos, was. Mrs. Obridos was a kind and gentle woman who calmly told me to sit down and explain what happened. When I told her my side of the story she sort of rolled her eyes and shook her head—she knew exactly what kind of person Hurricane Elna was, and she knew exactly how irrational Hurricane Elna could be. I sat there for the rest of the morning, and then went to lunch. Mrs. Obridos told me she would handle it with Biggy Rat, and I never heard another word about the incident. Suffice it to say that Sister Mary Elna hated me even more from that day forward.

Another incident that happened in 7th grade involved singing in church. The entire school attended Mass every Friday morning. Every student sat with his/her class and was expected to listen and participate in the church service. It is important to note that I come from a family of very terrible singers. Terrible. Most of us are so bad that we can actually ruin the singing of someone next to us if we actually sing. Being the conscientious student that I was, I sang along with every song during the weekly Masses. One Friday I was singing along when I heard someone behind me hiss, "Sssssssshut up." I kept singing. I heard it again. "Sssssssut up." I turned around and it was Hurricane Elna. She looked me right in the eye and "Shut up. Don't sing." I stopped singing.

A few minutes later Biggy Rat was patrolling the center aisle of the church making sure that everyone was where they were supposed to be. She saw me not singing. She leaned in the aisle and asked, "Mr. Francis. Why aren't you singing?"

I turned around slightly and caught a look coming from Hurricane Elna that told me that if I said anything I would die. "I, I don't know Mother Mary Donald."

"I want you to sing every song at every Mass as loud as you can sing," she instructed.

I didn't turn around, but a sly smile crept across my face. "Yes, Sister, I will do that every Mass from now on."

From then on I made sure that I sat as close to Hurricane Elna as I could, and I sang my heart out. I was darn near screaming as I sang. Everybody else wondered why I would sing so loudly, but Hurricane Elna and I knew. My terrible singing absolutely drove her crazy.

4

Introducing Conor Flanary

Let's talk for a minute about Conor Flanary. Conor was, and still is, one of my best friends. We spent hours and hours and hours growing up, playing basketball, kicking the football around, just hanging out. One incident in 7th grade sort of reflects the kind of kid Conor Flanary was.

First, Conor's dad, Bill, was one of the greatest people I've ever met. Fun, jovial, always in a good mood and always ready with a snappy, funny line. We always knew we were welcome at Conor's house, which was really on the west edge of Lorain. One day after school in the spring of our 7th grade year I was over Conor's house. We were kicking the football around—we both were straight-ahead kickers, with Conor being much better than I. Heck, he ended up kicking for Kent State University and was on the same team as NFL Hall of Famer Jack Lambert. Anyway, on that afternoon we were kicking the ball and Conor's dad got home from work. I had never seen Mr. Flanary mad, but he was mad that day. He got out of the car and said, "Conor! I thought I told you to mow the lawn after school today."

"Oh, yeah, sorry dad," Conor explained. "I, I sorta forgot."

"You FORGOT! And what would happen if I FORGOT to go to work tomorrow?"

Conor thought for a second, and only a second, before answering, "I guess you'd have time to mow the lawn."

I got sent home right then and I imagine Conor in big trouble.

5

My Very First Tennis Tournament

My entire family played tennis. My father had played for years and years, and he got all of us started in the game. My oldest brother, Bob, might have been the best junior player in the family, as he traveled around to numerous tournaments in the northern Ohio area and played. He was left-handed and had lots of natural ability, even if he never really developed it. He played number one singles for St. Mary's Academy for three years. Jack, my next oldest brother, probably had the most natural ability, but he was never very serious about the game. He had some incredible, natural shots, shots that you really can't teach in the game. He was also fiercely competitive, and he just really, really hated to lose.

I was the youngest boy, but got the most out of my ability. I loved the game back then, and played every day during the summer. The very first tournament my parents let me enter was the Lorain City Tournament, which I entered when I was thirteen years old. The tournament was divided into age-groups, and I played in the 14 & Under bracket. I won my first two matches and was scheduled to play for the tournament championship at noon on a Sunday in August. My family returned from 9:00 o'clock Mass and ate our brunch, as always. I promptly went to the front porch and threw up everything I had just eaten.

My mother saw me throw up and told me that if I was sick I couldn't play in the tournament. "I'm not sick," I told her. "I'm just really nervous."

"Well, if you're that nervous you shouldn't be playing in a tennis tournament," was her response.

My oldest brother told her that he had been through these things before and he took me for a walk down to the lake to relax. It actually helped a little bit, and when I returned I was pretty confident. I had won my first two matches pretty easily, but now I had to play 14-year-old Wade Kozich, who had been playing tennis for a few years already. He was bigger than me and probably a better athlete at the time, but I had some of the "moxie" that my dad always played with. I was pretty natural as an athlete and a competitor, and even then I could analyze a game and figure out how to win.

I won the 1965 Lorain City 14 & Under Singles Championship, 6-3, 7-5. It was the first tournament I had entered and the first that I won. It was very exciting when I returned home.

6

8th Grade Horrors

Our first 8th grade teacher was Sister Mary Lucita. No one seems to remember what happened to her, but, by the middle of the year we were being taught by Mrs. Edna Gruelich. I am not making that name up. Her name was Edna Gruelich. Just picture, if you will, what an Edna Greulich would look like and you probably have her appearance pegged pretty well. She was an old lady who wore her glasses around her neck on a chain. She pretty much had no control over the class.

At the very beginning of the year, I think the first day of school, I noticed that my parents were out in the hallway. I didn't know why they were there, but I just figured that my brother Jack had gotten into trouble already, so I didn't think anything of it. Sister Lucita told three of my classmates and me to stay after school for a short meeting. My parents walked in to the meeting and I had no idea what was happening.

Biggy Rat spoke first: "Your children have demonstrated outstanding ability in the classroom and we are going to offer a special program this year. This year we are going to allow your children to skip their lunch period and recess and go up into the high school and take a class."

Whoa! I thought. That's not cool at all. When you're in 8th grade, let's face it, you're the King of the Playground. I was gonna do what? Give up my lunch period and recess to go up into the high school and take a class? No way in hell am I gonna do that!

"That sounds like a wonderful opportunity for Stephen," my father said. "What are the classes he can take during that time period?"

Again, whoa! Time out! What's going on here?

"His choices during that period," explained Biggy Rat, ". . . are Algebra I or Latin I. Which of those do you think he might like to take?"

"Stephen will take Latin I," my father said. "I took four years of Latin here at St. Mary's, you know."

So, for my entire 8th grade year three classmates and I left 8th grade at 11:05 and went to the cafeteria for lunch. We were the only people in the entire cafeteria, and we were given about eight minutes to eat our lunch. Once the bell rang at 11:15, we had to head upstairs to take a class in the high school. Mackie MacGregor, Conor Flanary, and all of my friends went to lunch and then out on the playground for a half hour while I was up in the high school taking Latin I from Sister Mary Rita "The Rabbit."

Just about all of the nuns, and most of the lay teachers, for that matter, had nicknames, and Sister Mary Rita was dubbed "Rita The Rabbit." She was a small woman with huge teeth that stuck out from her face, and, thus, the nickname. It should also be pointed out that there was another Sister Rita, Sister Helen Rita, better know as "Tubby Rita," also on the staff. So, you had Rabbit and Tubby, which was a helluva lot easier than saying Sister Mary Rita or Sister Helen Rita.

There I was, every day, up on the third floor of St. Mary's Academy, trying to learn something about Latin. Guess what? Most studies indicate that if a student really doesn't like a class then he/she probably won't learn much. Well, I absolutely hated Latin I. I hated everything about it. I hated the fact that Mackie MacGregor and Conor Flanary would be down below throwing things up at our classroom. I hated the fact that those guys and my other friends would actually yell up from down below, reminding me to pay attention to Rita The Rabbit. With my attitude you can imagine that I learned very little about Latin.

Once Mrs. Gruelich took over teaching for Sister Lucita, another terrible incident occurred. Since Mrs. Gruelich was not a religious person (priest or nun) she couldn't teach us Religion class, and every Catholic school has Religion class every day. Thus, we had to have a different teacher for religion. Oh no! Can you guess who came in to our room once a day for Religion class? That's right, Hurricane Elna. I thought I was completely finished with her for my career, and here she was, back in my nightmares.

One day I was sitting near the back of the room and I was trying to pass a note to a girl I liked. The girl was sitting three rows over, but that wasn't going to stop me. The classic way for a junior high kid to pass a note is to write it, fold it up very small, and then go "Pssst," to the student sitting next to him/her. Patsy Conrad was sitting next to me, Margaret Hernandez was next to him, and Linda Cole was next to her. The note was intended for Linda.

I wrote the note, folded it up tightly, and went "Pssst," to Patsy. He just reached out his hand and I put the note in his hand. He did the same to Margaret, and she did the same to Linda. Linda opened the note and read it, wrote an answer, and started the chain sending it back. I have since learned that some teachers have supersonic hearing, and Hurricane Elna was one of those. She kept hearing those "Pssst's" and she really wanted to catch whoever was doing it.

I got the note back, opened it, read it, and answered it. I folded it back up and tried to hand it back to Patsy. I did the usual "Psssst," and he reached out his hand, never even looking at me. I must have "Pssst" too loudly, because Hurricane Elna heard it and spun around just as I was about to put the note into Patsy's hand. Since he was not looking at me, he saw the nun spin around. I looked at his hand and went to put the note in it, but, instead of him taking the note, he took my whole hand. I was a bit startled for a second until I looked to the front of the room, where Hurricane Elna was staring back at us. Patsy was now sort of swinging my hand, much as a couple would do. I looked back at his hand and slowly turned my head back to Hurricane Elna and just gave my sweetest, biggest smile and kept swinging his hand. She continued to stare back at us. I swear to God that they never taught her at "nun school" what to do if she caught two 8th-grade boys holding hands in the back of the room.

No one else in the class knew why she had stopped in mid-sentence to stare at the back of the room, but Patsy and I did. You know what she eventually did? She totally ignored it. She turned around and went on teaching. She had no response to two 8th-grade boys holding hands in the back of the room.

As I've already mentioned, our 8th grade football team was awesome. We crushed everybody and won the championship. It was fun being one of the biggest kids in the league and winning every game, especially after the previous year when we got shut out and lost every game.

I also had an outstanding basketball season in 8th grade, as I led our team in scoring and actually scored 23 points in one CYO game. The season ended on a sort of bitter note, however. You see, St. Mary's always had nice banquets at the end of the sports' seasons, and our 8th grade basketball season was no exception. The coaches handed out awards that had been voted on by the players. Even though I was clearly the best basketball player in our class (this really became clear in high school), I was not awarded the Most Valuable Player Award. Since the players voted for the awards, it was sort of easy to influence or fix the election. That's exactly what happened. Mackie MacGregor threatened David Fedor that he would beat him up if he didn't vote for him for MVP. David Fedor voted for Mackie and he won the award by a vote of, like, 5-4. I really shouldn't complain, though, because in

7th grade I won the award that surely should have gone to Timmy McDivitt, a small 8th grader who played on the 7th grade team. I should explain that basketball was just like football in that there were two divisions, with the bigger kids playing in the "A" division and the others playing "B." Timmy McDivitt, who was really a fine player, played "B" Basketball as an 8th grader because he was small.

By the way, every once in awhile Mackie MacGregor reminds me who was the MVP our 8th grade year. He thinks it's really cute to rub it in. He also admits threatening David Fedor in order to win the award. Mackie actually gave me the trophy in 2001 when we were 49, which was 35 years too late. I think his conscience was bothering him so much over the years that he felt he had to make things right.

One other thing that happened our 8th grade year that affected all of us at St. Mary's Academy was the hiring of Mr. Bill Phillips as the new football coach. He brought a new attitude and spirit to the Fighting Irish. St. Mary's Academy had not been very good in football the previous few years, even when they had talent. Bill Phillips brought a new, energized approach to the program.

Bob, my oldest brother, was the captain of the 1965 St. Mary team, the first coached by Bill Phillips. That team started the season 2-2, and then reeled off victories in their last five games, which was the start of the 24 game winning streak. Coach Phillips wasn't a very big guy, but he was a bundle of energy, and he really was at his best when he was in front of the student body at pep rallies. He even brought a new song to St. Mary's, a song that lived throughout the last years of the school.

> *Oh St. Mary's, Oh St. Mary's with your home by the lake,*
> *How you make me quiver and you make me shake.*
> *Oh I love you with my heart and whatever it takes,*
> *'Cuz your Fighting Irish spirit is so done gone great!*
> *Da-datta-da-dat-da, beat . . . . (fill in the next team we were playing)*

We loved singing that song, and the whole school would really crank it up at pep rallies. It should be pointed out that as good a coach as Coach Bill Phillips was, he couldn't hold a candle to John Flowers, still the most intense individual I have ever met. Coach Flowers arrived at the beginning of my sophomore year, so you'll hear lots more about him later.

Since I've already introduced Conor Flanary, I need to tell another story about him. In the middle of our 8th grade year Conor came to school one day with a large bandage on his ear. We all wanted to know what the bandage was for, but he was rather reluctant to tell us. Finally, he said simply, "My brother tried to punch my ear." We didn't understand until he took off the bandage. We all thought he meant that his brother, who was a junior in high school at the time, had tried to hit him (punch) in the ear. Nope! When Conor took the bandage off we soon realized that his brother had tried to use a single-hole paper punch through the top part of Conor's ear. The colors were brilliant. There was red, pink, blueish-green, purple, and black around the quarter-inch whole. Actually, there was no hole, just the colors and the bruising. The paper punch was only a quarter of an inch, but the bruising and the colors were way more than an inch in diameter. It was one of the greatest bruises I've ever seen.

7

22 Hotdogs & A Fabulous (and Frightening!) Kiss

At the end of our 8th grade year we had a class picnic at one of the girl's houses. There were about 30 kids there and we played games, threw some water balloons, and ate. As the day wore on there had been too much food cooked, especially hot dogs. Conor Flanary made some comment about me finishing all of the extras, and I felt a bit of a challenge. Over the course of the previous five hours I had already eaten seven hotdogs, but there were plenty left. I ate the last fifteen, for a grand total of 22 hotdogs consumed in about six hours. It was a race, but I just kept eating them, bun and all, and Flanary kept counting them. Twenty-two hotdogs, all with mustard. They all almost came back up a short time later.

The mother of the girl who hosted the party was going to give a bunch of kids rides home. She had this huge old station wagon. Kids piled in the front seat and the middle seat, and four of us layed down on the platform way in the back of the station wagon. The platform sort of covered the third row of seats. Anyway, two of the first kids to be dropped off were two of the kids back in the back with me—and Kristine Kline. Now, you have to understand who Kristine Kline was—let's just say she was a bit more mature than all of the rest of the girls in our class. Heck, she had dated high school boys already, so she was obviously more, how shall I say, "wordly." Anyway, she and I were now alone in the back of this station wagon, lying next to each other. Pretty soon she was a little closer to me. Now she's sort of rubbing up against me. I had never even kissed a girl, and now she was awfully close. I was incredibly nervous. I could feel the 22 hotdogs coming back up. It was unbelievable. The back window of the station wagon was open, and I was really happy about that, since I was sure there was going to be an awful accident caused by my nerves. I never did throw up, but I came really close. It's easy to remember that story, because Kristine Kline was one helluva kisser. Those weren't little pecks on the cheek she was giving me! Her tongue was so far down my throat she might have been able to taste the mustard from the last hotdog! What a way to end 8th grade and head in to high school!

8

Some Great Traditions At
St. Mary's High School

High school in the 1960's was really scary. My oldest brother, Bob, had graduated in 1966, and my brother Jack was a junior and my sister Veronica a sophomore when I entered St. Mary's High School as a full-time freshman. I didn't really count going upstairs and taking one class as being a real high school student, even though I did have a tiny bit of an advantage over my classmates in that regard.

There are lots of things that are scary in high school. First, the upperclassmen. St. Mary's High School had all kinds of interesting traditions, most of which are rather secret and would never be allowed in this day and age. Perhaps even more frightening than the upperclassmen were the new students in our class. That takes some explaining. In each class at St. Mary's Academy grade school there are approximately 40 students. Each class at St. Mary's High School has exactly 80 students. Therefore, the other 40 kids in each class came from the other Catholic grade schools in Lorain and the surrounding area. Each class thus got an influx of 40 new kids. It was a strange situation, because you already had cliques and friendships, and then here come these other 40 kids in your class that you sort of have to include in things.

One of the best traditions at St. Mary's was the football program, which had been legendary over the years, even though we hadn't won too many games in the past few seasons. Being a Catholic school, St. Mary's didn't actually own any buses, but that didn't stop huge numbers of fans traveling to every away game. There were always two student fan buses to every football game. Tradition dictated that the freshmen had to ride with the seniors and the juniors rode with the sophomores.

Once on the bus, the seniors pretty much had free rein over the frosh students. They did things like put make-up on the guys, make everyone sing stupid songs, and even take freshmen to the back of the bus to make out. That's right, back in the 60's things like that happened on a regular basis. Since I had older brothers and a sister at St. Mary's, I knew just about everyone. There was one girl I really wanted to go to the back of the bus with. It was Debbie Summerhill, a girl who lived in Avon Lake but drove all the way to St. Mary's every day. Debbie's brother, Marc, was, arguably, the greatest athlete to ever attend our school. The underground story was always that he was paid to go to St. Mary's, or at least had his tuition waived. It would have made sense, since he was the best football player, the best basketball player, and the best baseball player in the school. He was 6-3 and weighed 190, the perfect size for an outstanding high school athlete. He could do anything, and he even looked awesome with his perfect body and perfect blond hair. Marc was a great quarterback and the best pitcher on the baseball team. He quit basketball his senior year, and didn't get to play in all of the football games because he was suspended at times. Unfortunately, Marc Summerhill didn't possess the greatest amount of discipline or common sense. He did earn a full athletic scholarship to Miami University, but he never finished, getting in to all sorts of trouble as his career went on.

Debbie Summerhill, however, was absolutely awesome. She was incredibly hot, which isn't always the same thing as incredibly good-looking. In her case, however, she was both. Even as a freshman she had an amazing body and strawberry-blond hair. I always thought her hair was red, but she always referred to it as strawberry-blond, which was fine with me. Even more than her looks, however, Debbie Summerhill was really nice. She was friendly and always had a cutesy-but-somehow-mysterious smile. I was certainly enamored and infatuated with Debbie Summerhill.

The first football game that year was a Sunday afternoon game at Fremont St. Joseph. My parents drove to the game, but I convinced them that I should pay the extra money and get to ride on the students' bus since I was now in high school. I had other reasons to ride the bus. I tried to get my sister Veronica and my brother Jack to arrange things with the seniors on the bus for me to go to the back of the bus with Debbie Summerhill. On the way to the game I finally got called to the back of the bus. My stomach began to feel like it had with Kristine Kline. The first person they called to the back was definitely NOT Debbie Summerhill. Anna Kleinhetz came to the back and I had to kiss her. Not so exciting. Then things got lots better.

Debbie Summerhill was called to the back of the bus. They had her sit on my lap first. She was sitting with her arms sort of hanging in front of her. When they finally said, "OK, it's time to kiss her," I leaned forward to really lay one on her. Debbie tried to get her arms around me, but as she did she had to bring them from the front of her body. It appeared that she brought her hands up to push me away, not hug me. The seniors all started yelling and screaming, "Whoa, she doesn't want this guy! She's pushing him away!"

Debbie's face, and mine, got very red. I didn't know what to think. Well, I was just as mistaken as the seniors were. Once she got her arms around me I thought I was in heaven. I stayed back there as long as the seniors allowed, as I was kissing Debbie Summerhill. It was awesome, one of the most memorable moments in high school. After high school there was another memorable moment with Debbie Summerhill, but that's for another book.

Meeting the new kids on the football team wasn't too tough, because you were out on the field together, in the locker room together, etc. The city of Lorain had numerous Catholic grade schools, some within a block or two of each other. Holy Trinity School, for example, isn't more than two blocks from St. Stanislaus, which was one of the bigger grade schools. St. Joseph's School was right down Reid Avenue from St. Mary's.

The two biggest grade schools were St. Anthony's on the east side and St. Peter's on the west side. I should also point out that there were many, many Catholic churches in Lorain, and each one represented a certain nationality, and, thus, culture. St. Mary's, for example, was the Irish church. St. Peter's was the Italian church, St. Stanislaus the Polish church, Holy Trinity the Hungarian church, Sacred Heart the Puerto Rican church, etc. Members of each church were extremely loyal to their nationality and church, and people from Holy Trinity would never even dream of attending St. Stan's. It just wasn't done. I have never been to a regular church service at any Catholic Church in Lorain except St. Mary's. Obviously, if you had to go to a wedding or a funeral you might have to go into one of the other churches, but otherwise, it just wasn't done. Traditions like that certainly didn't help when the Cleveland Diocese was eventually forced to close some churches and consolidate others. The age-old fierce loyalties to one's church were very difficult to overcome.

So, coming in from south Lorain were football players like Robbie Cavellini and Jimmy Sullivan who had played for St. John's. Coming from Holy Trinity was JD Szollzy. St. Anthony's sent us a quarterback named Will Fitzpatrick and a good lineman named Jeff Brent. St. Joseph's gave us Bert Knouwer. Even with this influx of players we still only had about 20 guys out for football in our freshman class. Of course, that meant that half of the boys in the class were playing football. We actually didn't play any freshman games. We were combined with the sophomores and we played a JV schedule, which meant we were going to get crushed most of the time.

We had a new coach that year, a first-year teacher named Joe McComb. Coach McComb ended up coaching us in both football and basketball, and he also took over the baseball program and eventually turned it into a powerhouse. Let's just say that in Coach McComb's first year he wasn't the sharpest knife in the drawer, if you know what I mean. He has always been a fun guy to be around, but he learned an awful lot about coaching kids from working with our class, and he became an excellent coach in every sport. He just wasn't ready for having a team by himself that first year.

We only played five games, and, as I said, they were all against local JV teams. The public schools in Lorain were huge, and they would field JV teams of 35 or 40 guys back then, and we basically got beat up. I think we won one game and tied another, so our record was 1-3-1. We were also cannon fodder in practice. Speaking of practice, St. Mary's had no practice field. As I've already mentioned, the property owned by the school was in downtown Lorain, and we were lucky to have a playground, much less a practice field. We had to change clothes after school and walk/jog to City Field, a distance of about eight blocks, to practice. On the way to practice we had to always be on the watch for upperclassmen, since hazing was not only acceptable back then, it was a tradition!

One day after school it was pouring rain. I mean it was a torrential downpour. The varsity decided to stay in the gym to practice. We asked Coach McComb if we were going to cancel practice, and he said, "No way. It's just a little rain. We're tough enough to go out and practice." So, we headed to City Field. When we got there Coach McComb wasn't there yet. Conor Flanary and I decided that if we were going to get totally soaked we might as well have some fun. The practice football field was actually the outfield of the baseball field at City Park, so Conor and I started playing in the mud. We got running starts dove into the mud to see how far we could slide on our bellies. We were having a great time when Coach McComb finally arrived. Conor and I were totally caked in mud from head to toe. We lined up, did a few calisthenics, then Coach McComb called us together and said something like, "I just wanted you guys to realize that you're tough enough to come out and play football in any weather. Now let's take it in." What? We got totally covered in mud and now let's take it in? You've got to be kidding me! That wasn't the last time Conor Flanary talked me into doing something crazy that would backfire.

The varsity football team in the fall of 1966 was very, very good. They ended up 10-0, extending the winning streak at St. Mary's to 15 games.

They won quite a few very close games, including an incredible game at Elyria Catholic in the finale.

Both Elyria Catholic (our absolutely hated arch-rival) and St. Mary's entered the game undefeated. My brother Jack had started at quarterback in a few of the games that year and did a great job leading the senior-dominated team. The reason Jack was starting, though, was because Marc Summerhill was suspended for breaking curfew or other training rules. My brother Jack was a heckuva player, but Marc Summerhill was an athlete way beyond most of the other guys, and thank heavens he was allowed to play against EC.

The 1966 game was played on a Saturday night at Ely Stadium in Elyria. Elyria Catholic had its own stadium, but when we played them there was always a huge crowd, so we always played at the huge public-school stadium. I was sitting in the stands sharing a blanket with Dawn Piaget, a cute, nice freshman girl from Amherst who had caught my eye when she arrived at St. Mary's two months earlier. I had taken Dawn to the Homecoming Dance that year, and we were the only two freshmen allowed to attend the dance. St. Mary's had a rule back then that didn't allow freshmen to attend any dances or upperclassmen social events until AFTER the Freshmen Dance, which was actually in the spring. However, the Freshmen Homecoming Attendant could go to the dance with an escort. That escort was me. (I've got to interject here that I actually escorted the Freshmen Homecoming Attendant to the Homecoming Dance three years in a row. I took Dawn Piaget when we were freshmen, Maggie Coughlin my sophomore year, and Sandra Buscilli my junior year. I thought it might be a little strange taking the frosh attendant when I was a senior, so . . . . more on that later.

Dawn was, as I have described Kristin Kline, more mature than most high school freshmen. She had dated older guys, etc. I didn't care, since I was sitting in the bleachers at Ely Stadium holding hands under the blanket with the Homecoming Attendant and one of the hottest new girls in the school.

Elyria Catholic kicked off and Marc Summerhill was one of our deep returners. I know it sounds crazy to have your quarterback return kickoffs, but that's the kind of athlete Marc Summerhill was. He moved forward to catch the kickoff and then started his sprint right up the middle. No one touched him as he sprinted 87 yards for a touchdown before most of the crowd had even sat down. The place was going crazy! I stood up, dropped the blanket, and hugged Dawn Piaget. After the hug she broke away an inch or two and pulled me close and kissed me. Not a great kiss, but damn, it was a kiss from Dawn Piaget. I knew I liked Marc Summerhill returning kickoffs!

We lined up for the PAT kick and faked the kick and threw a pass into the corner of the end zone, good for two points. We led the hated Panthers, 8-0. What happened the rest of the game is absolutely legendary. Elyria Catholic's defense was tremendous. We played the entire game and never got a first down. We never got a first down. Not one. The entire game. Our defense was pretty good, too, and we held EC to a single touchdown, and they missed the extra point. We won the game, 8-6. We had defeated our arch-rivals in a huge game without getting a single first down!

By the way, I snuck another kiss from Dawn Piaget as the clock wound down at the end of the game and everybody was standing and yelling. Another memorable night for Stephen Francis.

On the last day of football practice we had to all be very aware of the seniors, since, as I have already mentioned, hazing was not only allowed, it was encouraged and traditional. Right near the end of practice, Coach McComb had moved us close to the opening in the fence near the corner of City Field. All of a sudden we looked over and saw the seniors sprinting towards us. There were all kinds of nasty "traditions" that we had heard about, so we started running to the only way out, the hole in the fence near the corner. The hole opened up into a ditch. It had been raining for a few days before the final practice, so the ditch was full of water at least three feet deep. I was one of the first guys through the fence, along with Mackie MacGregor and Gar Yunker. I almost got knocked out of the opening by Coach McComb. Why was he running? I guess he feared the seniors as much as we did. We ended up going to Gar's house, which was only about two blocks away from the practice field. Coach McComb went with us. We were wet from the ditch, but we got away.

The guys who didn't get away got taped to the goalposts, heat balm put in their jockstraps, and other "traditions." I'm glad I got away.

9

Mr. Rafsky Tries To Teach Latin

Remember that I took Latin I as an 8th grader. That meant that I had to move on to Latin II as a freshman. Most of the freshmen guys, my buddies, were in Latin I 3rd period. We had a new Latin teacher that year, a young guy named Mr. Mike Rafsky. Mr. Rafsky had this nasally, sort of whiny voice. He wasn't a very big guy, and he was a first-year teacher. Guess what? He had absolutely no control over his classes. I was scheduled for Study Hall 3rd period, and I was the only freshman in the study hall. Every freshmen girl had Religion 3rd period. Religion classes were not co-ed back then, since "things" were discussed in religion class that, well, were, sort of, how-shall-I-say, sensitive? Yeah, right. That means that sometimes sex questions were asked, and, since we were Catholic high school kids and didn't do that stuff, we shouldn't be talking about it with girls!

The twenty or so freshmen guys in Latin I with Mr. Rafsky quickly realized that he had no control of the class. It became an absolute zoo in that room every day 3rd period. Robbie Cavellini decided that the class should watch TV during that period, so he got up and turned on "Andy of Mayberry" every day. Mr. Rafsky tried to turn the TV off, but Robbie kept getting up and turning it back on. I think one day someone got Mr. Rafsky's attention and JD Szollzy hoisted a desk chair out the window, where it crashed three floors below on the sidewalk on 7th Street. It was totally crazy in the room during that period. It was so bad that Biggy Rat would go every day to check on the class. Once everyone realized that she was going to be checking in on them every day, a new plan sprang into action. Someone would get Mr. Rafsky's attention and someone else would go over and lock the door from the inside. That meant that when Biggy Rat arrived to check on the class, the door was locked from the inside. You could see her hulking figure through the frosted glass as she reached into her nun's habit and got her keys. That gave everyone a chance to rush back to their seats and act like they were behaving. It's incredible how fast someone can settle down and act normal when being threatened by a huge nun!

Three weeks into school I was so totally bored in study hall 3rd period that I had to do something. Conor Flanary told me to just skip study hall and go into the Latin I class. I wasn't that bold, but what I did was just as good. I went to Biggy Rat's office and explained to her that I was really struggling in Latin II. I wondered if there was a Latin I class I might be able to sit in on during my study hall. I knew, of course, that there was indeed that Latin I class 3rd period. She thought it was a great idea that I would be willing to give up my study hall to learn more about Latin. Yeah right!

After filling out the paperwork and taking the transfer to the study hall teacher, I headed to Mr. Rafsky's room. I tried the door. It was locked, but it sounded like something crazy was going on inside. I knocked a couple of times, and then the room grew quiet. Mr. Rafsky opened the door and I stepped in, just as an eraser went flying past Mr. Rafsky's head. My buddies started throwing all sorts of things at me. Mr. Rafsky went to his desk to get a pen to sign the paperwork, and Gary James calmly walked past me and re-locked the door.

Every day during 3rd Period it was absolutely crazy in that room. There were guys in the back flipping coins in two different games, guys playing cards, just not very much Latin being learned. Probably the most memorable day was in December when Conor Flanary brought in a block of tobacco. This is chewing tobacco, but it's not loose leaves. It's compressed into a square. He suggested we all try to chew some of it during Latin class. We were stupid and crazy, so most guys took a bite of the chaw as it was passed around. There we were, chewing tobacco in class. That stuff is disgusting. Most of us were spitting the juice on the old wooden floor, just trying to act macho and not get sick. Gary James finally stood up and said, in his best mimic, whiny, nasally voice, "Rafsky, I gotta go to the john." He left, unlocking the classroom door.

Moments later, Biggy Rat arrived for her daily check-in, and she didn't have to unlock the door, since it was already unlocked. She walked right in. Most of us sort of saw her coming and reached up and took the wet, nasty chaw from our mouths, holding the dripping goo in our hands, which was disgusting enough. Conor Flanary, however, was turned toward the back of the room when she entered and he didn't see her coming. She walked in and walked right up to him. He turned around, looked up at her and, and, and . . . . gulp! He swallowed the whole chaw of tobacco. Unbelievable! How disgusting! She stood in the front of the room and yelled at us for awhile, and we sat behind Flanary and watched as his neck and then ears turned a sort of greenish color. He was sort of rocking back and forth and we were trying to stifle our laughs. Once Biggy Rat left the room, Conor immediately headed to the nearest restroom, but I don't think he made it. He threw up into his cupped hands. Again, disgusting! Later, he asked us if we wanted to smell his hands, which, being the idiots that we were, we did. Disgusting times three!

10

". . . . and all you little rats . . . ."

One day in January Biggy Rat was administering a standardized test to all of the freshmen girls. They were in one room during 3rd period for Religion class, so she thought that would be an excellent time to administer the test. Unfortunately, the test took longer than one period. As all of the freshmen boys arrived at the room for our Religion class, the door was locked. We knew the frosh girls were in there, but we didn't know that Biggy Rat was. Someone pounded on the door and JD Szollzy actually kicked the door. All of a sudden, Biggy Rat appeared from within the room. We sort of backed away from the door when she opened it.

"You boys just wait out there until the girls in here are finished. It should only take a few more minutes," she said in her typical, nasty tone.

OK, so you leave 40 freshmen boys in the hallway unsupervised. Recipe for disaster? All of the other doors in the hallway closed as classes began. JD Szollzy turned and faced all of us. Considering that he was the toughest kid in the class (either he or Robbie Cavellini), we were going to listen to him.

"Here's what we're going to do," he said. "I'm gonna count to three, and when I get to three we're all gonna yell, 'Rat sucks!' as loud as we can. Got it?" We had it.

"One, two, three,"

"RAT SUCKS," we screamed. The sound echoed down the hallway and several teachers stuck their heads out to see about the commotion. All of a sudden we saw the hulking figure of Biggy Rat on the other side of the door. Again we backed up as the door opened and she stepped out. She looked at us for just a second or two and said, honest to God, she said in a low, almost-gutteral voice, "And all you little rats suck too." She turned and went back into the room. It may be difficult to believe that a nun said that to us, but that is absolutely the truth. We were stunned. Shocked. I think, in a small way, we admired her for saying something like that. Of course, we also admired her a bit because she had a better moustache than any of us!

11

88 Kids In A Cloakroom

There was never much supervision in the cafeteria during the lunch period. At times the upperclassmen would meet freshmen at the door of the cafeteria and "borrow" some lunch money from them. Right next to the door of the cafeteria was the door to the Home Economics room. Sister Mary Aloysius was the Home Economics teacher. Everyone called her either "Shakes" or "Snakes." We called her "Shakes" because she was a very elderly nun who was afflicted with Parkinson's disease, and she shook all of the time. You would talk to her and her head would be bobbing around uncontrollably. Students used to talk to her and say all sorts of disgusting things within the conversation. They also frequently did the old, "Eat me" cough.

One thing that Sister Aloysius was responsible for was keeping the cloakroom door unlocked and open. There was a cloakroom, approximately 10 X 12, just outside the cafeteria, which meant it was only a few steps away from her room. The door of the cloakroom was supposed to stay open at all times—you never know what could happen if a boy and a girl went into that cloakroom. Hey, Catholic kids were not only filled with guilt in the 60's, we were also filled with curiosity and raging hormones!

One day, as we entered the cafeteria, some seniors stood at the doorway and told us that we had to be at the cloakroom at noon. I originally thought that the seniors were just going to "borrow" money from me, but, instead, they just told all of us to report to the cloakroom at noon.

At noon I left the cafeteria and stepped towards the cloakroom. There were all kinds of students, boys and girls, just standing there. The seniors began stuffing us into the cloakroom. Once the floor area was full, they began to lift students off the ground and sort of pass them by hand into the room. I got a great place in the room. There was a coat-rack and hat-rack around three sides of the cloakroom. I was laying on top of the hat-rack near the ceiling in the corner. They just kept stuffing people in that tiny room. Finally, they decided the room was full. Someone actually closed and latched the door, and someone else went to get Sister Aloysius. She hobbled over to the door, put her key ring in, and unlocked the door. She then turned the knob and opened the door. As she did this, the door exploded open, almost crushing her, but she backed up as 88 students tumbled out at her feet. It was awesome. She just looked at the students as they tumbled out and shook her head a little more.

By the way, as much as students gave Sister Aloysius a hard time, they also took care of her. I saw Sister Aloysius have a seizure one day, and to watch the senior guys take care of her with great care and concern really taught me something about the kids at St. Mary's. We might do all sorts of crazy things, but, deep down, we were good kids who learned a tremendous amount about honor and charity and character and tradition from our attending St. Mary's. There is hardly a person I know who is sorry he/she attended St. Mary's.

12

The Fights

Our freshman year was also a year of lots of fights. It just seemed like fighting was an acceptable after-school source of entertainment. Robbie Cavellini was in quite a few of the fights, including several with a great sophomore athlete named Fred Knillen. You have to understand that in a downtown school setting there are all kinds of places to have fights. There are alleys behind big buildings, empty buildings, etc. The best places for the fights were across the street from the school behind DeLuca's Bakery, and out the back door and down the alley to "the barn," which was really just an old garage.

One day there was a fight out on the playground. I don't even remember who fought, but I do remember Coach Phillips and Coach Englund running out of the school toward the fight. Everybody scattered and I remember hearing Coach Phillips yell to us as we ran away, "Wait, we just want to watch."

Two freshmen, Jimmy Sullivan and Jim DaNucci, had already fought twice. The general consensus was that each had won one of the fights. Something happened in lunch one day that caused them to swear at each other and get ready to square off again for the third time. They decided to fight after school Friday in the barn down the alley. Since my older brother Jack and older sister Veronica were students at St. Mary's, I knew just about every kid in the school. Being outgoing and willing to talk to people, I became the unofficial promoter for the fight. Robbie Cavellini actually took bets on the fight, which was going to be a big deal.

I told everyone in the school to meet in the gym right after school on Friday to head to the barn. When I got to the gym I have to say that I was very disappointed in the number of people who were there. There were about twenty students waiting to go to this fight. I thought that I had failed as the promoter. However, when we reached the barn there were already about thirty people in there, most of them smoking. The scene was incredible. The barn, as I have said, was really just a big double garage with very old bi-fold doors. There were no windows in the structure, so the only light coming in was from the sun streaming in through the open bi-fold doors. The barn had a dirt floor, and when you combined the dust from the floor with all of the cigarette smoke, you could barely see. Yet, the scene was awesome, just like something from a movie. The haze really added a great deal.

Sullivan and DaNucci took their shirts off and the fight started. Both of those guys were pretty mature for freshmen, but the upperclassmen still were much bigger and stronger, and they kept the fight in the center of the barn. If the two combatants got close to one side or the other, the upperclassmen just pushed them back to the center. There was lots of yelling and screaming. Not long into the fight Sullivan had DaNucci in a headlock and was pounding him. Greg Skettle, a junior football player, had placed a bet on DaNucci, and he was losing. Skettle rushed up behind Sullivan, and, with his hands clasped together, swung both arms and hit Sullivan right on the back of the neck. Sullivan was both surprised and hurt, and he crumpled to the floor. Just then we heard sirens from the end of the alley. "Cops!" someone screamed, and all hell broke loose.

The alley separated the church and the school, the rectory and the convent, and houses on 7th Street and 8th Street. We had to choose where to run. We could go back down the alley towards the cops (no one in his/her right mind would head in that direction!), south through yards towards 8th Street (a sharp, but low, white picket fence would have to be crossed), toward yards on 7th Street (running past one of the meanest, ugliest dogs in history—he was chained, and I do mean chained, to a clothesline, but the chain was pretty long), or head to the end of the alley and climb a six-foot high chain-link fence. I chose that option.

I've always wondered what would have happened if everyone would have just stepped into the alley, a public road. Could we have been arrested for standing in an alley? Of course the fun was the running from the cops.

I don't recall if Robbie Cavellini paid back the bets he had taken, but my guess is he didn't.

Another fight that occurred during my freshman year was between my brother Jack and Jerome Casselle. Jerome Casselle was a senior who was not really an athlete. He did, however, participate in martial arts classes. I think he actually entered some Karate and Judo tournaments. Basically, though, he was a smart kid who didn't really do much around the school. He worked in the office during 1st Period, and went around and picked up the absence sheets from the teachers. Every day he would go in to my brother's class to pick up the absence list and every day my brother and his friends, who were really jerks and ruffians, gave him a hard time. They called him "Judo Jerry" and made fun of him because he wasn't a tough-guy jock like my brother and his friends—remember Greg Skettle who jumped in to destroy the Sullivan-DaNucci fight—he was one of my brother's tough-guy friends.

So, one day Jerome Casselle came to pick up the absence list and my brother, as he did on a regular basis, said, "Hey Judo Jerry, how's it hangin'?" Jerome Casselle had heard enough. He looked at my brother and said, and this is how he talked, "You, I do not like. You, I am going to kill."

My brother looked at him and said, "What are you gonna do, fight me?" My brother laughed.

"Yes," Jerome said. "After lunch today. I am going to kill you."

On the way out of the building after lunch my brother let Judo Jerry walk out first. As he headed up the steps to get out the door, my brother jumped up, grabbed Judo Jerry by the back of the collar, and pulled him back down the steps, tripped him, and kicked him in the face twice. As Judo Jerry lay on the ground holding his face and sort of whimpering/screaming, my brother looked down at him and said, "Where's all that judo you know now?" Not really much of a fight, huh?

Robbie Cavellini was in quite a few fights, including one with Phil Feller, and two with Fred Knillen. Most of the time, guys were friends after the fights.

The closest I ever got to a fight came at freshman basketball practice. Our class just wasn't a very good basketball class, and our frosh team, coached by Mr. Jack McComb, went 1-7. Coach McComb brought down the house at the banquet when he made an absolutely tremendous remark. He said, "We were 1-7 this year, but that is a very deceiving record. We weren't nearly that good."

Anyway, we're at practice, and JD Szollzy did something wrong and Coach McComb told him to start running laps. We were doing a passing drill, and he cut right in front of the line as he was running his laps. I hit him right in the head with the ball. He got very mad. On his next lap I was in the back part of the line and he came over and tried to run me over. I saw it coming and set my feet and we had a big collision. Coach McComb saw it and started yelling at JD. JD said something back at Coach McComb and that just got the coach more upset. He eventually told JD to, ". . . take it in," meaning he just got kicked out of practice. The frosh dressed in the visitors' locker room, and we could see when somebody left the building. JD was waiting for me in the locker room. I knew it, but that didn't take away from how scared I was. He was going to kick the crap out of me. When I got in the locker room he came from around a set of lockers and attacked me. Since I was ready for it, I sorta grabbed his arms and tackled him, all the while screaming for someone to go get Coach McComb. Someone eventually got Coach McComb, and JD got into even more trouble, but not enough trouble, if you ask me.

Speaking of getting in trouble at basketball practice, one of the greatest incidents ever happened one day when we were scrimmaging against the JVs. Our class was bad in basketball, and the sophomore class was very good in basketball, so we were getting crushed in this scrimmage. The head varsity basketball coach, Mr. James Englund, was sitting up in the bleachers watching the scrimmage. Coach McComb took Cavellini out of the scrimmage and started yelling at him because he wasn't guarding his man. Cavellini yelled right back at the coach and told him he WAS guarding his man and it wasn't the guy Coach McComb thought it was.

Coach McComb finally said, "Awww be quiet and go sit down." Coach McComb then turned away. Cavellini promptly made an obscene gesture at the coach's back. Yeah, that's right, he flipped him off. Well, Mr. Englund saw that and came rushing down from the top of the bleachers to yell at Cavellini. He got there and started yelling at Cavellini, who stood up and faced the angry coach. Mr. Englund was waving his finger in Cavellini's face, and Cavellini sort of waved the hand away. The older man got really mad and took a swing at Cavellini, who ducked out of the way. Another swing followed, and now Cavellini was backing up blocking punches. It should be pointed out that Cavellini was a Golden Gloves boxer who could really fight, so he had been trained how to slip a punch.

Later, we heard that Coach Phillips heard about the incident and asked Coach Englund why he hadn't hit Cavellini. Supposedly, Coach Englund said, "I tried. I couldn't get to the son of a gun."

In the summer of 2005 Coach Englund was asked about this incident. Everyone present remembers the incident as I just reported it. Everyone, that is, except Coach Englund. Here is his version, with the statements from the summer of 2005. Remember, this incident occurred in December of 1966.

Coach Englund's version: *"That's not what happened at all. The only part that's right about your version is that I was sitting in the stands and saw Cavellini flip off McComb. I was sitting near the top of the bleachers eating an apple. I actually had a small knife which I was using to cut off pieces of the apple. I went down the bleachers as fast as I could to get at Cavellini. I did start yelling at him, but never took a swing at him. Hell, I had a knife in my hand. I'm not gonna swing at a freshman in high school with a knife in my hand. Not even back then. Cavellini did mouth off to me, but that's it. There were no punches thrown by anyone."*

In the fall of 2005 Robbie Cavellini told his version via phone from California, where he is a prominent lawyer: *Coach Englund was furious. He came racing down the bleachers and got in my face. He was definitely trying to hit me, but I was bobbing and weaving and he never touched me. The more I backed up and stayed away from the punches the madder he got. That ended my basketball career at St. Mary's, though. I got kicked off the team for that incident."*

As mentioned, I stand by my version of the story, which happens to be the same version Cavellini tells. I don't remember any knife, and I do remember punches being thrown—but none connecting, and that's just about the best part of the story.

Speaking of fights or fight-type things, I was the only male student at St. Mary's not in attendance for one of the most spectacular incidents.

The Home Economics classes, and all girls took Home Ec, hosted an annual "Fashion Show" each spring. All the girls who had made outfits during the school year got to show them off at a Fashion Show. I was very active in all of the aspects of the drama department, including designing and running the lights for the drama productions. Our stage at St. Mary's was at the end of the basketball court, and the "auditorium" was simply setting up chairs on the gym floor. One of the side baskets has a platform attached to it with a spotlight. I was asked by Sr. Mary Lambert if I could go to the Fashion Show and run the lights. That meant setting some lights before the show and then running the spotlight during the show. By the way, all the rest of the boys in the entire high school were going to sit in the cafeteria. That, in itself, is trouble.

While I was upstairs in the gym running the lights, there were about 150 high school boys sitting in the cafeteria with nothing to do. Unsupervised. That's right, unsupervised. In today's day and age you can never leave a single student unsupervised, and, back then, there were 150 high school boys unsupervised. My brother Jack's class, the juniors, were sort of "feeling their oats." They believed, and probably rightfully so, that their class was tougher than the senior class of 1967. That class had some really tough guys like Ralph MacGregor (Mackie's older brother) and Marc Summerhill and Big Bill Wilson, but Jack's class had some really crazy dudes. The toughest kid in the school had to be Matt Mears. He was about 6-4 240, and got in fights all over the city all the time. Lorain was a city of almost 90,000 people then, and Matt Mears was known by everyone. Mick Dunning was just about as tough and as crazy, and Morgan Place was as intense and scary as anyone. The point I'm making is that it would have been an interesting fight, had it actually come to that.

Since the Fashion Show took place right after lunch, there were still some milk bottles around in the cafeteria. Some of them still had milk in them. The juniors started a contest to see who could slide a milk bottle, keeping it upright, across a table to the very end of the table, without having it fall off. They were taking turns doing that when a senior walked over and said that he could get it closer. One thing led to another, and some milk was spilled and thrown. All of a sudden the juniors were sort of huddling up around a table. They turned and shouted, "Seniors Suck!" It didn't take long before the seniors responded with "Juniors Suck!" It got louder and louder—I could hear it up in the gym, above the soft music that was playing during the Fashion Show.

After going back and forth a few times with the "Seniors Suck," "Juniors Suck," etc., they decided to go ahead and escalate the proceedings into a communal shouting match that was going to lead to numerous fisticuffs. The juniors were standing up on one side of the middle aisle in the cafeteria, and the seniors were on the other side of the aisle. Someone actually overturned a cafeteria table and things were really ready to explode. Guys were inching closer and closer, when in raced Coach Englund and another male teacher. They couldn't believe what they were hearing and seeing. This was moments away from being a riot at a small Catholic school. And I was upstairs in the gym running the lights for a Fashion Show!

Speaking of Mick Dunning, he was an outstanding football player. He was a great running back and defensive back my freshman year, and unstoppable and first-team All-Ohio as a senior. He was in a few fights himself, one of which could hardly be called a fight.

Mick Dunning was a tough character who was pretty much a law unto himself. He did just about anything he wanted to do. One night during the summer between his sophomore and junior years he decided to sneak out of his parents' house to go visit a girlfriend of his. The Dunnings lived in Avon Lake, and his girlfriend lived in Westlake, just a few miles away. He tried to hitchhike over to see her, but it was too late in the evening, so he jogged over. His girlfriend's bedroom was on the back of the house and had a porch out from the bedroom. He climbed up the porch railing and was ready to enter the house when the girl's dad met him at the door on the second-story porch. Mick Dunning jumped down from the second story porch! He got up and started running.

A few blocks away he had started walking home when a police car pulled up next to him. The girl's dad had called the police. Westlake had a curfew even back in the 60's, and he was walking the streets of their fair city way past that curfew. They took him to the Westlake police station, where he called his dad. Mr. Dunning was a tough old Irishman who had moved

to northern Ohio from the Boston area. He was the Director of Quality
Control at the then-huge Ford Motor Company assembly plant in Lorain.
He was one tough guy. Mr. Dunning isn't very big, but he is wiry and one of
those people you just don't want to piss off. Well, when his son called him
at 3:00 in the morning and asked if he could come and pick him up in the
Westlake Police Office, old Mr. Dunning arrived in a very bad mood.

After talking to the police about the situation he calmly asked if there
was a room where he could talk to his son alone. Although a bit reluctant,
the police showed Mr. Dunning into a room and then brought in Mick.
Mr. Dunning asked the officer to please leave the room because he wanted
a few minutes alone with his son. Those few minutes became legendary
around Lorain. Mr. Dunning beat the shit out of Mick Dunning in those
few minutes. Today he probably would be charged with child molesting
or brutality, but, back in the 60's, the Westlake police not only knew it was
happening, they supplied the room! There are a lot of people in the United
States today who think we need to go back to discipline like that provided
by Mr. Dunning that night.

Mr. Dunning's version of the story is pretty close, but, when asked about
it during the summer of 2005, he added that Mick was actually with an old
friend of his from Boston. The friend was visiting Avon Lake for a week or
so. The friend was with Mick when he got "arrested" and taken to the police
station. Mr. Dunning explained that he not only beat up his son, but he
also hit the friend a few times and explained to the kid, "I know your dad
and he would want me to handle it this way." How times have changed!

13

Freshman English With Sr. Chantal

One of our most memorable teachers ever was Sister Mary Chantal. She was our freshman English teacher, and she was hard of hearing. Basically, she was damn near deaf. Now before you accuse me of making fun of people who are hearing impaired, understand that my mother Tillie has worn a hearing aid since I can remember. I grew up in a house with someone who is hearing impaired, so I am very sensitive to the situation. With that in mind, we just about tortured Sr. Chantal.

Once we found out that she was hearing impaired, we pretty much did anything we wanted with our voices. Sr. Chantal could read lips very well. She just couldn't hear very well. There were times (many times) when someone would keep his mouth closed and make some strange noise that everyone could hear. Sr. Chantal wore hearing aids in both ears, and she could hear (with the hearing aids) pretty well. However, if she just heard a sound, she couldn't tell where it was coming from if she couldn't see someone's lips moving. Every day we had bird sounds, train whistles, just about any sound you could make with your mouth. Everyone would laugh, answer, whatever, and Sr. Chantal could hear the sound somewhat, but could never tell where it was coming from. It was pretty crazy in that English classroom.

The meanest thing anyone ever did was the time Conor Flanary, as he often did, spread the word as we entered the classroom, to "play along" with him. We asked him what he was going to do, and he just said, "You'll see." We were reading aloud that day in class, and Sr. Chantal would just go up and down the rows and we would read a paragraph or two from our literature books. When it got to be Conor Flanary's turn he opened his mouth. Now remember, his mouth was moving, but there was complete silence. This, of course, was the exact opposite of what Sr. Chantal (and the rest of the class!) was used to. Everybody looked at Conor then looked up at Sr. Chantal, who reached up and spun the little wheel-type gear to turn up the sound on her hearing aids. As soon as she did this, Conor let loose and began to yell as loudly as he could while reading. The sound had to echo in her head, because she jerked her head up, her eyes got wide, and she started shaking. She couldn't reach up and turn down her hearing aids fast enough. That is one mean thing to do to a person!

The best thing about Sr. Chantal was the fact that she was easy-going. Our class and other classes picked on her lots of times and she just sort of rolled with the punches. Flanary was constantly thinking of things to do to bug the nuns, including Sr. Chantal. One day he stood at the door of the classroom and just said, "Snakin' the cough today, got it?" No one knew what he meant until he started the "cough snake." Everyone in the room took turns coughing. The turns were decided by going up and down the rows, from front to back and then back to front, thus the turn "snaking." It was absolutely hilarious. Even the girls participated. Of course their "coughs" were little baby-sounding-throat—clearing noises, but they all did it. Once in awhile, and usually when it got back to Flanary, he would let loose with a huge, loud, disgusting, phlegm-drawing cough that startled everyone and just made everyone lose control with laughter. Listening to the many kinds of coughs was, in itself, very funny. On one of the funniest days, Sr. Chantal actually joined in the coughing snake. She timed it right after the front person in row three coughed. We all laughed our asses off about that. We also respected her even more

Flanary might meet us at the door of Sr. Chantal's room and say something like "Crossin' the legs on the knock." After a month or so with Flanary in the class, we all kind of figured out what he meant. Conor would rap his knuckles on the desk and everyone would cross their legs, right over left, even if it was only at the ankles. On the next rap, we would go left over right, then right over left, etc. This might go on for fifteen minutes and it might go on for the whole period. Sometimes Conor would knock on his desk every fifteen seconds and sometimes he would knock only once every five minutes. You had to listen very carefully, which meant, of course, that you weren't paying any attention at all to Sr. Chantal. If you missed the knock and didn't cross your legs immediately, you were out of the game, sort of like musical chairs.

14

The Static Sound & The Freshmen Dance

Every spring St. Mary's Academy would hold a dance for ninth-graders only. This dance was very traditional, and it meant the freshmen were gaining maturity and were then able to attend other high school social functions. No one took a date to The Freshmen Dance, and every freshman was there. There were no upperclassmen and no students from other schools.

Some guys in our class had formed a band, and they were going to be the entertainment for the dance. Bert Knouwer and Patsy Conrad were two members of the band, which called itself "The Static Sound." I know that it's virtually impossible to believe this, but "The Static Sound" knew three songs. That's it. They knew three songs. They knew "Wipeout," "Louie, Louie," and "A Little Bit of Soul." That's it. They played the same three songs over and over and over, for about three hours. When they took their breaks there was a record player squeaking out a little music, but "The Static Sound" was the featured attraction. They eventually changed the name of the band from "The Static Sound" to "The Brig," which I thought was a terrible name compared to "The Static Sound."

Very few people, especially guys, danced back then. The girls basically went out on the floor and danced, but most of the guys were too shy or too macho to do that. By the end of the night, though, every student in the class was out of the floor dancing, jumping up and down, whatever, to the great sounds of "The Static Sound."

15

Getting A Ride To The Class Picnic

At the very end of school someone came up with the idea to have a class picnic. We decided we would travel about 30 miles down Route 58 to Findley State Park. The trouble was, no one in our class had a driver's license, and not enough parents were willing or able to take a day off work to drive us there.

We met at St. Mary's at about 8:00 in the morning, and half the class showed up to go to the class picnic. Unfortunately, there were only three adults to take kids. As many kids as possible climbed into those cars, leaving at least ten of us left standing on the corner of 7th Street and Reid Avenue. We looked around and said, "What are we gonna do?" No one seemed to have an answer. Just then an old guy with a beat-up brown station wagon was stopped at the light at Reid and 7th. His window was down and he was smoking a cigarette.

I thought, what the heck, and I yelled to him, "Hey Mister, wanna take a group of kids to Findley State Park for our class picnic? We need a ride." He looked over at me, put his blinker on, and turned left onto 7th Street, where he promptly turned around in a driveway and came back to where we were standing. He looked out the passenger window, which was also down, and asked me, "Where am I takin' you kids?"

I explained to him where Findley State Park was, and he agreed to drive us out there. Remember, this made for a full morning trip for him, when you count the distance, traffic, returning, etc. Anyway, we climbed in and he took off. Remember, this was a total stranger we had just gotten into the car with. In the spring of 1967, we never thought twice about it. We just wanted a ride to the class picnic. There had to be at least ten of us squashed into that old guy's station wagon.

Once we got to Findley State Park we got out of the car and began to look for the rest of our classmates. Even though Findley state Park is very large, we found our classmates pretty easily. Some of them had rented canoes for an hour or so. Findley State Park has a huge lake with numerous inlets and channels. Our driver, by the way, turned his car off and took a walk in the sand at one of the beach areas. Later, much later, I noticed him trying to start his car. It was dead. He had some other people in the parking lot trying to help him start the car, but it was really dead. So, he tried to help people and it killed his car.

Danny "The Rapper" Jackson was out in a canoe with the ever-popular Kristine Kline. "The Rapper" got his nickname from a popular song back then. It was not Rap music, but talked about a guy who hit on women all the time and considered himself pretty suave. That pretty much identified Danny Jackson. Everyone called him "The Rapper," especially the girls. Anyway, Will Fitzgerald and I rented a canoe and went out to try and find Danny Jackson and Kristin Kline. We thought we might be in for a little visual treat. Hey, we were freshmen, and it's OK to dream, right?

We paddled around the lake and actually found Jackson and Kline "parked" in one of the inlets. Sure enough, they were making out. We really didn't get to see much, but it was still sort of a thrill spying on someone making out. Isn't that against the law? In the spring of 1967 it was just fun. Later we got together and played some tackle football in knee-to-waist deep water. Some girls played, and it was once again a thrill to tackle a girl and throw her down in the water and land on her. Suffice to say that there were roaming hands as the tackles were made, and there certainly wasn't any "shrinkage" in the water that day.

Since the old guy's car had died and I didn't have a ride home, I searched out someone to hitchhike home with. It ended up being Will Fitzpatrick, and it took us awhile to get a ride, but we eventually made it home. I think it's somewhat important to point out that in the late 1960's and even well in to the 70's hitchhiking was a common form of transportation. During our freshmen year, for example, it wasn't unusual for me to stick my thumb out and hitch a ride to Avon Lake to go see Debbie Summerhill.

16

What's The Worst That Could Happen?

The last day of school my freshman year was a day that will, in stealing a line from FDR, ". . . . live in infamy." My brother Jack was expelled from St. Mary's Academy.

That's right, expelled.

Jack and three other guys, members of that crazy class of 1968, were expelled from school. Supposedly, they reached under a uniform skirt and grabbed some girl's butt. 1968 was way before the term "sexual harassment" was coined, but that's basically what it was. A girl in their class who had been pinched hundreds of times before, finally got tired of it and complained to Biggy Rat. She called the four guys in on the last day of school and kicked them out. That was a huge deal at my house. Huge! Remember that my father had graduated from St. Mary's in 1937, my brother had graduated the year before, in 1966, and my sisters and I were students there at the time. Biggy Rat just thought she had seen and heard enough about Jack Francis and his buddies and the trouble they had caused. She kicked him out.

Jack was grounded for the entire summer of 1967, the summer before his senior year. He never went anywhere the entire summer without my parents. Never. Anywhere. Every day they left a list of jobs for him to do around the house. He did the jobs and then sat on the front porch or the front steps and watched cars go by on West Erie Avenue. The other three guys who got expelled enrolled at Lorain Senior High School, but my parents refused to enroll Jack in a public school. They just refused to do that. They refused to accept the punishment Biggy Rat had handed down.

Something else happened in the summer of 1967. Bill Phillips, our football coach, left. He was in the midst of a 15-game winning streak, and his record at St. Mary's had been a sparkling 17-2. Coach Phillips was replaced by a young man with roots in Cleveland, John Flowers. Coach Flowers came to us after graduating from Xavier University in Cincinnati. He had been an assistant for a few years at Catholic high schools in Cinci, but St. Mary's was going to be the 26-year-old's first head coaching job. St. Mary's and Lorain would never be the same.

17

The Legendary John Flowers Arrives

My first 'John Flowers sighting' came at a meeting in Johnston Hall, the gym at St. Mary's. I had been a reporter for The Lorain Journal for two years already, and I found out when Coach Flowers was going to meet the St. Mary kids for the first time. I guess it's important to point out that my brother Jack was still expelled, and I was not going to be allowed to play football at St. Mary's unless my brother got to return. Like that was any reason to let him back in—his punk sophomore brother wouldn't play unless Jack Francis got to.

So, I got assigned an article for The Lorain Journal to cover this first-ever meeting of Coach John Flowers and The Fighting Irish, owners of a 15-game winning streak with plenty of talent returning.

Since I wasn't going out for football, I didn't sit with the players. They were seated in the bleachers in the gym, and I sat on the bottom row of the bleachers a section away from them. In strode Coach John Flowers. What an impressive figure! Tall, lean, tough-looking, with jet-black hair. He just looked intense and mean.

The meeting had just started when Morgan Place walked in the back door. Coach Flowers just stared at him and said, "When I say we meet at 7:00, that means you have to be here at ten til seven. Don't ever be late again." Morgan Place, one of the scariest, toughest kids I've ever met, just looked at Coach Flowers. There wasn't really a stare-down, but there were a few tense moments. A few minutes later Coach Flowers was talking about intensity (as he often did) and he mentioned how we were going to work quick and hard. The workouts were going to be in 30-second bursts of energy. He mentioned pushups and said that he wanted us to be able to do 25 pushups in 30 seconds. Mick Dunning, the team's best player, was sitting on the bottom row of the bleachers, leaning back to the second row. He mumbled something to one of the other guys about how he could probably do that right then. Coach Flowers quickly looked over at him and said, forcefully, "Hey. You got something to say? Sit up straight! I don't know who you think you are and I don't care. Sit up straight!"

Needless to say, that got everyone's attention.

Coach Flowers then looked over at me, sitting away from everyone else, 'Move over here." I got up and started walking towards the rest of the team and said, "I, I'm not coming out for football."

"Then why are you here?" he snarled.

"I'm here covering this meeting for the newspaper," I said in a rather meek voice.

"All right, then," he pointed at the bleachers. "Sit right there."

That was the first time, but not nearly the last time, Coach Flowers yelled at me.

Coach Flowers addressed the team in a very strict, straight-forward manner that night. I went home and my brother wanted to know who was there and what the new coach was like. I told him about the new coach yelling at Morgan Place and Mick Dunning, and my brother just expressed awe in the "guts" of the new guy.

I didn't go to any of the football pre-season workouts, but I did go to the scrimmages. The first scrimmage was at Loudonville. I was down on the field jotting down notes for an article for the newspaper. Since I wasn't dressed to play, Coach Flowers called me over and told me to hold this clipboard and write down the plays and how many yards were gained. I did as he had told me for awhile and then sort of drifted over towards the players, specifically the sophomores. I was standing there talking to Mackie MacGregor when Coach Flowers yelled over at me. He told me to get away from the players and to get closer to him so I could write the plays down. It was a very bright, glaring morning, and I was squinting in the sun. He thought I was smiling at him after he yelled at me. He yelled at me again and told me to wipe the smile off my face and get my butt over near the huddle. I wasn't even on the team and he was yelling at me. Once I did get on the team, it got much worse.

My parents refused to send my brother to the public school, and school actually started and my brother was still sitting on the front porch watching the cars go by. My mother finally got a chance to see Monsignor Duffy and she appealed to him one more time to let my brother back in St. Mary's. There are several stories as to how my brother actually got back into St. Mary's since the other three guys were already enrolled and attending the public school. The best version of what happened was told to me years later . . . . My mother supposedly reminded Father Duffy that before she got married to my father they had to take classes together, since my mother was not Catholic at that time. (My mother is 100% Macedonian and she was Greek Orthodox at the time. She eventually took classes and converted to Catholicism, much to the surprise of my father and the rest of us!) Anyway, before a Catholic could marry a non-Catholic, the couple had to meet with the priest and basically promise to raise the kids Catholic. My mother reminded Monsignor Duffy that she was required, as she had promised, to raise the kids Catholic, and now, Biggy Rat (my mother probably didn't call her that in front of Monsignor Duffy, but who knows!?) wouldn't let my mother raise the child in the Catholic school. That's a pretty strong and pretty persuasive and perceptive argument. My mother is, and always has been, very, very smart. Perhaps the thing that finally made a difference was when Coach Englund or someone else reminded Monsignor Duffy what a great quarterback my brother was. The old Monsignor really loved his football, so that may have been it. Whatever, three days after we started school my brother was re-admitted to St. Mary's Academy.

Perhaps I should mention that Biggy Rat, Sr. Mary Donald, was no longer the Principal of St. Mary's Academy, and that might also have had something to do with the Monsignor's decision to let my brother back in school.

Sister Mary Neumann was the new Principal of St. Mary's, and she called my brother in and, "read him the riot act," and threatened to kick him out once and for all if he even looked sideways at someone. The bottom line was this . . . . my brother was back in school and he and I could go out for football!

Let's go back to the very first day of school my sophomore year. It was, of course, the first day Coach John Flowers was a teacher at our school. He also had the title of Dean of Discipline. I had Coach Flowers in first period Biology class. The first day, as he was calling out the attendance, I was sitting right near the front of the room. He called the name of a new girl in the school, and she was sitting two seats behind me and one row over. As she said, "Here," I turned around and started talking to her, telling her that I would be happy to show her around the school so that she didn't get lost, etc.

As I was turned around talking to her a large hand grabbed me by the front of my white shirt and tie and pulled me right over the black laboratory table. Coach Flowers got on top of me and started slapping my face while yelling, "No one talks in my class unless they raise their hand!" I was so shocked (and scared!) of this wild man that I kept saying, "I'm sorry, I'm sorry, I'm sorry." He was on top of me like a bully gets on top of a weakling, and he was slapping my face. It was crazy! This guy was nuts.

Three days later, when my brother was re-admitted to St. Mary's I had to meet with Coach Flowers in the coaches' office to ask him if I could come out for football. He sort of hesitated, but Coach Englund told him that I was actually a good kid and would work hard for him. He never hesitated about accepting my brother on the team, but he also gave my brother a talk about responsibility and teamwork, etc. Basically, I think he threatened my brother within an inch of his life if my brother screwed up.

The St. Mary's Fighting Irish had already defeated Fremont St. Joseph's in the first game of the season when my brother and I joined the team. The second game was against Norwalk, and my brother didn't start, but he played the second half and was off and running. Fran Dunning, the junior brother of superstar Mick Dunning, played quarterback when my brother wasn't there, and he did a great job. It's sorta strange, because the next year Fran Dunning took his brother's spot at running back and didn't play quarterback.

Halfway through the season The Fighting Irish were 5-0, and they hadn't given up a touchdown yet. I had worked my way up to being on the kickoff coverage team, which I thought was pretty cool. Mick Dunning and Conor Flanary shared the kickoff duties, and some underclassmen got to play just to give the starters a breather. We were playing Our Lady of Lourdes High School in Cleveland on a Sunday afternoon. It's important to understand that most small Catholic high schools do not have their own stadiums. We had to share them with the public schools, which meant we played some games at unusual times. In this case, we played Our Lady of Lourdes on a Sunday afternoon at Cleveland Rhodes High School.

On the opening kickoff I was lined up as the third player from the left sideline. It's important to run down the field and "stay in your lane." If a single player gets out of his lane, a great big hole opens up for the kick returner to run through. Well, I sprinted down the field and a guy came to block me. I ran around him to avoid the block. Just as I ran around him to avoid the block, the ball carrier ran right into the area where I was supposed to be. There was a gaping hole there and he ran the ball back for a touchdown. Our safety on the kickoff team was Dan Shine, a senior defensive back who was very, very reliable. He fought off a blocker basically all the way down the field, and eventually turned to make the tackle at around the ten-yard line. The blocker actually fell into the back of Shine's legs, and a flag was thrown. Clipping was called, and Our Lady of Lourdes started the drive on our 25-yard line. They did go in to score, and it was the very first touchdown we had given up that season.

We returned home from the game that afternoon, went home and had dinner, and returned to St. Mary's for a film session from that afternoon's game. We were in the Johnston Hall cafeteria set to watch the film. There was a screen set up, and the projector was on a cafeteria table. Due to Coach Flowers' violent nature, the seniors all sat way near the front of the group, close to the screen. You see, on the old projectors there is a cord about three feet long that everyone called the clicker. It had one button on the top. Let the button go and the movie went forward. Push the button in and the movie rewinds. Coaches love to hold film sessions and run one play numerous times, watching each player one or more times on each play. I have no idea why I didn't sit someplace else, but I was sitting directly in front of Coach Flowers when the film started.

He ran the kickoff once, in silence. He ran it again, in silence. Then he screamed, "Who's 30?" (my number) I raised my hand. He smacked me on the back of the head. I jerked forward. He ran the play back 22 times, and hit me 22 times. He hit me in different ways: open hand, fist, with his ring sticking out (maybe the worst), on the neck, on the shoulders, on the head, etc. After 22 hits he screamed, "Francis, you will NEVER be on a kickoff team again as long as I'm the coach. You got that?"

I had it.

After the film session, my brother came to me and said, "I'll go get the car." He left the cafeteria. It was just the seniors and me. My brother just didn't want to be in the room when the other seniors beat me up. They didn't really beat me up, but they surrounded me and started in with, "You owe a lot to this team. Don't you ever let us down again!" They were all poking me with their fingers. They weren't really hitting me, they were just poking me. If I had been a bit braver, I would have pointed out to them that Lourdes didn't really score on the kickoff, because of the clipping penalty. They still had to drive 25 yards for the touchdown, and I wasn't on the field for any of those 25 yards. The seniors could have stopped them, and they didn't. I wasn't that brave, though. When they were yelling at me and poking me it didn't seem like a very good time to be a wise guy and mouth off to a bunch of pissed off seniors.

One of the meanest things I ever saw Coach Flowers do was during a practice session that year. My brother Jack was the starting quarterback. Fran Dunning, a junior who had started the season as a quarterback but hadn't played QB much at all since my brother returned, was probably the second team guy. The quarterback of the future was one of my best friends, Will Fitzpatrick. He would eventually set school records as a passer and play four years in college as a quarterback, but when he was a sophomore he was a very nervous, obviously-intimidated-by-John-Flowers sophomore.

We practiced at Lakeview Park in Lorain, which is about a mile and three-quarters from St. Mary's Academy in downtown Lorain. Fitzpatrick had trouble holding on to the ball, especially on the snap from center. He was used to taking snaps from Mackie MacGregor, the sophomore center. When he got on the practice field and had to take snaps from Richie Brillhart, the senior center, he just couldn't hang on to the ball. He kept fumbling the damn thing and Coach Flowers kept getting madder and madder. Fitzpatrick was a sophomore and really scared. When Coach Flowers yelled at him it only made matters worse. Finally, at practice one day Fitzpatrick fumbled a snap and Coach Flowers went nuts. He started yelling at him and screamed, "Fitzpatrick, if you fumble another snap you're walking back to school!"

Oops. Two plays later Fitzpatrick fumbled a snap from center and Coach Flowers absolutely HAD to be true to his word. "Get out of here," he yelled at Fitzpatrick. "Get the hell out of here." If Coach Flowers hadn't sent him back to school the coach might have lost some credibility, but, by sending him back to school he lost some respect from us. We thought that was just about the meanest thing we had ever seen.

Fitzpatrick had to walk back to school and wait for the rest of us to return. He was sitting on the steps waiting for us when we got back.

We completed the season 9-0, which included a big 34-6 win over our rivals from Elyria Catholic and a crushing victory over Midview in the final game of the year. Mick Dunning had an incredible year both rushing and scoring touchdowns. Tackle Joe Allen and Dunning were named first-team All-Ohio. My brother ended up completing 33-56 passes for 11 touchdowns. That is real efficiency. One out of every five passes he threw went for a touchdown. He was a great ball-handler and a great leader. Of course, his job was made a little easier by the fact that Mick Dunning was behind him, and any fake to Dunning meant a defense would collapse around him, allowing my brother to throw all those touchdown passes. It was an absolutely tremendous season. St. Mary's scored 279 points that year, and gave up 26. Four sophomores played enough minutes to letter that year: Robbie Cavellini in the secondary, Bert Knouwer on special teams, Mackie MacGregor as the punt snapper, and Jeff Brent who played some on the offensive and defensive lines.

The team ended up ranked 5th in Ohio, but I really believe that if the present playoff system had been in existence in 1967 that team would have won the state championship. It was a great, great high school football team. There were only 32 guys on the team, and 14 of them played college football. That's an incredible statistic considering the size of the school. We had a great running game, a great quarterback, great receivers, and the defense was almost unbelievable.

By the way, that 1967 St. Mary's team was inducted into the Lorain Sports' Hall of Fame in May 2005. Coach Flowers came back and was there for the induction, along with 21 of the players. It was a special night to remember that great of a team.

Back to Coach Flowers . . . . One of the most memorable situations of the year occurred during the winter. There is a large restroom on the bottom floor of St. Mary's. It has probably 15 urinals and ten stalls. The urinals are along the outside wall and the stalls are sort of an island in the middle of the room. I was in the restroom using the facilities when three junior guys, Tommy McDivitt, Terry Louis, and Paul Downing, walked in and lit up cigarettes. Obviously, they shouldn't have been smoking. They were standing near the corner of the urinals when in walked the new Dean of Discipline, Mr. John Flowers. None of the three guys smoking played football, so they really hadn't seen Coach Flowers at his best like I had. Even so, McDivitt and Downing flicked their cigarettes down into the urinals quickly and tried to flush them. Louis, whose father was the band director at our school, looked at Coach Flowers, took a puff off the cigarette, slowly flicked it into the urinal, and then turned and blew the smoke towards a suddenly-enraged Coach Flowers.

Coach Flowers displayed great control at that point. The veins were bulging on the sides of his neck, but he didn't kill anybody. He did grab Terry Louis and lift him up by the lapels of his sport coat and slammed him against the wall above the urinal. I was watching all this, and I couldn't believe that Louis had the guts to respond verbally. He said, "Take a break, Jake. Watch the threads, man." Oh my God! I thought he was dead. I'm not totally sure, but I think I saw smoke come out of Coach Flowers' ears. He dropped Louis. Coach Flowers' hands were shaking. It was an awesome sight to see someone control himself like that when he wanted to and certainly could have killed Terry Louis. All Coach Flowers said was, "Coaches' Office. Three o'clock. After school." What great patience and control! I also knew that I wanted to be near the Coaches' Office after school, because something exciting was sure to happen then.

I told some people what I had seen, and their eyes got very large when I told them that Terry Louis had actually said the Coach Flowers, "Take a break, Jake. Watch the threads, man."

I wasn't in the Coaches' Office that day, but I was just outside the door, listening. The three juniors went in, and Tommy McDivitt and Paul Downing got paddled and sent out of the room. Coach Englund was also in the room as sort of a witness to the paddlings. When it was Terry Louis' turn, he refused to bend over. Coach Flowers got in his face and was pointing his finger at Louis. Louis, who wasn't a very big kid but was a very big punk, reached out and knocked Coach Flowers' hand away from him, saying something like, "Get that hand out of my face." Coach Flowers grabbed him, and Terry Louis fought to get away. It was like a fight. There was grabbing, pushing, shoving, and, eventually, from what I understand, punches thrown. A high school kid in 1967 actually fought back against a teacher/coach/administrator in a Catholic school. I do remember hearing the set of steel lockers in the middle of the room go tumbling over. Have you ever heard steel lockers tumble over? It's a very loud sound. That just added to the entire atmosphere.

Eventually Terry Louis emerged from the Coaches' Office. He had a bloody nose and a welt/bump above his eye. For days he told the story of how he fought back against Coach Flowers. He was still a punk, but we all sort of respected him a little more for fighting back. Respect, of course, is one thing. We also thought he was pretty stupid for getting into a fight with Coach Flowers.

Terry Louis' dad, the school's band director, went to Monsignor Duffy to complain. Supposedly, when Coach Flowers went in to see Monsignor Duffy about the incident, Monsignor Duffy told him that paddling in school was OK, but fist fights with students weren't. As the Dean of Discipline he could paddle kids, but he couldn't beat them up. The funny part of that is Coach Flowers supposedly said, "OK, as the Dean of Discipline I will keep my hands off kids. How about as the football coach?" Monsignor Duffy looked at him and said, "That's completely different. Do what you have to do when you're coaching our football team." That consent would come back to haunt me in a big way in the next few years.

18

The Story of Big Bob Franks

Early in the football season we got a new kid in school. He was a sophomore, and he was immediately the biggest kid we had in our class. The kid was huge. He was about 6-3 and weighed about 185 or 190. He was a transfer from one of the small schools in the southern part of the county. We couldn't understand why such a big kid, an obvious athlete, would transfer to our school. Because he was a transfer he wasn't eligible to play varsity athletics. He probably wasn't eligible to play any athletics, but I guess our school figured that if he played in some JV games it wouldn't hurt anything.

I befriended Big Bob Franks basically right away, as soon as I realized that he was an athlete, particularly when I asked him if he played basketball. Remember, the Class of 1970 was NOT filled with many basketball players, and a good, big guy was a great addition.

Big Bob used to come over my house after school when the JV basketball team didn't practice until 4:30. Sometimes we would shoot baskets and sometimes we would just sit around for awhile and watch TV before heading back to practice. One day he was over after school and I called up some girl to talk to her. Bob wanted to listen to the conversation and asked if we had another phone. I pointed him in the direction of my oldest brother's "shop" area in the basement. My brother was pretty handy and he had added his own phone extension in his area in the basement.

There was no big deal about the phone call, but when I got home from practice hours later my brother was hot. He asked me if I had been in his shop. I told him no. He asked me if I had seen the $80 sitting on the desk. I couldn't believe what I was hearing. He told me that he had cashed his check from work and had put four $20 bills on the desk. I knew right where they were.

I went upstairs and called Bob. He wasn't home, but his mother was. I told her about the $80 and how, if Bob didn't bring it back that night we were going to call the police. I told her that I didn't know why he was attending St. Mary's, but stealing $80 certainly wasn't going to help his reputation.

Bob called me back about an hour later. At first he tried to lie about it and he denied taking the money. When I threatened to call the police he told me that he didn't have all the money, that he had already spent some of it. I told him to get it back from his mother, because if he didn't pay it back by the next day we were calling the police.

The next day at school Bob gave me the $80, but it wasn't in four $20 bills.

The JV basketball players would often go to a little restaurant just down the street from St. Mary's after school. We often didn't practice until 4:30, which meant we had over an hour after school to sit around or get into trouble. It's really funny, because the JV basketball team that year was made up mostly of juniors, with just a few sophomores (me, Will Fitzpatrick, JD Szollzy, Conor Flanary, and Big Bob Franks) thrown in for good measure. The juniors, guys like Paul Downey, Lenny Abecedo, and others, were like grown men to us. They used to go to Ral-Mar's Restaurant after school and have a cup of coffee and a cigarette before practice. I know that sounds crazy, but they really did. The rest of us would have a plate of home fries, toast, and water. That cost about 30 cents back in 1967.

So, one day we are sitting in Ral-Mar's having our after-school treat, when the door opened and in walked two men. Both had on long overcoats. We were sitting at the counter just eating our home fries when the two guys walked up to me. They stood right behind me, one on each shoulder.

"Are you Bob Franks?" They asked me.

I was actually pretty scared for a moment, and then said, "No. He is," and pointed to the guy sitting next to me.

The guys in the overcoats quickly shifted down one stool. "Are you Bob Franks," they asked Bob Franks.

"Yeah, why?"

"We need you to stand up and come with us, Mr. Franks." They then introduced themselves as Lorain City Police Detectives.

Whoa! This was our teammate they were arresting. Bob got up and walked out with the two guys we now knew were policemen. The rest of us just sat there with our mouths hanging open. We couldn't believe what we had just witnessed.

Later, we had a good laugh about the whole incident, as we had to explain to Coach McComb why Bob Franks was not at practice and might never be back to practice. I have not seen or heard from Bob Franks since that day. Mackie MacGregor says that he saw Franks a few years ago at a junior high volleyball or football game, and that he still lived in the area.

19

The Great B-B Gun War Games

This was absolutely crazy. My brother Jack's class liked to fight. They liked to fight with their fists or anything else handy. They got this great idea that it would be fun to play "war games." That meant going out into a woods, dividing up teams, and playing a version of capture the flag. Once they got this brilliant idea they decided they needed some flags, so they went to a local putt-putt golf course late at night, climbed the tower, and stole two large, brightly-colored flags.

I was roped into playing, of course, even though I didn't own a b-b gun. Since I didn't own a gun, I was always given the worst leftover gun. That was OK, though, because I couldn't shoot very well anyway.

The field of battle was a park area out in Sheffield Lake, The French Creek Reservoir Park. This place was beautiful. It had great woods—deep and rolling hills. It had the French Creek running through it. The French Creek was 30-40 feet wide at its widest, and only about 10 feet wide at its narrowest. There was even a big cliff overlooking the creek. It was and is a beautiful area, even though it has now been ruined somewhat by the addition of a little kids' baseball field and a soccer field. Back then it was wilderness and the perfect place for war games.

After we divided up teams we would separate for 20 or 30 minutes so that each team could go into the woods or wherever and hang the flag. The one rule we had was that the flag had to be hanging where we could see it.

I played twice in these idiot war games. One time I was "captured" and taken to the other team's camp. I was actually tied to a tree. I started yelling to my teammates to give them some direction to the opponent's camp. Guarding me was Danny "The Rapper" Jackson. He told me to shut up or he was going to shoot me. I kept yelling. He shot me. He shot me. The sonuvabitch shot me. He shot me right in the leg, just below the butt. He shot me. I couldn't believe it.

The only other time I played, I was looking over the edge of a large hill at the opponent's camp. I had once again found the flag. It's important to understand that there were all kinds of b-b guns out there. Some guys had a single-shot gun while others had a pump action rifle that needed a C02 cartridge. These were the most brutal, and my brother naturally had one of these. You had to pump the rifle before you shot it. A few pumps were plenty to get it to shoot, but some guys would pump it 20 times or more, which made the weapon damn-near dangerous.

So, there I was, peering over the edge of the hill looking down at the camp. I never heard or saw it coming, but I was hit with a b-b about ¼ inch below my left eye. I was incredibly lucky. It could have easily put my eye out. Whoever shot that rifle had the C02 cranked up big-time. After I got hit just below the eye I quit the game and haven't played since.

During one game one of our big junior tackles, Stosh Kurek, actually fell off one of the cliffs. He dropped about 40 feet, and he was lucky to land just on the edge of the water, in rather soft sand. He jammed his back a bit, but, otherwise, he just laughed it off. Stosh was one big, strong character you just had to love.

The biggest and best war game ever was held the third Friday in October. There was no school scheduled that day because it was the Northeast Ohio Teachers' Association Day. That meant that teachers from all over northeast Ohio got together for meetings, workshops, etc. It's basically a day off for the students. Well, a day off for the kids at St. Mary's meant nothing but more time to get in trouble.

We didn't have a football game that night because we were playing Cleveland St. Stanislaus on Saturday evening at home. The juniors and the seniors had planned this huge war game for early that day until about 2:30, when we would have to call it off and head to practice. The juniors actually spent four days before the war games scouting out just the right place to make a camp. They decided to establish their base on the only island in the French Creek, a land mass about 25 yards wide and about 60-70 yards long. They went out the two previous weekends to begin moving around some trees, build a bridge to the island, etc. They were really going to be organized, and their entire strategy was going to be, "Let the seniors find us." The juniors were not going to search out the senior camp. They were going to just sit on their island and wait. And smoke. And drink beer.

The seniors arrived that day ready to rumble. Some of the crazier guys in my brother's class had actually taken nails and taped them around cherry bombs (explosive fireworks). They were going to light the cherry bombs, throw them, and watch for shrapnel flying.

The juniors had made great plans for the island and had taken just about everything into account except one thing: the weather. It had rained for three straight days leading up to the war games, and the French Creek was swollen and swift. As the juniors arrived they used their bridge to get across. At least one guy did. After he got across, while the other 25 guys stood and watched, the bridge broke loose and floated away down the French Creek. Most of them did wade across the four-to-five-feet-deep water onto their island.

Once the seniors found where the juniors were encamped, they got together to plan the invasion strategy. According to my brother, after a little bickering they decided, "What the hell? We want to win. Let's just attack from all sides and go right across the French Creek. We know we're going to get wet and we know we're going to get shot, so let's just protect ourselves." That was it. They waded across from all sides and tried to keep their arms and b-b rifles in front of their faces. The juniors, probably tired of sitting there and somewhat drunk, only offered token resistance, and the battle was quickly won.

Many of the "soldiers" had to go to football practice after that, and someone told Coach Flowers about the battle. He really lit into the juniors and seniors about responsibility and taking care of themselves and their teammates. For once I wasn't the focus of his anger.

20

Crazy Times With JV Basketball

The 1967-68 Junior Varsity Basketball team was comprised of almost all juniors and just a few sophomores. I have already explained that the class of 1970 was thought of as a better football class than basketball. Basically, it was just Will Fitzgerald and me playing basketball from our class. The juniors, guys like Fran Dunning, Paul Downey, Stosh Kurek, Mark Campole, and others made up the rest of the team. Obviously, if you have a JV team comprised mostly of juniors and you are playing other JV teams comprised mostly of sophomores, the more veteran team is going to win most of its games. And we did.

The coach of that team was Mr. Jack McComb, the same guy who had coached us to that fine 1-7 season the previous year. A few things stand out from that season. First, the after school time spent at Ral-Mar's that I have already described. The other two incidents both happened during Christmas Break.

One day during Christmas break we were scheduled to play Cleveland St. John Cantius, a team that was always horrible in basketball. We had an outstanding JV team, so what we did during the day of the game was going to be pretty irrelevant to the outcome of the game. We played hockey for about six hours. That's right. The day was one of those perfect winter days. It was about 25 degrees, crisp, cold, sunny, breezy. The hockey rink at Lakeview Park had been frozen for a week or so, and it had a great layer of ice. Since it was Christmas Break and we didn't have school, we decided to meet at 9:00 to play hockey. It was one of those pick-up games, one where whoever showed up would get to play. We had twelve guys show up to play, about eight of them from the JV basketball team. We divided up teams and started to play. None of us had skated yet that winter, so we all had to get the kinks out, so to speak.

We played right through lunch-time and played until around 3:00. If anyone was tired while we were playing, he didn't mention it. We were having such a good time with great and fair teams, that we lost track of how long we played. We were supposed to be at the school by 5:30 to get ready to play a basketball game. Most of us went home, took a nap, and had something to eat. The amount of time between the last hockey game and when we had to be ready to play basketball was just long enough to remind us how stupid and how sore we were all going to be.

I walked in the locker room around 5:20, and Fran Dunning and Mark Campole were laying on the benches in the locker room. Unless you have skated and played hockey, you can't appreciate how sore our legs were after playing for six hours the first time out that winter. Our hands were sore, our legs were sore, our necks were sore, and everyone's face was bright red. It looked like sunburn, but it was actually windburn. Some of the sorest guys were the starters on the JV team, and we led a horrible St. John's team by two at halftime. Coach McComb was really steamed at halftime. He had never seen us play this poorly. He couldn't understand why we couldn't guard anybody, couldn't handle the ball, couldn't even hit the rim with our shots, and certainly couldn't jump to rebound. He yelled at us and told the starters that he was going to play the second-teamers (most of whom had NOT played hockey for six hours that day!).

The team we were playing was so bad that our second team guys killed them in the second half and we didn't even have to get off the bench.

The other incident occurred the day after Christmas. We got to the gym for a morning practice two hours before the varsity was supposed to come in. We started shooting layups and everyone was talking about what they had gotten for Christmas. It was an innocent conversation, but Coach McComb obviously thought we should be concentrating more on basketball. He just lost it. He blew the whistle, called us all together, and started yelling at us. He eventually said, "If you want to talk about what you got for Christmas, go ahead. I'll be in the Coaches' Office. Come and get me when you want to get serious about practice." He walked away and went into the Coaches' Office, slamming the door.

We all looked at each other, sort of shrugged our shoulders, and went over and sat down against the bleachers. We sat there and talked for about twenty minutes. Mostly, we giggled about Coach McComb's action. We actually discussed getting dressed and leaving completely, but eventually Fran Dunning, who was our captain and the first one to suggest we leave, went in and got Coach McComb and we continued practice.

The varsity team that year was pretty good. They were led by one of the best players to ever play at St. Mary's. Liam Downey was an awesome scorer. I won't say he was an awesome shooter, because he only shot about 38% from the field, but he could really score. If you know anything about basketball you will know that there is a difference between a shooter and a scorer. Liam was a scorer. He obliterated the school single game scoring record that year when he rang up 48 points versus Parma Byzantine. He averaged about 26 points a game, and it's important to remember that he scored those points before the establishment of the three-point line. Liam had great range on his shot, which simply meant that he would shoot the ball anytime he came over half-court. Of course, half-court at some of those tiny gyms wasn't too far away from the basket. He could get a shot just about anytime he wanted to, and he never saw a shot he didn't like.

Everything wasn't all that pleasant on the varsity team that year. My brother Jack and Mick Dunning were two guys on the team who never got to play. They weren't real happy about that. They decided that they wouldn't dress in the regular locker room, so they established their own dressing area in the equipment room. If any of the starters tried to come in their area, they pretty much threw them out. That included Liam Downey, who was their close friend at all times except during basketball season. When Jack and Mick Dunning would get into games, which was always in the fourth quarter of blowouts, they would play this incredibly physical brand of basketball, hip-checking guys into the stage at one end of the floor, or running guys into the walls which were much-too-close to the sidelines. It was almost scary watching those guys play. There was always a chance someone was going to be hurt. Maybe that's why Coach Englund hardly ever put them in.

One of the highlights of my entire athletic career came at the end of that sophomore season. After the regular season ended, the varsity squad got to play in the sectional tournament. Three JVs were "moved up" to join the varsity for the tournament run. I was the only sophomore asked to move up. I wore a warm-up that didn't match the other guys', but it was still a thrill to go out on the floor for warm-ups my sophomore year.

21

St. Mary's versus Admiral King Tennis (Englund versus Hicks)

Lorain St. Mary's had a very limited number of sports. It offered football, basketball, baseball, tennis, and golf. Girls' athletics hadn't started yet, so "gym-time" was lots easier to get. I've already talked about football and basketball my sophomore year, and in the spring we played tennis.

Lorain St. Mary's had a pretty fine tradition in tennis. The tradition went way back into the '30s, I think, and continued through the 60's and even until the school closed in 1969. My oldest brother Bob was a very fine player for St. Mary's in the early 60's. He graduated in 1966, after playing #1 singles all four years. My brother Jack, who was never a serious player, but an outstanding natural athlete and tennis player, played #1 singles for two years when Bob graduated. When Jack was a senior he played #1 singles, Jim Thiesman played #2, I played #3, and Fran Dunning and Joe Wendell played #4 and #5. Back then a team match consisted of five singles' matches and two doubles' matches. Thus there was a total of seven points, and whichever team won at least four of those points won the team match. By the way, players could play both singles and doubles, which meant that a team only needed five players to play a full match.

The state of Ohio was just on the verge of changing the match format to three singles and two doubles that year. The major difference between five singles and two doubles and three singles and two doubles was the fact that in three singles and two doubles each player could only play singles OR doubles. That meant you needed seven players to play a match instead of the traditional five players. Well, at St. Mary's we had five really good players. We didn't have seven.

We went to Central Park to play Lorain Admiral King, one of the very large public high schools in Lorain. Coach Englund was still coaching our team, while a guy named Frank Hicks was coaching Admiral King. Frank Hicks is a legendary tennis coach. His teams won over 600 high school matches in Ohio, but he was really still quite early in his career in the spring of 1968.

We arrived at Central Park with our five players, expecting to play five singles and two doubles, as we had in every match we had ever played. Coach Hicks asked Coach Englund as we walked up, "Where are the rest of your players?"

Coach Englund responded, "We have our five."

Coach Hicks said, "We're playing three and two today, so you need seven guys."

"We've never played three and two. We've always played five and two."

As he opened a can of balls Coach Hicks responded, "Well today we're playing three and two, so you need two more guys."

Coach Englund was absolutely right. We had never played three and two. You see, with my brother playing #1 singles and #1 doubles, and with me playing #3 singles and #2 doubles, we had a chance to win just about every match. I don't want to make it sound wrong—Jim Thiesman was not a very strong #2 player, but he was a pretty good doubles' player when he played with my brother and the other guys on the team, Fran Dunning and Joe Wendell, were excellent players. It wasn't the Jack and Steve Francis show. We were very deep and very good. We didn't, however, have two other players nearly as strong.

The five high school kids stood there and watched these two adults argue about the format of a high school tennis match. Both of them are fiery guys, and neither would back down. Coach Englund eventually sent us to the car so we wouldn't have to witness any more bickering. He eventually came to the car, which was a big, old station wagon, got in, and explained what was happening. He finally asked us whether we should go try to round up two other players and come back and play the match.

My brother Jack, the captain, was the only one to speak. "Screw Admiral King. Let's go home." We never played them, and it was years before we re-established athletic relations with Admiral King.

It would be unfair for me to not explain that Coaches Englund and Hicks are two of the most influential people in my life. I learned all sorts of things from both of them. Coach Englund remains a very close friend and a mentor. He was one of the greatest coaches and people I have ever been blessed to know. Coach Hicks influenced my coaching life more than anyone, and he was truly a mentor to me in coaching tennis throughout my career. Despite the fact that they don't really like each other too much, both are in the Lorain Sports Hall of Fame, and deservedly so.

One other incident happened during that sophomore tennis season. Early in April it rained for a few days straight, and Coach Englund wanted his tennis team to stay sharp physically, so he would have us hit a few balls against the wall in the gym and then he would get the basketballs out to play. That was our conditioning: playing basketball. I loved basketball, and I was pretty good, too. My brother Jack didn't really like basketball that much, but he was a decent player and was very, very competitive. He didn't care what the game was, he was going to play it as hard as he could to win.

One day after one of those indoor tennis practices Coach Flowers was still around and we all decided to play a pickup game of basketball. My brother and I were on the same team, and we gave Coach Flowers some of the other guys. The only guy I've ever met who is as competitive as my brother is Coach Flowers. My brother was guarding Coach Flowers and was really giving him the business—elbows were flying and forearms being delivered on just about every shot and rebound. There was a loose ball and the two of them starting to go for it and my brother sort of pushed Coach Flowers out of the way. Before we knew it, Coach Flowers tackled my brother and got on top of him. I thought he was going to beat him up, but he just started yelling.

"I don't know what the hell you're trying to do, but if you think you're such a tough guy and are looking for a fight, then let's go, or else let's play basketball," he yelled. Things calmed down right away, but the fierceness of the game and the play wasn't lost on anyone: those two guys really loved to compete and to win.

By the way, the very next morning Coach Flowers drove my brother, Morgan Place, and Dan Shine all the way out to Wartburg College in Iowa for a recruiting visit. All three ended up getting scholarship money and all three graduated from Wartburg College. The conflict the night before had been forgotten. Well, maybe not forgotten, but certainly my brother and Coach Flowers had gotten over it.

22

Heartbreak For Veronica And I Fall In Love

In the spring of 1968 St. Mary's Academy was getting ready for an annual tradition: cheerleading tryouts. My sister Veronica had been a cheerleader since seventh grade. She was a good cheerleader, serious about the position. Veronica had been a junior varsity cheerleader her junior year, and the only question for her senior year seemed to be whether she or Sharon Strubanski would be the captain of the varsity squad. Oops, something happened to destroy those plans.

My sister didn't even make the varsity squad. She tried out and everything supposedly went well. She was offered the captain position for the next year's JV squad. There was simply no way she would accept that position. The surprise member of the next year's varsity squad was Bridgett Mulroney, a girl in my class who hadn't been a cheerleader for a few years. Bridgett's brother had recently been killed in Vietnam, which was a terrible, heart-wrenching situation for everyone at St. Mary's.

Bridgett was a very thin girl, with long, straight black hair. She was actually pretty athletic, but hadn't been a cheerleader before that year. My sister, her friends, and my mother all were terribly disappointed that Bridgett had made the varsity squad as a junior, and my sister hadn't. Needless to say, there was never any love loss between my sister and Bridgett Mulroney.

In October of 1968 the Student Council sponsored a Halloween Dance at school. Early in the week leading up to the dance I talked to Dawn Piaget, who had become the school "matchmaker." She was the person you could depend on to set you up with another person or possibly find you a date. I went to Dawn and said, "I need to find a girlfriend. Any ideas?"

Dawn looked at me and said, "Do YOU have any ideas?"

I said, "How about Jane Writing or Bridgett Mulroney?"

She said, "Ill see what I can do."

Dawn came back to me the next day and said, "Remember what you asked me yesterday?" I nodded. She said, "One just laughed and the other said, 'Tell him to go to hell.' Which one do you think said what?"

I said, "Bridgett obviously said, 'Go to hell,' and Jane just laughed, right?"

Dawn looked at me with a puzzled look. "No, it was the other way around. Jane said 'Go to hell' and Bridgett just sort of laughed."

Everyone decided to go to the Halloween Dance, and everyone even decided to dress up. I went as a witch. I had black make-up on, a black wig, long black gloves, a black turtleneck, black pants, etc. Everyone seemed to have a good time, and we left around 10:00. All of the juniors went to McDonald's while still in costume. We hung around there for awhile. Earlier in the evening, I had danced with Bridgett a couple of times and told her that I would meet her at McDonald's. At McDonald's I sat and talked to her for awhile. I had not driven that night, and I was riding with Bert Knouwer. Bridgett invited me over to her house. The three of us, Bert, Bridgett, and me, climbed into Bert's car and went to Bridgett's. After we got there Bert watched TV while Bridgett and I, well, I guess there's no other way to say this: we made out. Nothing heavy, just lots of kissing.

I started dating Bridgett Mulroney, much to the chagrin of my mother and my sister. Bridgett became my steady girlfriend for several months. In fact, she was probably my very first love. You can't really count my infatuation with Debbie Summerhill, since I never got too close to her, much to my chagrin!

In the middle of January the Student Council hosted an evening of fun and games called "Flunk and Forget It Night." I was the Vice-President of Student Council, so I probably should have gone to the event. Mackie MacGregor was always fighting Will Fitzpatrick for the attention of Grace Orsini. Grace's dad was a doctor and a very strict father. I'm not sure he ever liked either Mackie or Will, but those guys seemed to be always competing for her attention. Grace was one of Bridgett's best friends, and was always one of my best friends. She is a great lady even today. Back then she was fun-loving, friendly, and just nice. She was also the Secretary of Student Council. As Student Council officers, we both should have gone to Flunk and Forget It Night, but we decided to go to Bridgett's house with Bridgett and Mackie and play our own cards. We met at Bridgett's and sat there for three hours and played Hearts.

At around 10:15 we decided that we should probably go to the end of the Student Council event and help clean up. The event was supposed to get over at 10:30. Grace and I left to go to the school together, and, as we walked in, there was Sister Mary Neumann, the Principal and Student Council Advisor. She was waiting for us at the door. She was very upset. She sort of yelled at us, even after we explained where we were and the fact that we had come to clean up, which is the least desirable job. I thought that that should have calmed her down, but it sure didn't. She actually asked us if our parents knew where we were. To me, that was a tip-off that she was going to call our parents the next day. We helped clean up and then went home.

The next morning at breakfast I explained to my mother what had happened. I explained that we had gone to Mulroney's to play cards, and then went to school to help clean up. Grace never told her parents what had happened, probably because she wasn't supposed to be out with Mackie. Sure enough, Sister Mary Neumann called our homes that day, and my mother told her that she knew that I had gone to Mulroney's and that I had then gone to help clean up. Everything was cool with my mom—my mom has always been pretty cool.

Grace's dad was enraged when he found out his daughter wasn't where she was supposed to be. I think she was grounded for a month or so. I might ground my daughter if she dated Mackie MacGregor too.

23

"Dem mosquitoes is treacherous,"
&
"No Such Word As Slave"

My summer job for four summers in a row was to take care of the brown clay tennis courts at Lakeview Park. I earned $1.62 an hour, which was a decent wage back then, and I was responsible for getting up and being to work at 6:00 every morning. There were four old, clay courts at Lakeview Park, and each morning I would drag a very large push broom over the courts to spread out the sand and dirt evenly. I would then spray all of the courts with water to further get the sand and dirt spread. I would then drive a roller over the courts to flatten and make the courts harder. Finally, I would mix up white lime and water and line the courts (paint the lines on) each morning. It was really a fun job, except for the early morning hours. Around Lorain I was known as "the kid who took care of the clay courts."

If it rained while I was supposed to be working, I obviously couldn't do any work on the courts, as they would be all muddy, so the Parks and Recreation Department foreman would come over and re-assign me for the day. I might have to mow or weed the rose garden, trim around parking lots, whatever they needed me to do that day.

One day it had rained all night, so the courts were basically flooded with water, so there was no way I would be working on them. The foreman came and told me to meet him across the street at the other side of Lakeview Park. When I got there a little while later, the foreman was there with two young black guys. The foreman went to the back of the truck and pulled out three hand-held hedge trimmers. He told us to go into this area between these hedges to trim the large bushes.

The day was one of those absolutely steamy days where you can see humidity rise off of the road. By 9:00 in the morning it was about 85 degrees with 90 percent humidity. A person would sweat profusely just standing still. All three of us waded into the weeds and grass that we were supposed to trim. There were hundreds, no make that thousands, of mosquitoes present in the area. One of the black kids was rather fat, and he had already taken his shirt off when he went into the hedge. He was basically attacked by mosquitoes, which we all were, but at least I had a shirt on. He was only in there for a few minutes when he walked out and sat down by the curb. He didn't do anything the rest of the morning.

When the foreman arrived about two hours later, two of us were working and the one fat kid was sitting by the curb. I headed out of the area when the foreman arrived, since he had already seen me working. He asked the kid who was just sitting what the problem was. The kid said, "It's dem mosquitoes. Dey is fuckin' treacherous." I started laughing because he was right, but just the way he said it was funny, and it was a line that I knew Conor Flannery and Mackie MacGregor would really enjoy, and I was right. For years after that, and, even to this day, we say, once in awhile, "Boss, dem mosquitoes is fuckin' treacherous."

Another incident that occurred in the summer of 1968 came from the creative, brilliant, and warped mind of Fran Dunning. He called me up one evening and said, "Be behind Fitzpatrick's house at 7:00 Saturday morning. I asked why, and he just said, "You'll see. Oh, by the way, wear shorts and bring a sheet. We're making a movie."

"What?" I asked. "Making a movie? What do you mean?"

"We're making a movie, a gladiator movie. You'll see when you get there." I reminded Fran that I had to work that day, but I told him I would finish the courts and get there as soon as I could. If I started my job earlier than usual and cut a few corners (such as only re-painting the lines that really needed it) I could finish on a Saturday in about two-and-a-half hours. I did that and drove across town to Fitzpatrick's house.

When I got there they had already begun. Fitzpatrick's back yard overlooks Lake Erie, and there was a long stairway which went right down to the beach. There were several chairs set up in the backyard, including one director's chair which even had the word "Director" printed on the back. I could hear everyone else down on the beach, so that's where I went.

Fran was already directing a scene. There were five guys tied together: Tommy Jackson, Conor Flannery, Robbie Cavellini, Bert Knouwer, and Julian Holliday, who just happened to be the five guys with the best physiques. They were supposed to be five brothers who had been enslaved by the evil emperor. The scene involved the emperor, played with a certain pizzazz by Mackie MacGregor, arriving by boat. The boat was tied up at a neighboring dock, and the emperor got out of the boat and walked along the dock. I arrived in time to become one of the emperor's guards, and four of us led the emperor from the boat to the beach, where he was supposed to look over his newest slaves.

The leader of the guards was played by the biggest guy there, Jeff Brent. He was an awesome actor. Even though we were filming this in 1968 with an old eight millimeter camera which had no sound, Brent talked and acted all the way through each scene. It was really funny, and we all tried not to laugh, but we often failed in that regard, and then Fran would get all upset because once something is filmed, you can't just go back and erase it. It's on the film, and someone is paying for it. Anyway, we led the emperor to the beach and the five brothers were brought to him. One of the brothers, Julian Holiday, disrespected the emperor and was killed right there on the beach. That caused the other slaves to go crazy. Naturally, a huge fight ensued.

The second major scene was filmed at an empty George Daniel Stadium. The emperor was shown sitting up in the bleachers of the ancient coliseum (OK, so there was also a press box and chain link fence in the shot. We were doing the best we could). The remaining four brothers were brought in and told to fight to the death to entertain the emperor. There were some great fight scenes, and, in the end the brothers refused to kill each other. When the mean leader of the guards (Jeff Brent) went out on the field to make sure the brothers would kill each other, the brothers overwhelmed him and escaped.

The final big scenes were filmed at French Creek Reservoir Park, which was also the site of the many b-b gun wars we had fought. The guards and the emperor chased the brothers and eventually caught them in an open area, and further fights ensued. One of the remaining brothers was killed, but the other brothers killed the emperor and raced off into the forest, no longer slaves. The movie was an integral part of not only our friendship with each other, but just the idea of working together and creating something unique and original was great. We still watch the movie once in awhile, and still absolutely crack up with laughter.

One other thing happened during the filming of the movie. One of our friends and a performer in the movie, Dan "The Cat" White, had a seizure. Most of us had not realized that Cat was an epileptic, so we really didn't know what to do when he had the seizure. A few guys stepped in and responded brilliantly, and we all were aware from then on about how to handle the situation. Our friendship for Cat came through several other times in our high school career, and we all knew how to respond. He was our friend, and we were going to take care of him.

24

1968 . . . . The End Of The Streak

When my brother's class of 1968 left St. Mary's they left behind quite a legacy. They had been a large part of the 24-game winning streak the Irish had accumulated. Several of the players from the 1967 undefeated team went on to play in college, including my brother Jack. Jack and two of his friends, Morgan Place and Dan Shine, went to Wartburg College, a small Division III college in Waverly, Iowa. Jack and Morgan actually received money in the form of football scholarships (Wartburg was NAIA then, not NCAA), and Shine just went to play football with the others and eventually received money for playing. All three had stellar careers playing for the Knights. Mick Dunning, our real stud, earned a full-ride football scholarship to Northwestern University, where he played on a team that beat a fabled Ohio State team. Joe Allen, the other first-team All-Ohioan, was recruited by Woody Hayes at Ohio State, but he chose to accept a football scholarship to Duke. Jake Jurevicious, one of the best defensive players as a linebacker, played football at Akron, while Ted Krupski played at Culver-Stockton College in Kansas. The bottom line was . . . . there were plenty of really good football players on the 1967 team. Unfortunately, most of them had graduated. We had to start anew.

Coach Flowers started his second season with a renewed vigor. He was as intense as ever. We were definitely going to be smaller in 1968, and we were going to be missing, not only experience, but also talent. We made up for those deficiencies by playing with lots of heart.

Our summer conditioning workouts were held at Longfellow Park on the east side of Lorain. The park had plenty of space for us to spread out and run a lot. Everything we did was based on quickness, since that was truly one of our strengths. Coach Flowers continually emphasized doing things as quickly as possible.

Will Fitzpatrick had stepped up to earn the starting quarterback position, and Fran Dunning and Robbie Cavellini looked great as halfbacks. Bert Knouwer had worked incredibly hard and was very strong at fullback, even though he only weighed about 160 pounds. Of course, 160 pounds made him the biggest of the backs, as Cavellini and Dunning were both about 150 pounds. All we needed was a line. Our best returning linemen were tackle Stosh Kurek and end Mike Campole, both returning senior lettermen. Jeff Brent had grown up enough to man one tackle spot, while Tom Jackson, a guy who hadn't played football the year before but was one of the best athletes in the school, looked to be the other end.

The center of the line had to be rebuilt. Coach Flowers really didn't like Mackie MacGregor. No one ever knew why, because Mackie was a fine football player. Coach Flowers just didn't like him very much. At the start of practice Coach Flowers told me that he wanted me to become the center. I had hoped to play either end or guard, but you tend to do what Coach Flowers says, so I tried to play center. It was a disaster. I hated it. I loved to pull and lead sweeps, and I knew I could catch passes, but snapping the ball and stepping with the proper foot was a skill I neither had nor wanted to acquire. I think that Coach Flowers either wanted to try and make MacGregor a tackle, since he was one of our biggest kids, weighing about 210, or he just wanted him out of the lineup. Maybe he just wanted MacGregor to see that there was some competition for his position so that he would work harder, but if that competition was supposed to come from me it wasn't a very smart move.

One day at practice I was really struggling trying to be a center, and Coach Flowers started yelling at me. He eventually told me to go off away from the team and work on my stance and step. He sent the sophomore quarterback over with a sophomore defensive lineman. I was supposed to snap and step into live blocking. Well, I did that drill for about fifteen minutes, and then I realized that every other snap was laying on the ground, which meant the sophomore quarterback wasn't getting the ball from me when I was supposed to be snapping it up to him. I told the defensive lineman to take a break and that the quarterback and I were going to work on our exchanges. The defensive lineman moved off to the side while I just snapped a few up to the quarterback. One of the assistant coaches, Bill Dunning (Mick and Fran's older brother who had played at Notre Dame), saw what was going on and he went nuts. He ran over to us and started yelling at me for not stepping and blocking like Coach Flowers had told us to do. Bill Dunning was a mean assistant football coach and he never liked me. I guess he was just demanding. Anyway, he got down on all fours and started yelling at me and told me that I had to block HIM, not the sophomore defensive lineman. I started snapping and stepping. Snapping and stepping. He was hitting me with forearm shiver after forearm shiver. I didn't really like it too much, but what was I going to do? Everyone sort of started watching the excitement of Stephen Francis versus another coach. The other players, most of whom didn't like Coach Dunning any more than I did, started cheering me on. It got a bit vicious. Eventually, I snapped and stepped and blocked him and my arm (fully padded) came up right between his legs with a pretty good shot. It wasn't really dirty (well, OK, maybe it was sort of dirty), but it ended the drill one play later.

We had some incredible practices during the summer. Our conditioning was held at Longfellow Park on the east side of Lorain. Our practices during the season were held at Lakeview Park on the west side of town. We continued to work very hard and we continually emphasized quickness, which is what we were going to have to do in order to be successful, since our team was so small.

The great experiment of trying to make me a center just didn't work, and I ended up starting at guard. The other guard was another junior, Ryan Stoyanoff. We actually had about five guards who ran plays in and took turns giving each other breaks.

The defense was spearheaded by two seniors, Jon Kramer and Danny Seroka. Kramer was really small, probably about 5-7 and 150 pounds. He played defensive tackle. He was very quick and very tough to block. Seroka was a really mean kid who didn't even play football all four years. He wasn't very big either, about 5-9 and 160, and he played inside linebacker. As you can see, we were not very big at all.

We had a few interscholastic scrimmages, and we performed okay, but we were really trying to put things all together. We had lost so many seniors from the previous team, and we also had a number of guys playing football for the very first time or playing new positions. We opened the season on a Sunday afternoon at Fremont St. Joseph's. They had defeated St. Mary's about 20 times in a row until the '66 and '67 teams had knocked off the Crimson Streaks. St. Joe's ran the single wing offense and had this huge fullback (who eventually got a scholarship to Notre Dame). We knew that this was going to be one of the toughest games of the entire year.

St. Joe's scored two touchdowns in the first half, converting both, for a 14-0 lead. We were having one heck of a time moving the ball. We scored on a touchdown pass in the second half and went for a two-point conversion, which we made, cutting the score to 14-8. Now, we had them reeling. Our defense was really stepping up and making plays and the offense was moving the ball just enough.

Late in the fourth quarter we got a nice drive going and reached the St. Joe one-yard line. On 4th down Will Fitzgerald tried a quarterback sneak. I thought the line surge got him well over the goal line, but the officials didn't see it that way. They had stopped us, and the Crimson Streaks had ended the Fighting Irish's 24-game win streak. I can remember my brother Jack yelling at me on the phone that night, complaining that we couldn't keep the streak going.

That game actually taught us a few things about ourselves. First, we could move the ball once we settled down. We had three very good running backs, any of which could gain over 100 yards rushing in any game. Second, Will Fitzpatrick was going to be just fine at quarterback. Third, the defense could get downright nasty, especially once we got a little more experience and confidence.

One of our more unique games we played early in that season was against Xenia Woodrow Wilson School. Xenia is in southern Ohio, which meant a long, long bus trip. The game was scheduled on a Saturday afternoon, not just because of the distance, but also because their field did not have any lights. Coach Flowers had scheduled the game in southern Ohio in order to get us some publicity in that part of the state. We were all kind of upset that the undefeated 1967 team only finished fifth in the state, and he thought that if we traveled to that part of the state we might actually get some votes.

Woodrow Wilson School was actually an orphanage. It was sort of a military school with a campus-type atmosphere. When we arrived there we got to walk through some of the buildings and they actually had a pool that we hoped we could use following the game. The scouting report said that Woodrow Wilson was a tough team led by a big, mean fullback/linebacker. Once the game started we kept looking for this big, mean fullback/linebacker. We never saw him. He had run away from the school the night before. That's right, he had run away from the orphanage. It helped that they didn't have too many other great players, and we won, 34-6.

One thing that really upset everybody after the game was the fact that Coach Flowers wouldn't let us go swimming in their swimming pool. He was so mad that we had given up a touchdown after leading 34-0 that he refused to allow us to go swimming. Fran Dunning always told everybody that we wouldn't have wanted to go swimming in that pool anyway. It wasn't very nice.

By the way, the play that Woodrow Wilson scored on was a defensive miscue by the coaches. They had the ball very deep in our territory, and Coach Flowers called for our inside linebackers to blitz. One of the few things that can hurt a blitz from a 4-4 is a short little pass over the middle to the tight end into the area vacated by the blitzing linebacker. We always sort of thought that the coaches should have taken responsibility for that touchdown, instead of blaming us.

We won our next few games, and we were all set to play one of our rivals, Lorain Clearview. Clearview had great athletes. They were big and fast and rugged. Their fullback/linebacker, Joe Toth, was as brutal as they come. Their running backs were quick and slippery, especially the aptly named Money Goines. That was actually his name. They were 6-1 too, with their only loss coming in the first game of the season versus our biggest rival, the hated Panthers of Elyria Catholic.

The game was played at Lorain's George Daniel Stadium, a huge, classic, Depression-era stadium that seats about 6000 fans. We actually got to use the Lorain Senior locker room, something that we hadn't gotten to do very often. Usually, we dressed in one of the visitor locker rooms under the west side of the concrete bleachers. We were in the locker room just before the game when an old guy, at least 50 years old, stumbled into our locker room. We had no idea who he was. The coaches were going over the very final game plan, and it was quiet when he stumbled in. Everybody looked at him, and then everybody looked at Coach Flowers to see what he was going to do. He was sort of shocked and frozen in time.

"I wanna talk to you guys," mumbled the obviously-drunk intruder. "I wan you guys to remember one thing . . . . if they're bigger'n you, then . . . . then . . . . then yer bigger'n them." We couldn't believe that this guy had actually made it all the way into the locker room and that the coaches hadn't killed him yet. Coach Flowers finally said, Get him outta here."

Coaches McComb and Dunning grabbed the guy and started pulling him towards the door. Right near the door he grabbed the frame and sort of pulled himself back into the room. He yelled, "Hey, I got twenty bucks on this goddamn game." What an incredible sight. We pretty much lost our edge right then, and some of us started laughing to ourselves.

Clearview scored first. They led 6-0, and they lined up for their extra point. They were going for two. Their quarterback sprinted down the line and ran an option. He kept the ball and was stopped short. Our defensive end on that side, JD Szollzy, tackled the pitch man, Money Goines, even though he didn't have the ball. Defenses, by the way, are coached to do that—on an option, both guys need to get hit. Goines didn't like getting hit when he didn't have the ball (Hell, he didn't like getting hit when he DID have the ball!), and he sort of kicked at JD when the two of them were on the ground. JD kicked back. Both players jumped up and started fighting. The officials threw flags, separated the players, and then kicked both JD Szollzy and Money Goines out of the game. We have been accused many times over the years that JD started the fight with Money just to get them both kicked out. JD, after all, was a defensive end for us, and just an average one at that. Goines, on the other hand, was truly one of Clearview's stars.

It was really good for me that JD was kicked out, since that allowed me to play the rest of the game on defense, as well as right and left guard on offense. I actually earned two helmet awards for sacks on the Clearview quarterback that game, and I had a great time playing defense.

Clearview scored another touchdown, and we also scored two touchdowns. Conor Flanary missed both extra points, including the second one with just minutes left in the game. We had to settle for a 12-12 tie. The game itself was sort of a bummer, but with the drunk guy coming in before the game, it did make for unusual and an interesting story.

By the way, the drunk guy was actually Joe Wojohowicz' uncle. Joe was a reserve defensive tackle on our team.

After the Clearview game we had to get ready to play Elyria Catholic, which would be for the conference championship. Both teams were unbeaten in the North Central Conference. We had defeated EC the last three years, and they had had great teams all three years. My oldest brother Bob had scored a touchdown in the 1965 game. The 1966 game was the epic 8-6 upset, and the 1967 game was a resounding 34-6 Irish win. My brother Jack threw two touchdowns against the Panthers that year, and Mick Dunning had run roughshod over a Panther defense that was highly-touted but overrated. The 1968 game was another one for the ages.

The week leading up to the EC game was always special, with a great pep rally and bonfire. The schools hated each other so much that vandalism often accompanied the EC-St. Mary's week, and 1968 would be no different. The game was scheduled for Saturday evening at Ely Stadium in Elyria.

We had some absolutely crazy guys in St. Mary's, and they had formed their own little club, the NFP, or Non-Football Players. Just because they didn't play football didn't mean they liked Elyria Catholic any more than the rest of us. In fact, BECAUSE they didn't play football allowed them to wreak a little more havoc and add to the rivalry by doing some crazy things. Imagine a football player going over to EC and then getting caught vandalizing. Coach Flowers would have killed us!

Someone at our school had heard that the EC students were going to come over and drive past our school on Friday morning, shouting insults, honking horns, and waving signs. The NFP's got prepped for the visit. They arrived at school with pumpkins, eggs, tomatoes, etc. You may not believe this, but there were plenty of witnesses. When the EC students, at least six or eight carloads, arrived at our school, the NFP's were ready. They had placed their items on top of the building, and they rushed into position. The blocks on Reid Avenue aren't very long, and there are traffic lights at each corner. If eight cars are stopped by a traffic light and the kids in the cars are yelling, waving, holding signs, etc., they are sitting ducks for vandalism.

Here were these EC cars, just sitting in front of our school. The NFP's began pelting the cars with the eggs, tomatoes, pumpkins, etc. Someone even ran out in front of our school with a baseball bat and broke out a few headlights and taillights on the cars. It was quite a scene.

Of course if the EC students were going to attack our school, our kids were going to reciprocate. When the NFP's arrived at EC that night they noticed that there were all kinds of people standing guard. They drove around the school from a distance a few times before trying to decide what to do. One of the great acts of vandalism ever done involved the best golfer at our school, Vic Holdish. He could really hit a ball. Our guys parked on the other side of the EC football field. Too far away to do any harm or vandalism, right? Wrong. Vic took some golf balls and started hitting them over the fence towards the school. He actually broke a couple of windows, I heard, and also scared the hell out of some of the "guards" who were standing there. Imagine a golf ball flying at you in the dark, especially after you've heard one hit and break a window just moments before.

When we received the scouting report on EC that year we couldn't believe how big they were. Not just in weight, but also in height. Their defensive ends were 6-4 225 and 6-5 210. We didn't have anybody on our team that tall. In their white uniforms they looked even bigger. Their fullback was Jerry "The Baby Bull" McHugh. His older brother, Tom "The Bull" McHugh, had been a great player for the Panthers a few years before. The Baby Bull broke all of his brother's rushing records. The Baby Bull was 6-1 230, and he wasn't that fast, but he ran really hard, and he loved to lower his head and run right over little defensive backs in the secondary. You had to get to The Baby Bull before he got his speed up. I actually wondered how our tiny defensive players were going to stop him. Our secondary went 150, 155, 160. Our inside linebackers were 155 and 165, and, remember, we had a defensive tackle who only weighed about 160.

Elyria Catholic kicked off and we started moving the ball with beautiful efficiency. Our quick traps and sweeps were being blocked to near perfection. We went down the field and scored on our first possession. We led, 7-0. We kicked off and the Panthers fumbled the ball on the kickoff and we recovered. We went in and scored, went for a two-point conversion, and led, 15-0. We led this huge, arch-rival game 15-0 and the favored Panthers had not run a play from scrimmage yet. We kicked off, and they ran three plays and we stopped them, forcing them to punt. We took the punt and went right down the field and scored and converted for a 22-0 lead. They had run three plays and we were ahead, 22-0. This was absolutely a shocker, and boy was it fun.

Elyria Catholic gained some first downs in the second quarter, but they couldn't score, and, late in the half, we scored again for a 30-0 lead at the half. It was an absolutely beautiful sweep. Fran Dunning took the pitch, I pulled from my right guard position and led the way, fullback Bert Knouwer kicked out the end, I kicked out the cornerback, and the other guard turned up and sealed the safety. There was a wide lane for Fran Dunning to run through, and he went 68 yards for a touchdown to put us up, 30-0 at halftime.

We went into the locker room and Coach Flowers had written on the blackboard in huge numbers, "0-0." His point was we had a second half to play, and if we scored 30 points against them in one half, they could score 30 against us in the second half. No way. There wasn't one guy in that locker room who believed we would give up 30 points to the Panthers in the second half. Despite Coach Flowers' warning, we all relaxed a little.

The Baby Bull and his mates got going in the second half, but we already had the game won. He scored one touchdown late in the game, but we still won, 30-6.

There are few things better in life than defeating a hated arch-rival like Elyria Catholic.

25

A Huge Surprise At Midview

Our record stood at 7-1-1, which was pretty darn good considering how small we were and how many guys we had lost from that great 1967 team. We had only one game left to play. The last game was against Grafton Midview, a team with a 3-6 record that year. They hadn't been good in football for quite awhile, and we had defeated them the year before, 52-6. We were in for a huge surprise.

Have you ever heard of a team preparing for one game all season? Sure, Army prepares for Navy all season, and vice versa. We pointed towards Elyria Catholic all season. Ohio State points to Michigan all season. Those are huge, arch-rival games however. We certainly weren't "rivals" with Midview. Heck, I think the year before was the very first time we had ever played them.

Midview, for whatever reason, had started preparing for the 1968 Lorain St. Mary's game a year earlier, right after we beat them, 52-6. I remember carrying Coach Flowers off the field after that game, and the story was that he never shook the Midview coach's hand after the game. I find that very difficult-if-not-impossible to believe. Coach Flowers had always been the consummate sportsman. As I said, though, I do remember carrying the first-year coach off the field the year before after completing the undefeated season. Maybe Midview thought we ran the score up on them the previous year. I don't know what got in to them, but they supposedly prepped for our game the entire season.

The game was played at Midview, and the team was going to go out to eat after the game at a very nice restaurant, so everyone dressed up on the way to the game. The locker room was one of the strangest I can remember. It was almost like no one wanted to play the game. We took the field for the pre-game, and it was bitterly cold. Every blade of grass was covered with ice, as if it had rained a bit and then the temperature dropped and everything froze. It was cold as hell, and that just added to the poor attitude. Perhaps the fact that we had defeated our arch-rival the previous week had taken the edge off, but we just didn't want to play this game. Our starting center, Mackie MacGregor, never one of Coach Flowers' favorites, had been benched for the game in favor of a senior center who had played very little. Mackie was one of us. He had been out there on the field the entire season at center, and now Coach Flowers was benching him. No one really knew why. That didn't help our attitude, either.

We actually played pretty well early in the game, and we led 15-12 at halftime. Ever play in a game where you were winning at halftime but didn't think you had any chance to win the game? This was one of those nights. Our locker room was in the school, and we had to cross paths with the Midview Middies as they headed to their locker room at halftime. As we sifted our way through them, their players were all saying things like, "We're gonna kick your ass in the second half." Again, it was a very strange feeling, because we believed they were right.

Midview had changed their entire offense for this game. They came out in a double-slot formation with two split ends, two slotbacks, and one running back. They put one of the slotbacks in motion every play. We had never seen this type of offense. They had never run this in any game film we had seen of them. They practiced this offense all year just to run against us. It was incredible. Actually, it was really the Run-and-Shoot offense that became popular in college football a few years later. Our 4-4 defense wasn't really designed to stop this offense. We had to change numerous assignments, especially our outside linebackers and defensive ends. We were pretty much screwed up the entire game.

We scored one more touchdown in the second half, but Midview scored 18 points and beat us, 30-23. The ultimate insult occurred late in the game when Midview punted deep in to our territory. We ran one play, and, on second down, we ran a sweep to the left. Their linebacker blitzed and tackled Robbie Cavellini for a safety. No team ever wants to give up a safety, and we just got tackled our endzone. The new center was supposed to step hard playside and pick up a blitz, but he didn't, and that's where the blitzing linebacker came through. Had Mackie MacGregor been in the game instead of standing on the sideline freezing we might not have given up the safety.

One other bad thing happened late in the game. We ran another sweep to the left, and Robbie Cavellini broke off a long run. He gained 37 yards. The play was called back, however, because an official had detected me clipping. I had pulled to the left, headed up the field and tried to seal the safety. He turned just as I left my feet for the cross-body block, and I sort of rolled onto the back of his legs. Not only did it bring back a long gain for our team, but Robbie Cavellini ended up the season with 969 yards rushing. If I didn't clip, he would have rushed for over 1000 yards in the season. He hasn't forgotten that in all the years since then. By the way, Fran Dunning rushed for 914 yards, which meant we had two guys who averaged almost 100 yards rushing per game. We were quick and very efficient. Will Fitzpatrick, the quarterback who was sent walking back to school the year before, threw for over 1200 yards and 13 touchdowns. Those were remarkable figures for a first-year varsity quarterback.

After that Midview game we still went out for dinner, but it wasn't really the same. There was very little talk, and it was just a matter of eating our nice dinner and going home. Losing to that team, that was so fired up to play us, was definitely not a good way to end the season. Our record, 7-2-1, was pretty darn good, but the season ended the same way it had started—with a loss.

So the season was over. Several of the seniors got football scholarships, or at least some aid to play. Tackle Stosh Kurek went to the University of Akron on a scholarship. End Mike Campole played for a couple of years at Miami University of Ohio. Fran Dunning and Tom Jackson both went to Wartburg College in Iowa and joined my brother Jack and Morgan Place and Dan Shine.

26

Cafeteria Hi-jinks & The Imperial Wizards

The cafeteria at St. Mary's was full of long tables. They were set up pretty close to each other, as the cafeteria needed room for students in twelve grades. Just inside the cafeteria there was a long table where students would dump their books when they came in to eat. They would pick their books up from that table on the way out of the cafeteria after eating. The long table also served another purpose.

After eating lunch couples would sit together at the table. It was just a place to not be bothered by the other hundred or so kids in the cafeteria at the time. Naturally, when I was dating Bridgett Mulroney we spent some time at the "Couples' Table."

One day we were sitting there talking quietly and holding hands on top of the table. I looked behind Bridgett and there was Fran Dunning and about twenty other guys. They were standing about fifteen feet away from us with their arms crossed just shaking their heads as if to say, "C'mon Francis, you should be sitting with us over on the other side of the cafeteria." Fran didn't particularly like Bridgett, but, even more than that, he couldn't stand the whole "high-school-couples-holding-hands-in-school-routine." I was leaning forward talking to Bridgett when I noticed Fran and the other guys standing there. He had obviously orchestrated this little act.

I looked up, started to laugh a bit and then looked back down. I did this a few times before Bridgett asked me what was up. I looked up behind her one more time and she spun around and looked at the collection of guys standing there with their arms crossed shaking their heads as if they didn't approve of what we were doing.

Bridgett got very upset and got up right away and started crying and ran to the restroom. As she was running away the assembled guys started laughing, which added to the problem of the situation.

As mentioned, people only sat at the "Couples' Table" if they wanted privacy. You could actually find some people sitting there by themselves studying for an afternoon quiz. Granted, that sight was rather rare, but it did occur once in awhile.

One day early in the school year I noticed Fran Dunning sitting by himself reading something. He was actually reading with his lips moving and his head was sort of bobbing around. I asked everybody at our table what he was doing and no one seemed to know, so I thought I better find out. I walked over to Fran and noticed that what he had in his hand was actually sheet music. He was reading music. That was really strange.

"Fran, what are you doing," I asked.

"I'm working on the lyrics to a song I need to sing," he told me without looking up.

"Why do you need to learn a song," I asked.

Without looking up he said, "I'm the lead singer in a rock band and I need to work on some songs."

Yeah, right, I thought. Fran Dunning, who no one had ever heard sing, was the lead singer in a band. "OK, Fran," I said. "I'll bite. What's the name of this band?"

Without batting an eye he said, "The Imperial Wizards. It's a group out of Westlake with some guys I went to grade school with. Do you mind if I get back to my concentrating?"

I turned around and went back to the other guys and explained that Fran had said he was the lead singer in a band. Everybody thought this was pretty funny, because we didn't think Fran had any musical ability at all. Fran spent days and days sitting by himself acting like he was singing. He didn't spend as much time with us on the weekends because he said the band was rehearsing, getting ready for their first big gig. The entire school bought this story, and it lasted for months and months. He really had us going.

Finally, when it came time to hire a band for the Senior Farewell and everyone wanted to hear The Imperial Wizards, Fran told us that he had never been in a band and that the whole story was made up. We couldn't believe it. Everyone, and I mean everyone, in our school had thought that Fran Dunning, really the school leader, was in a band. The band never existed and he was just pulling a practical joke on everyone.

27

A Great, Great (Yet Disappointing) Basketball Season

As soon as football ended Tom Jackson, Will Fitzpatrick and I reported to basketball. Coach James Englund had returned to St. Mary's after a coaching stint at Brookside High School, and he was getting the Fighting Irish back to basketball prominence.

Gone from the '67-'68 team were some great players like Liam Downey, but back were outstanding players like Fred Knillen, George Rivers, and Earl Winters, big guys who could really play. There were plenty of other seniors, but Paul Downey, Liam's brother, had grown to about 6-2 or 6-3 and improved enough to guarantee him a starting position. That meant there were four outstanding players. Power forward George Rivers, who was 6-4 and very steady, consistent, fundamental, and the team captain, would handle lots of the rebounding chores. The center was going to be Earl Winters, all thin and wiry and a rough 6-5. The shooting forward would be the afore-mentioned Paul Downey, who had great range and never let a shot go by. The best player on a team of outstanding players was Fred Knillen. Knillen, despite a rather strange attitude and some erratic behavior, was a tremendous player. He was a big-time scorer, and he could play every position on the floor. He was about 6-1 ½, and he could slash to the basket, stop and shoot, back up and shoot long-range, and even go inside and bang with people. He also got lots of lay-ups when we pressed and even when we played a 1-3-1 half-court zone. He was the point man on the zone, and he was very difficult to pass around or over. He had long arms and was very quick flicking the ball away from other teams and then heading the other way for a lay-up.

So, there were four outstanding starters. The fifth guy was going to be a guy who wouldn't make many mistakes. He wouldn't have to do much, maybe take the ball out of bounds once in awhile and hold up his own on defense, generally not get in the way and mess up the other four good players. Heck, that sounded like a job description I could fill.

When the season started there were three guys vying for that other starting position: senior Tom Jackson, sophomore Joey Laszoff, and me. Jackson, as I have already pointed out, was a great athlete—a runner, jumper, pole vaulter. I was also a pretty decent three-sport athlete. Laszoff was a kid who had pretty much given up everything else to concentrate on basketball, and he had improved a great deal over the summer. Still, I didn't think that Coach Englund would start a sophomore in front of a senior or a junior, which Jackson and I were.

The season started and Laszoff was the starting point guard. When Coach Englund announced the starting line-up on Monday before the first game, both Jackson and I were pissed. We both thought that we should be in front of Laszoff.

I asked to talk to Coach Englund privately after practice, and I went into the coaches' office pretty upset. I explained to him that I was a better basketball player than either Jackson or Laszoff, and that I thought I should be playing. Coach Englund listened to me, sort of nodded his head, and then said the immortal words every coach has memorized. "Keep working hard and you'll get your chance." That wasn't really good enough for me, and I was really ticked.

We got off to a good start as a team and won our first three games, including an exciting 72-68 win over Sandusky Perkins. The next night, a Saturday, we traveled to Mansfield St. Peter's, the defending Ohio state champion. They were led by the legendary Whitey Varga, a great player.

St. Peter's gym is actually a stage. Many of the smaller gyms in the old days were built like this. The stage floor was actually the basketball court. There were several hundred folding theatre seats on one side of the stage, pretty much below the stage floor. There was also a sort-of cat-walk on the other side of the court. This balcony actually stuck out over the floor a bit, so you had to be careful when throwing the ball in if you were under the cat-walk. The balcony (cat-walk) was actually the St. Peter's student section. All the students in the school stood on this balcony, and I'll tell you, if you got too close to the sideline you were liable to get hit by some popcorn, or at least a big, gooey spit-wad. I actually loved the atmosphere in that gym. It was hostile. I can't imagine any high school basketball team going into that gym and winning a close game. It was extremely intimidating to go in that gym, and I know that St. Peter's rarely, if ever, lost a home game. They didn't lose to us, either.

Mansfield St. Peter's 69, Lorain St. Mary's 31. That's right, 69-31. We got spanked. It was like men playing against boys. Even though St. Peter's wasn't very big, they boxed out for rebounds better than anyone we had ever played. We couldn't do anything against their defense. I got to play the last three or four minutes of the game, which I enjoyed, even though I thought I should have been playing more. In those minutes that I got in, I made two baskets, including banking one in from the top of the key, which was a really lucky shot, but one I thought might earn me some more playing time.

Monday at practice Coach Englund got us all together and said, "We're gonna make a change at point. Jackson, you're going to take over for Laszoff this week. Tommy, you'll be our new starter." Now I was really pissed. I asked to see Coach Englund in the coaches' office, and he told me to see him later. When I finally did go in after practice, he gave me the classic, "Keep working hard and you'll get your chance," speech.

We won our next three games to reach 6-1, and then we were going to play Avon High School on a Saturday night. We moved the game to the huge Admiral King gymnasium so that more people could get in to see the game. Admiral King's "The Shot Palace" seated about 3,000 fans, and the Avon-St. Mary's game was a huge game certain to draw lots of people, especially on a Saturday evening when a lot of the other area schools weren't playing. Avon, by the way, was outstanding. They were in the midst of a 66-game regular season win streak. It had been years since they had lost a regular—season game. They always seemed to have some bad luck in the tournament, but during their regular season they were darn near impossible to beat. The Eagles were led by Mark Wagar, a 6-8 center who went on to play at Ohio State.

We lost, 66-54. There was a huge crowd, and I got to play about two minutes in the entire game. I was really beginning to get upset about my lack of playing time.

The next Monday at practice Coach Englund got us all together and said, "We're gonna make a change at the point. Laszoff, you'll be starting this weekend against EC." As mad as I was right then, Tommy Jackson was at least that mad. He had worked hard, earned a starting position, and then lost it without really doing anything wrong. By changing the line-up it looks like the coach is blaming one guy for losing a game. The other four guys all stayed the same. Jackson and I both wanted to talk to Coach Englund, and we didn't want to wait until after practice. When I got my turn with him I said, "We win some games and then lose a game. We make a change. We win some games and then lose. We make a change. But this change isn't the one that should be made. When's it Francis' turn to get to start? This just isn't fair and I should be out there."

Guess what Coach Englund said? You guessed it . . . . "Keep working hard and you'll get your chance." I was beginning to believe that I might never get a chance to play.

All week at practice Jackson and I went full-go in every drill, every scrimmage, etc. We were both really trying to get more playing time. In my case, there were a few games where I had been trying to get ANY playing time. That would end soon.

We had a pep rally for every football game. Basketball, however, only merited pep rallies for special games, and the next game was special. We were going to go over to Elyria Catholic and play the Panthers. Remember when I told you that they had huge guys playing football? Most of those guys also played basketball, which meant they were going to be huge for that sport, too. Of course, we could battle them on the boards with George Rivers and Earl Winters and Fred Knillen. We might have been small in football, but we were plenty big in basketball. It's too bad these guys didn't play football, because they probably would have been pretty good.

At the pep rally on Friday afternoon Coach Englund was trying to get everyone really fired up. He was ranting and raving and shouted, "We're going to go over there and break that streak! We're going to go over there and win by ten!" The streak to which he was referring was this: the Panthers had NEVER lost a home game in their four-year old gym, called The Coliseum. It was a beautiful place. The building had been added to their school four or five years before. The building is a huge oval-shaped, light-colored brick building. When you walk in on ground level the playing floor is sunken into the ground. In fact, both sides of the gym have equal seating in upper and lower sections, and ground level is actually the split between the upper and the lower sections of seating. It has a large walkway all the way around the entire facility, so you could actually walk all around the gym at ground level and watch the game being played beneath you on the sunken floor. It's an awesome gym, and one that seemed to give the Panthers a great home-court advantage. The Panthers had this famous press that just gobbled teams up. That's how they won all those games in a row.

We started the game and were playing just OK. It was a pretty close game. In the middle of the second quarter Fred Knillen was called for his second foul. Fred had a pretty bad temper, and he could do some crazy things when he got mad. Within a few seconds after getting called for his second foul, he was called for his third foul. Officials didn't really like him very much, since he was sort of a hothead. Anyway, if you get called for three fouls in the first half you just have to sit down for a while. Coach Englund looked down the bench and HAD to put someone in. It was me. Now remember, we had four really good players, and when you took one of them out we were down to three really good players and two guys who weren't really expected to do much.

I had a pretty good game. I played the rest of the game and handled the pressure pretty well. Their supposedly unbeatable press really wasn't all that tough. I just dribbled through it and then passed the ball to someone else. EC did foul me a few times, and I hated shooting at The Coliseum. The clear glass backboards had a black pole running down through the back of the backboard. The pole was attached to the rest of the standard that hung from the wall. We never shot very well at EC, and we always blamed it on the "shooter's eye" backdrop with the black pole. I missed my first five free throws, and I missed them badly. The ball slipped off my hand and I shot five air balls. The shots did hit the backboard, but none of them drew iron (hit the rim).

We played very well as a team, and late in the game we led, 58-50. I was dribbling the ball up the floor against their press and I went all the way to the basket to shoot a lay-up. I made the shot, my only basket of the game, and I was fouled. I went to the free throw line and made the free throw, giving me three points for the game and one-out-of-six from the free throw line. Those were the last points of the game and we won, 61-50.

After the game everyone was all excited. We showered and got dressed and ready to leave. As I left the locker room I came through the door and saw Coach Englund being interviewed by several newspaper reporters. As I walked by I heard one guy ask our coach, "So, Jim, did you really think you were going to come over here and break the streak?"

Coach Englund answered him, "Yeah, I did. I told the kids at the pep rally today that we were going to come over here and win by ten." As he said this I walked past the interview area. "Hey, Francis," he said in front of the others, "You know if you would have missed that last foul shot instead of making it I would have been exactly right and we would have won by ten."

I never even thought about what I was going to say. It just came out. I looked back over my shoulder and said, "Maybe if I'd get to play a little more I would have made them all and we would have won by sixteen."

Oops. Coach Englund burst away from the reporters and attacked me. He grabbed me by the lapels of my sport coat and had me against the wall so fast it scared not only me, but also the newspaper guys. He had me up against the wall yelling, "Who do you think you are talking to me like that? You don't talk to a coach like that." He wasn't really raising his voice, but the intensity was clearly there. I WAS scared that time, and I clearly deserved everything I got.

The following Monday at practice Coach Englund announced the starting lineup for the next game. I was the starting point guard that week and started every game the rest of that year and the next year.

28

Biggy Rat Dies

We received word on January 13, 1969 that Sister Mary Donald (Biggy Rat) had died at the Immaculate Heart of Mary Mother House in Monroe, Michigan. To say that anyone at St. Mary's was terribly upset would probably be a bit of a lie. I don't think Sister Mary Donald had endeared herself to anyone at our school, particularly the students.

The funeral was going to be January 15, and the student body would be represented by the senior class officers: Leon Holiday, Tommy Jackson, my sister Veronica, and Fran Dunning. Fran, of course, was giving the rest of us lots of crap about how he was going to get to miss school for a day while the rest of us had to attend. Wrong! Enough of the nuns decided to attend the funeral that school was canceled for the day—and the four senior class officers were still expected to drive through the snow to Monroe to attend the funeral. Fran was pissed and we all laughed.

When the four students approached the casket, they walked up two-by-two and knelt at the little kneeler in front of the casket. My sister Veronica knelt next to Leon Holiday first. When Fran saw the emaciated body of Sister Mary Donald (she had died of cancer) he whispered, "That's Biggy Rat?" My sister and the others heard him say that and they then had to keep from laughing. My sister was trying very hard to stifle her laugh; her shoulders were actually shaking. A few other nuns came up to help Veronica because they thought she was sobbing and weeping. Boy were they wrong!

29

Slow-Down Basketball and a Stunning Upset

We averaged about 75 points a game, which meant we were really running and gunning. Teams tried to slow us down all sorts of ways, but it was usually pretty futile. St. John's Cantius, for example, really tried to stall. Their gym was in downtown Cleveland, and was actually upstairs above a bowling alley. It was the kind of place you probably think only existed in the movies. It had a stage at one end of the floor, and a huge pole right underneath the basket at the other end. The pole was wrapped in an old, gray tumbling mat so you didn't kill yourself if you went in too fast for a lay-up. The pole was just about on the playing floor, which was only about 60 or 65 feet long anyway. They tried to hold the ball on us and we eventually drilled them.

Our Lady of Lourdes had a gym that was actually a tile floor. It was very narrow and very short, too. Their gym had three rows of bleachers on each side, and that's it. When we played them we were playing our 1-3-1 zone, and on a small, narrow floor it was virtually impossible to get a good shot against an active 1-3-1 zone. We got the opening tip and went down the floor and scored, so we were ahead. They came down the floor and just stood there and held the ball. We let them. We eventually went out to try and pressure, but they had practiced holding the ball, so we couldn't get it away from them. At the end of the first quarter the score was 5-2. We were very anxious to play the game, but they were pretty good just passing the ball around. They played a tiny bit in the second quarter, and we led at the half, 12-7. They had to go to the basket a little bit in the third quarter, and that allowed us to get some things going, and we led, 24-12, at the end of the third quarter. Obviously, they had to play basketball in the fourth quarter or we were going to just sit back and let them hold the ball. Once they started running and shooting, they had no chance. We scored 30 points in the final quarter. Final score, 54-24.

As we got to the last week of the regular season, we had to play a league doubleheader. We had to travel to Cleveland St. Stanislaus on Friday evening and then return to Lorain and host Elyria Catholic in the league championship game. We had won every other league game, and so had Elyria Catholic, so all we had to do was beat St. Stan's to clinch at least a tie for the league championship. We never played EC in our gym because it was too small, so we always played them at Admiral King's big gym. We always played them on a Saturday night and there was always a huge crowd at the game.

Early in the next week Coach Englund called up the Admiral King coach and asked if we could get on their floor to practice. Remember that we were going to play for the league championship on that floor later in the week. Admiral King's Hall of Fame Coach, Mr. Elmer Meyers, wasn't really interested in St. Mary's just coming over to practice in his gym. He did know, however, that we were pretty good, as were his Admirals, the best public school team in Lorain. Rather than letting us just practice on the floor, he told Coach Englund that we could come over and scrimmage his public school kids during the week. The big, bad Admirals were in for quite a surprise.

We scrimmaged Admiral King High School on their court on Championship Week Tuesday. We all drove over to Admiral King and started warming up. Joey Laszoff was sick, so we only had nine guys ready to play. I played with both the first team and the second team that afternoon. We crushed the Admirals. We played six quarters and beat them, 120-90. I think we won all six quarters. They complained later that we had played our 1-3-1 zone against them, and that it was a defense they weren't prepared for, but the bottom line was we crushed the best public school team in Lorain late in the season. We were really hitting on all cylinders during that scrimmage, and things seemed to happen quite easily for us.

After the scrimmage I went in the locker room and just collapsed onto one of the benches. Coach Englund came in and talked to us and then dismissed the other guys to head home. I was still laying on the bench when he asked me what the problem was. I was almost in tears. I explained to him that I had played all six quarters and had not come off the floor. That meant six straight quarters of high-intensity, high pressure basketball against a tough public school team on a huge court. Coach Englund looked at Coach McComb and said, "Did he play the whole time?"

Coach McComb looked down at some papers he had been using to write down notes and said, "I think he did."

Coach Englund said to me, "Why didn't you say something? We could have given you a blow."

My answer was simple and direct. "I waited too long to get on the floor. I wasn't about to give up any of my time to someone else just to get off the floor." I think he understood.

Cleveland St. Stanislaus played a great game against us on Friday night. We weren't very sharp that night, and they pulled the huge upset, beating us, 38-37. We depended on our defense to lead us to lots of easy baskets, but that night they handled our defense pretty well, refused to give us any easy baskets, and held the ball on offense. Remember, we were averaging about 75 points a game, and they held us to half of that. It was a stunning upset. It also meant that we were now tied with EC for the league lead with 8-1 records. It meant that whoever won the Saturday night game at Admiral King would be the sole champion in the league.

There was a huge crowd on hand, with many fans coming from around the county to see this big game. We got the opening tip and Paul Downey ended up with the ball. He took about two dribbles towards our basket and jumped to shoot. I think he forgot where we were playing. In some of the small gyms we played in two dribbles from half-court would get you to about the free throw line. At Admiral King's "The Shot Palace" two dribbles got you about 28 feet away from the hoop. Nevertheless, Downey rose up and shot just about the most beautiful jump shot I've ever seen. Boom. Swish. St. Mary's 2, EC 0. (Remember, there was no three-point line in high school basketball in 1969) We then proceeded to outscore the Panthers 17-1 at the start of the game. They called two timeouts to try to slow us down, but we were on a roll.

As the game wore on the Panthers had an interesting game plan. They remembered that when we had played them a month before I was not a good free throw shooter. I actually wasn't a bad free throw shooter, just at their gym. When they were behind late in the game and they had to foul someone, it was me. During the game I made three baskets and eight foul shots for 14 points. It was my career high at the time and I actually led our team in scoring that night. All five starters scored in double figures that night, and we beat the Panthers.

After the game our students swarmed the floor, and it was a chaotic scene. There were lots of hugs, high-fives, etc. We had beaten our hated rivals in football and twice in basketball. The following week things turned around and weren't nearly so bright for the Fighting Irish.

30

Father Penny, Brenda Shine
& Bye-bye Fred Knillen

We finished the regular season 15-3 and were champions of the North Central Conference. Everyone was excited about the regular season and we were really ready to enter the tournament and go a long way. We were really rolling as a team. The history of St. Mary's basketball was about to change.

On Monday after the EC game and the end of the regular season, I was in a fourth period Religion class called *Christ, The Church, and Mary*. It was taught by a young priest named Father Nick Penny. He was sort of a jerk. He just thought he was a great teacher and he thought that because he was a priest he deserved respect. I guess I've always been bothered by people who think they DESERVE respect even if they haven't EARNED that respect. Father Penny was one of those people.

He was writing on the blackboard with a brand new piece of chalk. The chalk broke in half. He bent over, with his butt facing the class, to pick up the piece of chalk on the floor. At that moment Brenda Shine whistled. You know, the kind of whistle construction workers blow when a pretty girl goes by.

Father Penny turned around and stared at Fred Knillen, who was sitting right behind Brenda Shine and right next to me. "I heard that, Knillen. That will earn you a detention after school today," said the young priest.

"But, but, I didn't do anything," protested Knillen.

"You want to argue with me?" asked the priest.

"But I didn't do anything," said Knillen. "We've got the sectional basketball tournament this week. I can't stay after school. Besides that, I didn't do anything."

"That'll cost you another detention for tomorrow. You want to keep going? I've got all week," said the priest.

Knillen shut up for a few moments, but when Father Penny turned around and faced the board again Knillen said to Brenda Shine, "Fuck you." He told her that because she hadn't spoken up when he was in the argument with the priest.

Father Penny heard Knillen say "Fuck you." He assumed that the statement was aimed at him, and he blew up. He kicked Knillen out of the room and sent him to the office. The young priest then went and told Principal Sister Mary Neumann that Fred had said the words to him. Knillen was suspended from school and kicked off the basketball team. Our leading scorer (19.8 points per game) got kicked off the team. That wasn't right.

When I heard what had happened to Knillen I made an appointment with the Principal. I went in to her office and explained exactly what had happened, which, I'm sure was different than the story she had heard from the priest. I emphasized that Knillen was saying the bad words to Brenda, NOT Father Penny. That should have made a world of difference. It didn't. Sister Mary Neumann looked at me across the table and said, "People shouldn't be using language like that in a Catholic school no matter who they say it to." She was not being reasonable. I almost felt like saying it to her. Our season was ready to go down the drain because of something someone had said.

I explained what had happened to Coach Englund later in the day and he was really mad. He went and talked to Sister Mary Neumann and she wouldn't budge. Knillen was gone. Coach Englund actually went and talked to Monsignor Duffy, who really had the final say on everything involved with the parish and the school. The great Monsignor, who was really on his last legs, wouldn't just override Sister Mary Neumann's decision. He did, however, tell Coach Englund, "Professor, do what you think you have to do." (Coach Englund and most of the other coaches always had a unique relationship with the Monsignor. The Monsignor loved sports and he thought they were very important in young peoples' lives. Father Duffy, for whatever reason, called Coach Englund "Professor.")

Coach Englund, after his talk with Monsignor Duffy, had a really tough decision to make. Should he ignore the Principal's decision and go ahead and play Knillen? He probably could have gotten by doing that and saying that Father Duffy told him it was alright. The problem was this: The Diocese of Cleveland had already announced that St. Mary's Academy would close its doors at the end of that school year. The new Lorain Catholic High School was going to open its doors in the fall of 1969. Coach Englund obviously wanted to be a part of that new school. Sister Mary Neumann was in line to be the first Principal at Lorain Catholic. If Coach Englund ignored her decision now, could he even count on getting a job when the new school opened in a few months? The Monsignor told him to do what he had to do. He did. Fred Knillen was no longer part of the Fighting Irish basketball squad.

We won three tournament games, including a huge win over Clearview for the sectional championship, and we headed for the districts. We lost to a school called Badger. The remaining "Big Three" (Paul Downey, Earl Winters, and George Rivers) all scored in double figures, but without the defensive pressure and especially the scoring of Fred Knillen, we couldn't get it done. Coach Englund later took two teams to the state finals, but he still, to this day, claims the last St. Mary's team was as good as any team he coached and might have had a chance to make it to Columbus for state if Father Penny didn't misunderstand a whistle.

Just as a quick post script, Father Penny, within a few years, left the priesthood and married one of the nuns at our school. I don't recall her name because she was only there a year or so, but I do remember that everyone called her Sister Miniskirt, since she wore a habit that didn't reach the floor, but only went below her knees. She also was the first nun I can ever remember who actually showed hair. The habit around her face didn't cover her hair, and she had a large section of hair sticking out from the veil on top of her head.

31

Coach Flowers and the Football Workout

We lost to Badger on Tuesday night. Coach Flowers had started football workouts after school on Mondays-Wednesdays-Fridays. The guys who weren't playing basketball had spent time in the cafeteria lifting and conditioning for about two months. St. Mary's didn't have a weight room, but Coach Flowers had managed to gather plenty of free weights, benches and bars, and set up stations in the cafeteria for the guys to work out.

I came to school Wednesday without any workout clothes. I had just finished a tough basketball season which had followed a tough football campaign. Tennis was going to start practice the following Monday. I didn't see any reason to start football weight lifting and conditioning when I was only going to get to work out one or two days.

After school Coach Flowers saw me and asked, "Did you bring stuff to suit up for lifting and conditioning?"

"No, Coach, I didn't bring my workout clothes."

"Why not? You should be ready to work out for football," he asked.

"I haven't had a day off after school for three years. I've had a game or practice every day for every day I've been in high school. My mom told me she wanted me to come home after school for just a couple of days," I explained.

He looked at me with one of his very serious expressions. "A couple of days? A couple of days? Have your stuff here Friday to work out."

I really couldn't understand why he wanted me to work out on Friday. Tennis started Monday. All a Friday workout would do for me was to make me sore. However, you don't question Coach Flowers when he tells you to do something.

After school Friday everyone got dressed. Since basketball was over the football workouts had been moved up to the gym instead of in the cafeteria. I was matched up with Will Fitzpatrick. There were about ten "stations" lined up in the gym. Each group of two or three guys went from station to station. Coach Flowers moved from station to station with Will and me, showing us the proper technique for each lift and exercise. When we came to the Upright Rows, one of the funniest things ever happened.

Coach Flowers took the barbell with weights on it and was showing Will and me how to do it correctly. Coach always wore a white shirt and tie to school, and after school he simply removed the tie and changed shoes. So here he is, showing us how to do an upright row with a white shirt on. He did the exercise as he described it.

"Keep your hands very close to your chest. As you do the exercise, your hands have to remain close to your chest." As he said this and did it a second time, his thumb, as it was holding the barbell, hooked on his shirt pocket. As he lowered the weighted barbell, he tore his shirt pocket right off. The pocket just flapped down, still attached at the bottom of the pocket, but sort of just hanging there on his shirt.

I was standing right next to him. I saw the whole thing. My jaw was shaking and I was biting though my bottom lip trying not to laugh. I stood there and looked at him as he looked over at me. I was doing everything I could to not laugh. He looked at me doing this and said, "You think that's pretty damn funny, don't you Francis?"

I could barely get out the words. "Nuh, nuh, no sir." My whole face was shaking.

"You're damn right it's funny," he said. "Go ahead and laugh."

You know what? Once he told me it was OK to laugh I didn't really think it was very funny. I didn't laugh that day, but I've laughed about it plenty of times since.

One other thing happened that Friday after basketball ended. Coach Englund, who was also the school's athletic director, told me that Mr. Mike Parrish was going to be the new tennis coach. Mr. Parrish was a second-year teacher and had acted as the trainer for the football team. I approached him and said, "Hey, I hear you're going to be the new tennis coach this year. Are you a player? Do you know anything about the game?" My hope was that we had found a diamond in the rough who could really help our tennis team move to another level.

His answer? He smiled and said, "Nope. Never played. I'm gonna read up on it over the weekend."

The tennis season was sure to be interesting.

32

The Open-Minded Sister Tubby Rita

Sister Helen Rita Dorsey was our junior English teacher. I believe she thought she was one of the greatest teachers in the entire history of education. She was so old that she had been around for a significant portion of the history of education.

As mentioned earlier, there were two Sister Rita's at St. Mary's Academy. Rita The Rabbit taught Latin, English, French. She had these huge teeth that stuck out, hence the nickname Rita The Rabbit. Tubby Rita was this short, heavy-set nun. Picture a mailbox on a corner. Now put a face in it. That's what Tubby Rita looked like.

The absolute worst thing about Tubby Rita was that she actually thought she was a great teacher. Wait, that's only the second worst thing about Tubby Rita. The worst thing about her was that she was never, ever wrong. About anything. She was never wrong. She was also always right, which could be different than never wrong. She would ask us what we thought this poem or story might mean. Let's face it the meaning of a poem is pretty subjective and personal. It's not really objective. What one poem means to me might be completely different than what that poem means to you. Right? Wrong! She knew exactly what every poem and every symbol in every story meant. Hell, she was old enough that maybe she had known the poets we were studying personally, but that would be the only way she could absolutely tell us what a poem or story meant. I think that English teachers are notorious for interjecting their opinions into subjective topics like poems and stories.

I was the Vice-President of Student Council for the school year 1968-69. I thought it was very unfair (I still do) that teachers get to evaluate students every nine weeks (grading periods) but students never get to evaluate teachers. Virtually every college in America now has some form of student evaluation, but high schools usually don't, and no high school had an evaluation procedure which included students in 1969. I thought that was wrong and set out to do something about it.

One day at lunch another Student Council Representative, Bill Ducek, and I were talking about this very topic. He agreed with me that it could be very valuable for students to evaluate teachers. He and I sat down and wrote out a fifteen-statement evaluation for teachers. I took it home that night and typed it out. Each of the fifteen statement/questions had 5-4-3-2-1-0 next to it, allowing students to circle whichever number they deemed appropriate. One of the questions, number 5, said simple, "Is this teacher open-minded or close-minded?" Students were to circle "5" for Open-Minded and "0" for Close-Minded. That was just one of the questions, but it was the one question specifically written for Sister Tubby Rita.

I made an appointment with Sister Mary Neumann, the Principal, and went in and showed her to copy of the teacher evaluation. Bill Ducek went with me to talk to the Principal. "Well, Mr. Francis and Mr. Ducek, this is very interesting. I can't make the teachers be evaluated by the students, but if you go around and get permission from all the teachers, I will run off enough copies of this evaluation for you. I just want you to promise that the teachers get a copy of the results and so do I. Okay?" We then had to go around and ask every teacher in the building if he/she would be willing to be evaluated by the students. By asking them, I thought that it sort of defeated the whole idea, but, surprisingly, every teacher we asked said that it would be alright to evaluate them.

Tubby Rita, of course, thought that she was the greatest English teacher in the entire world, so she quickly and happily agreed. Sister Mary Neumann printed the copies of the evaluation form, and Bill Ducek and I helped pass them out. That also meant that we had to count them when they were returned. I began to think that this was a really foolish and time-consuming thing to do just to prove to Tubby Rita that she was close-minded. Finally, we completed the results.

On the day I handed them to Tubby Rita she gave our class a reading assignment and looked over the results. No one was reading, as we all watched her. When she got down to question number five, which was written just for her, she stopped and looked sort of puzzled.

"Mr. Francis, I don't understand these results," she said.

"What's the problem, Sister?" I responded.

"I don't understand the results for question number five."

"What was the question," I asked, faking ignorance. I knew exactly what the question was and what the results were.

"It's the question about being open-minded and close-minded," she said.

I again faked ignorance. "What were the results of the question and what's the problem?"

"It says here that 138 out of 151 students in my classes circled '5, Close-minded.' I'm not close-minded."

"Well, Sister," I tried to explain, "What I think people are saying is that sometimes they have ideas about poems and stories and you tell them they are wrong."

"That doesn't make me close-minded," she argued.

"Well, Sister," I tried to be diplomatic. "I think there are certain things in English that are open to opinion. What a story or a poem means is really sort of subjective, don't you think?"

"That doesn't make me close-minded!" She was beginning to get fired up.

"Well, Sister, I think . . . ."

"Listen to me," she screamed as she pounded on the podium in front of the class, "I am open-minded and that's all there is to it!!!!"

I think that pretty much summed up the students' feelings.

One other Tubby Rita story. We were studying Shakespeare's classic *Romeo and Juliet*. Tubby Rita was trying to get everyone to understand why the characters would act in the way they did. "Romeo and Juliet are in love. What does 'Love' mean?"

I usually answered questions in class, but even I wouldn't touch this one. Do you know any high school student who would answer this question? What are they supposed to say, "Well, Sister, I think that love means three things. There are actually three kinds of love, love of the mind, love of the body, and love of the heart." What high school student is going to answer that question? None that I know.

Sister Rita was also one of those teachers who became very upset when she asked a question and no one answered it. "What does 'Love' mean?" was one of those questions. She started to get upset. "C'mon," she said. "What does 'Love' mean?" Again, silence.

She looked over at JD Szollzy, who was dating Alexa Wheatley, and said, "Mr. Szollzy, I see you walking around with Miss Wheatley all the time. I see you carrying her books. Are you in love with her?"

JD was going to have none of this. "I don't know," he said quickly.

"Well don't give up so easily," she said. "What is love?"

JD, who carried a bit of attitude with him wherever he went said, "I said I don't know."

The nun kept on with him. "C'mon, tell me what you think love is. Are you in love with Miss Wheatley?"

JD had heard just about enough. "I said I don't know, so get off my back."

Sister Tubby Rita, in front of 25 high school juniors, said the classic line, "If you don't know what love is, go out and get some."

She obviously didn't want to say it quite like that. There was silence for a second or two, and then I sort of laughed. Everyone began to think about what she had said and then the single laugh turned into a full-class explosion. Sister Rita looked up, realized what she had said, and then tried to get us to get back on track. "Let's go on," she said. "Let's go on." There was no way. We went crazy. We had started a tradition that when someone, a teacher or a student, said something that was really off-the-wall, crazy or stupid or whatever, we would write down what he/she said on the back page of our notebook, and date it, keeping it for posterity.

Every guy in the class turned to the last page of his notebook and wrote down, "Tubby Rita says if you don't know what love is, go out and get some." We dated it. We then looked at the girls in the class and just pointed. "Don't you think we should listen to Sister Rita," we asked with our facial expressions.

33

How Did They Survive?
1969's Crazy Seniors

The St. Mary's baseball team practiced and played home games at Longfellow Park on the east side of Lorain. The Park is pretty large, with tennis courts, four baseball diamonds, a swimming pool, and plenty of room for Coach Flowers to just about kill us during pre-season football workouts.

Longfellow is about two miles from St. Mary's Academy, with the first five blocks through downtown Lorain. After crossing Broadway Avenue you have to go over the Lorain Bascule Bridge, which spans the Black River. The bridge is really awesome, as it opens straight up from each side when a large ship passes beneath. After crossing the bridge to the east side, there are numerous stoplights and stop signs.

Just like the football players had to get to Lakeview Park on our own to practice, so too did the baseball players have to get to Longfellow Park. Everyone shared rides, and it wasn't uncommon to see six or eight guys stuffed in to one guy's car. That's what happened on one of the legendary days.

Senior Jim Guinness had an old beat-up car that he drove to practice just about every day. One day, as seven guys piled in, he said, "Hold on today boys, cuz I ain't stoppin'." What he meant was that he was going to drive straight to Longfellow without stopping even once. He was going to drive through every stoplight and every stop sign without stopping. He did sort of slow down a few times, but he drove the entire way to Longfellow without stopping. There has to be at least ten traffic lights between St. Mary's and Longfellow, as well as numerous stop signs.

Another legendary baseball story involved Guinness and Fred Knillen. Knillen was allowed to play baseball even after he was kicked off the basketball team. He was the best basketball player in the school and the best baseball player in the school. He was long and lean and had a great whipping action on his arm as a pitcher. When he wasn't pitching he played centerfield.

One day it was drizzling rain. It was gray and misting, with fog and a low sky. Just a very dismal day. The Fighting Irish had a home game that afternoon at Longfellow. No one thought the game would get played because of the weather, but the game started. A few innings into the game it started raining a little heavier, so the umpire sent the players off the field. The visitors went and sat in their bus, while the St. Mary's kids went to their cars. A bunch of the players, Knillen included, went to Guinnness' car. They were totally bored and the windows were already fogged over, so one of them pulled out a couple of cigars. The players lit up the cigars and puffed away.

A short time later the rain slowed down enough to continue the game, and the coaches went around and knocked on car windows, telling players to report back to the field. Knillen was right in the middle of a great cigar. He took it with him. He went out to centerfield and was smoking the cigar, which was placed between the fingers of his glove. Between half innings he took the cigar out of the glove and left it in centerfield, where it stayed lit for a couple of innings. Incredible!

34

St. Mary's Last Undefeated Team

The 1969 St. Mary's Tennis Team was deep, balanced, and undefeated. We completed the season 13-0. Despite the fact that I had won the Lorain City Championship, I played number two singles and number two doubles. One of my classmates, Joe Wendell, came from an excellent tennis family, and he really wanted to play number one singles. Hey, good for him. He actually did beat me in the preseason, so he deserved to play that position.

I played number two, Fran Dunning played number three, Phil O'Keefe played number four, and Troy Dunnehy played number five. We handled every team we played. Of course we didn't have to play Admiral King, since we had already had the argument with them about playing format.

First-year coach Mr. Mike Parrish drove us to the matches. I can't really say that he coached, because he had never even played tennis, but he did open the cans of balls correctly and fill out the paperwork for the line-ups. One other thing—we convinced him that we had to have something to eat after school before matches. We told him that we often ran out of energy if we didn't have anything to eat from lunchtime until six or seven o'clock in the evening. It was a fun season, particularly since we had fun guys on the team and we ended the season undefeated, which is no small task for any team in any sport.

35

No Track Team? Says Who?

Lorain St. Mary's Academy did not sponsor a track team, but each spring a group of guys got together and asked to represent the school at the North Central Conference track meet. It's really amazing that, even though we didn't have a track team, we had crowned some NCC track champions in the previous few years. For example, Mick Dunning won the 100-yard dash one year, and Joe Allen had won the shot put. My junior year a bunch of us decided that we would represent St. Mary's at the league track meet.

Will Fitzpatrick and I decided that we would compete in the 880-yard run. I liked the 880 because it was two laps around the track, and it didn't seem like anyone actually sprinted the whole way. It was just a nice, middle-distance run. We actually went over to George Daniel Stadium to practice running the curves, and we seemed fairly confident that we could at least finish the race, if not place. While we were practicing at George Daniel Stadium, we noticed a teammate of ours practicing the pole vault. Tommy Jackson was working out with the public school kids, and he seemed to be better than any of them.

On the day of the league track meet, the dozen or so of us competing went to Elyria Catholic. We checked in with the meet officials to make sure we were entered properly, and then we began to warm up. Actually, I stretched a little and jogged up and back on the football field, and I was ready to go.

Another tennis player, a sophomore, Troy Dunnehy, was entered in the mile run. When it was just about time for him to get ready for the race, he took his sweatpants off and continued to stretch and jog. He jogged on the infield up and down the field a few times. Troy didn't realize that he didn't have any shorts on. All he had on under his sweatpants was his jockstrap. He jogged up and back in front of the grandstand a few times, not realizing that everyone was watching him. Will Fitzpatrick was the first to realize what was going on, and he rushed to Troy's side and gave him some shorts to wear.

Will and I both ran pretty hard in the 880, but, without proper training, we were blown away by the real track athletes. Actually, we thought we did pretty well. Will finished sixth with a time of 2:10, while I was right behind him in seventh place with a time of 2:12. Will almost placed and scored points in the race, and I was pleased because I hadn't finished last.

Tommy Jackson, by the way, won the pole vault easily. He went on to pole vault at the State Meet and finished in second place, vaulting 13-8 ½. That is a truly incredible height for a guy who wasn't even on a track team.

35

"When One Door Closes . . . . Another Opens"

That was actually the class motto for The Class of 1969. I gave them the idea. My oldest brother Bob had given me a book of proverbs and sayings, and I found that saying in the book. My sister Veronica was the class secretary, and she was sort of responsible for coming up with some possible class mottoes. I gave her that idea, she took it in to Sister Mary Neumann, and it was accepted shortly thereafter.

At the end of every school year St. Mary's sponsored an athletic banquet. A new face appeared at the banquet, and his announcement shocked us all, and disappointed most. Father Thomas Boone was the newly-appointed Director of the yet-to-be-opened Lorain Catholic High School. Father Boone came to the banquet and was introduced as the Lorain Catholic Director. He stood and made an announcement. He said that Lorain Catholic had great respect for St. Mary's and its tradition. He said that Lorain Catholic would never dream of stealing the colors or nickname of St. Mary's. We were stunned. We all just expected Lorain Catholic to continue using the Green and Gold and the nickname The Fighting Irish. We not only expected that to occur, we wanted it to occur. We weren't going to be The Fighting Irish? What was up with that? We were devastated. How could he do that? How could he make that decision? The next day at school everyone talked about the fact that we wouldn't be the Fighting Irish the next year. I don't know anybody who was pleased about that, but I guess they wanted new traditions to start at Lorain Catholic High School.

36

Another Great Cheerleading Controversy

I dated Bridgett Mulroney throughout my junior year. I didn't know any better, and I thought I was truly in love with that girl. In the spring of 1969 there was another controversial cheerleading situation. Once Father Boone announced that St. Mary's would officially close and Lorain Catholic would officially open in the fall, the enrollment doors to the new school swung open. St. Mary's had 80 students, 40 boys and 40 girls, in every class. No more. Lorain Catholic was going to admit more students than that, and, in fact, they were welcoming transfers in from other schools. The LC administration thought that it would only be fair if all students enrolled at the new school would be given the opportunity to try out for cheerleading, sports, etc. So, in the spring of 1969 there were girls trying out for cheerleading who were total strangers to us and the judges. These were girls who were going to be students at Lorain Catholic in the fall. No one thought that any of the strangers had a chance to actually make it, but several did. In fact, a senior-to-be, Dominique Pavlak, made varsity cheerleading for the next year. Guess who didn't make it? That's right, Bridgett Mulroney. My mother and my sister thought, "What goes around, comes around," but I was nearly as upset as Bridgett when she didn't make it. Who was this stranger coming in to our school and taking my girlfriend's spot on the cheerleading squad? Bridgett and her friends immediately hated Dominique, as you can imagine.

Early in the summer of 1969 I broke up with Bridgett. I heard she was going out on a date with Joe Wendell. I was pretty upset, because he was the number one man on the tennis team and I thought he was a friend of mine. Guys will be guys, however, so I really didn't blame him all that much. I was crushed that Bridgett would do this to me. I drove around looking for them the night they supposedly went out. I found them parked at Lakeview Park in the make-out area overlooking the lake. I actually pulled up behind Joe's red Camaro and flashed my lights. I was with Will Fitzpatrick, and I was pissed. The worst thing of all—the windows were all fogged over and I couldn't see them sitting up in the car. I was devastated!

When the football team started our summer workouts the cheerleaders would often bring us pop sickles or watermelon after the workouts. The first time they did that I noticed the new cheerleader, Dominique Pavlak. Wow. She had long blond hair and a great smile. That very night I asked the cheerleader captain and a very good friend of mine, Grace Orsini, who the new girl was. I had forgotten that she was the girl who took Bridgett's spot on the cheerleading squad. Grace introduced me to Dominique, and I was immediately attracted. She was an intriguing young lady. Nothing like Bridgett, she was outgoing and almost a bit of a smart-ass. I liked that. The second time she came to one of the workouts I asked her if I could call her up. She said yes and had Grace give me the number later.

I began a relationship with Dominique Pavlak.

37

Pre-Season Football Exploits

The 1969 Lorain Catholic football season for me actually began on June 30. That was the day I cut my sideburns, which I had always worn quite long. I didn't cut them voluntarily, because I thought I looked pretty good in sideburns. I cut them because Coach Flowers had said, "This year we're adding a new training rule. Well, it won't actually be a training rule, but it will be a rule and we will stick damn to it. No players will be allowed to wear long hair or long sideburns." Considering that Bert Knouwer and I were the only two guys on the team who had sideburns of any length, the rule was obviously directed right at us. Since Bert was one of our captains and a guy Coach Flowers really liked, it appeared that the rule was aimed right at me. I almost raised my hand when he told us about the rule and asked, "How long is long?"

The actual start of practice in the state of Ohio during the summer of 1969 was July 1. On that date coaches could begin preseason conditioning programs. Get this. No footballs or other equipment could be present, but coaches could work with athletes on conditioning programs. That just means it was legal for coaches to work the hell out of athletes without doing anything football-related. That sounds like fun, huh?

At Lorain Catholic we like to think we work harder than anyone in the state of Ohio. Our workouts are only about thirty-five or forty minutes long, but they are a very intense thirty-five or forty minutes. We never stopped moving the entire time. There was really no such thing as a rest period during a Coach Flowers-run conditioning period. We were extremely quick and in great shape, because that's how we worked.

I arrived at the field at Longfellow Park at 7:15 with Mackie MacGregor and Bert Knouwer. There were about 25 other guys there. There was also one coach: Bill Dunning. He hated me. He's the guy who had beaten the crap out of me at practice the previous year when they were trying to make me a center. He liked me about as much as I liked him. He thought I was a smart-ass, which I was.

Coach Flowers appeared at exactly 7:25. He always appeared at exactly 7:25. He blew his whistle and we assembled into rows of six players. We stretched and did our quickness drills. We are the only team I've ever seen do quickness drills like these, but it's really what we hang our hat on. Since we are usually so small, it's what we have to depend upon to be successful.

After the stretching and quickness drills, we went to stations. There were seven stations, and we spent two minutes at each station, with ten seconds to move to the next station. After every group had completed every station, we began the running portion. We started with twenty-yard sprints and advanced up to fifty-yarders, and then returned to twenty-yarders. At that point we were basically exhausted, and then and only then did we begin "Packer Drill." I don't know who invented Packer Drill, but Vince Lombardi made it famous in the 60's with the Packers. You run in place with your knees high, and on the coach's signal (usually the whistle) you dive onto the ground and jump to your feet running in place again. Every football team does it and everyone probably has a different name for it, but in the late 1960's the Packers were a team to emulate, and that's what we called it.

When we actually finished the workout, we gathered around Coach Flowers and knelt down on one knee. He gave us an inspirational talk that concluded the workout. He's a great speaker, and he never fails to pump us up. These workouts were going to continue ever Monday-Wednesday-Friday throughout the month of July. Helmets and football cleats could be worn starting August 1, and footballs could be used.

We found out that senior guard-defensive end JD Szollzy was out for a month with a hernia. That's JD's second hernia in two years. Everybody is wondering what JD is doing to get all those hernias.

38

A Big Gamble To Be Crazy

We had been working out for three full weeks, doing the same grind. I figured it was time to liven things up. I knew I had to time this crazy act just right or risk getting caught by Coach Flowers (and then getting killed!).

I drove to practice at Longfellow Park in my family's 1961 Buick convertible. The top was down. I brushed my longish hair into an afro-looking thing and tied a bright-red headband around my head. I had on a pair of sunglasses with only one lens, and I had on a pair of painted-white shoes. I drove around Longfellow Park and came in from the east so that I was coming towards the team and they could see me from several hundred yards away. The radio was blaring as loud as it could, and I drove right by everyone going about 70 miles an hour with a lit cigar in my mouth. I turned the corner and headed back onto the field and screeched to a halt on the middle of the practice field. I jumped from the car without opening the door and walked over to the rest of the team. They were all laughing hysterically. I simply said, with the lit cigar between my teeth, "I don't feel like practicing tonight, do you?" I then quickly ran back to my car and moved it to where it was supposed to be parked. I timed it just right and actually had time to change into my sneakers before the coaches arrived.

Obviously, had I not timed it exactly right and if Coach Flowers had seen me, I would have been killed on the spot. Was it worth it?

39

To The Moon!
My Only Date With Grace Orsini

One of my best female friends was Grace Orsini. She always seemed to be dating one of my best friends (either Mackie MacGregor or Will Fitzpatrick) and I always seemed to be dating one of her best friends (Bridgett Mulroney and, eventually, Dominique Pavlak). Well, even great friends need to try things out once in awhile.

On July 20, 1969 I took Grace Orsini out on a date. I remember saying that, "What the heck. We're such good friends we should probably go out on at least one date." We started the evening at The Ranch House, a restaurant in downtown Lorain. I had a Ranchburger, steak fries, and a tossed salad with blue cheese dressing. After dinner we went to the Amherst Theatre to watch the wonderful and romantic classic, *Romeo and Juliet.* After a wonderful dinner and great movie we went back to Grace's house where history was going to be made. (I wish I could say that I had some lurid details about something exciting between the two of us, but that just didn't happen) Instead, we sat in Grace's house, which overlooked Lake Erie, and watched television with her mother and little sister.

At 10:56 PM that evening Neil Armstrong became the first man to walk on the moon. I wish the night had been more historic for me, but things don't always work out in real life the way they do in your dreams. The worst thing about the evening occurred as I was leaving. Grace walked me out to my car. I was excited for a good night kiss at the very least. As she got close to me in my arms and I started to kiss her, she started laughing. What? What was this? I tried again. She started laughing again. A third try and the same results.

"What's wrong?" I asked. "Am I that bad of a kisser that it's funny?"

"Oh no," she said. "It's just that we're such good friends that I can't even think about kissing you for real."

I really wanted to tell her to try, but I just got in my car and drove home. At least the night was historic for one good reason. Grace really did everything she could to get Dominique Pavlak and me together after that, and I really wasn't one to argue about getting hooked up with someone as nice and as hot and as smart as Dominique.

40

Senior Weekend At Bay Point

Bay Point is a seasonal park across the Sandusky Bay from Cedar Point. It's basically a trailer park with campers, tents, and other places for people to stay. There's a nine-hole golf course, plenty of boat ramps, a fabulous white-sand beach, and good old Lake Erie. Bert Knouwer's parents owned a trailer at Bay Point, and Friday night, August 1, just about all of the seniors headed right there after practice.

The drive to Bay Point from Lorain was about an hour, so we really didn't arrive until almost 10:00. The Knouwer's had a small TV, and some of us watched the old college-all-star game. A team of college all-stars were playing the Joe Namath-led World Champion New York Jets, who had won the previous year's Super Bowl. They don't play this game anymore, but back then it was really the very first football game on television each year.

By midnight everyone was ready for bed. There were five beds available inside the trailer, and there were nine of us. I volunteered to sleep outside, and I quickly convinced Jimmy Sullivan to join me. The other two guys who slept outside were Will Fitzpatrick and Jeff Brent. They didn't volunteer, but I think they were sort of kicked out of the trailer. It might have had something to do with Jeff Brent's ability to fart on command, but I'm not sure.

The next day was filled with swimming, water-skiing, golfing, and sitting around. It was a great day. I thought we were really pulling together as a group of senior leaders for the upcoming football season. Since Bert Knouwer knew most of the people who spent the summer at Bay Point, he had arranged a big football game for the beach that evening. We had nine guys on our team, and we jogged to the field in single file, with our old St. Mary's jerseys on. We looked sharp. That was just about the only thing we had going for us. The self-titled Bay Point All-Stars were ready to play. They had brought some "ringers" in, college guys, to play us.

On the game's first play they sent this tall, geeky-looking kid down the field for a long pass. I was playing in the secondary with Robbie Cavellini and Conor Flanary. After the receiver got about 50 yards from the line of scrimmage I yelled over to Flanary, "Let him go. They can't throw it that far." Flanary stopped chasing the kid, and, just then, their quarterback uncorked a 60-yard pass that softly nestled into the hands of the tall, geeky-looking kid. Touchdown Bay Point All-Stars.

When we fell behind three touchdowns to one, we went to all extremes, inserting "The Golden Arm" (Mackie MacGregor) into the game at quarterback. We eventually tied the game at four touchdowns apiece, and it was almost getting dark on the beach. Some of their players just left. Some went down and went swimming. They had plenty of substitutes, so they just kept switching guys in and out. We decided that we wouldn't quit until we were ahead in the game.

Danny Jackson ran a pattern across the middle of the field and Mackie threw him the ball. Jackson dove for the ball just as a Bay Point All-Star dove from the other direction. The two players' heads collided. There was a loud-but-dull thud as they hit. Both players just stayed still, but the Bay Point All-Star rolled over a few seconds later. Jackson stayed pretty still. He was knocked out.

All the while we had been playing there had been some girls watching the game. They were very rude and had really been giving us a bad time. One of the girls went to get some cold water and some ice, but the others were still sitting around and mouthing off. One of them said something like, "I hope he's dead," or something like that.

Robbie Cavellini turned toward them and said something like, "Why don't you just shut the hell up over there?" The girl who had been mouthing off was the girlfriend of one of the Bay Point All-Stars, and he sort of got in Cavellini's face and told him to watch how he talked to the girls. Cavellini just said they had been hassling us the whole time and they were worthless.

Now, as Jackson still lay unconscious in the sand, the Bay Point kid and Cavellini were ready to fight. It was a very tense scene for a few minutes. Cavellini wasn't going to back down from anybody, and the other kid had numbers and size on his side, so he wasn't going to back down either. The other kid told us that he could get us kicked right out of the park if he wanted to. We were visitors, he reminded us, and he could kick us out. Cavellini said, "What, you can't say anything you want around here? What, do you own the place?"

The kid's answer was priceless. He said, "You betchum."

Cavellini looked at him and started to laugh right in his face. "You whatchum?"

"You betchum." None of us had ever heard that line before. "You betchum." What is that? We all just laughed at the kid and the fight was defused. We finally got Danny Jackson to wake up, but we were worried about him the rest of the evening. I thought it might be interesting to make up the story of how he got hurt, so Conor Flanary and I kept telling him everything BUT what actually happened. He had been knocked out cold, so he didn't remember anything.

After dinner that evening, just about all of us went back to the beach where there was a big bonfire. We watched the fireworks from the great Cedar Point amusement park, which is right across the Sandusky Bay from Bay Point. I ended up the evening at some girl's trailer. I had just met her at the bonfire, but, since I'm a friendly sort of guy, I ended up back at her place around a smaller campfire her parents had started. I must have stayed out pretty late, because eventually Mr. Knouwer sent Jimmy Sullivan and Will Fitzpatrick out to find me. I was sitting around the campfire having a great time talking to people I had just met a few hours before when the girl who had brought me to the trailer looked out onto the alley between rows of trailers and said, "Aren't those your friends standing over there?"

Sure enough, I looked out and there were Sullivan and Fitzpatrick peering in towards the fire. They told me that Mr. Knouwer was really upset. When I finally made it back to the Knouwer's trailer just about everyone was asleep. Mr. Knouwer sort of yelled at me for just wandering off without telling anyone where I was going.

Sunday morning at Bay Point was really interesting. We all got up and went to Mass, but no one had brought any dress clothes, so we were all dressed in shorts and sandals. We went to Marblehead, Ohio to this church that offered a "Vacation Mass," which meant that people were dressed like they were on vacation, which we were. Conor Flanary fell asleep out on the steps of the church and we had to wake him to bring him in for communion.

We finally all drove back to Lorain Sunday evening after a weekend that was supposed to draw us closer together as a group of seniors playing football.

The next day at practice we were all dragging a bit. We were all pretty tired from the weekend. The practice really sucked. It sucked not only because we were tired, but it sucked because another coach was there to yell at us. Assistant Coach Ken Havrady was there. I think Coach Havrady liked Mackie MacGregor less than Coach Flowers, which means he didn't like him at all. Unfortunately for me, Coach Havrady didn't like me either, so every single time he saw me not hustling he would start yelling. He seemed to catch me doing this a lot.

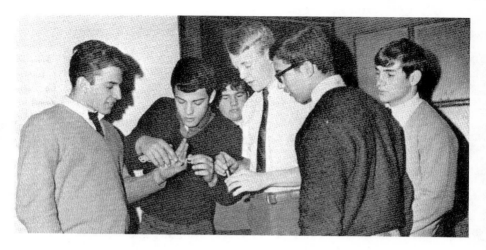

It may seem like we're just messing around in the hallway, but I am actually sizing Robbie Cavellini for his class ring. Will Fitzpatrick is in the white shirt, JD Szollzy is next to Will in the dark sweater, and Rod Achter is looking on.

This is Father Penny. He dropped the chalk and eventually got Fred Knillen kicked off the basketball team, ruining our chances to go to state. Thanks a lot.

The front door of St. Mary's Academy that we entered every day.

St. Mary's Academy at the corner of Reid and Seventh Street in Lorain, Ohio.

At the induction of the 1967 St, Mary's team into the Lorain Sports' Hall of Fame in May 2006. Coach Flowers is holding the t-shirt. To his left is Mick Dunning, our greatest player. Behind Dunning, holding the program is my brother Jack, the quarterback on that great team. I'm right behind Coach Flowers.

The era of Secondary education at St. Mary's ended with Commencement on June 3, 1969.

Another view of St. Mary's, specifically Johnston Hall. In that building we had the gym, the cafeteria, the library, and the Home Ec classroom.

Robbie Cavellini and me reading poetry as the emcees of the annual Senior Follies. We performed under the title "The Kings of Conceit." I can see that for Robbie, but for me?

Coach Englund making the first basket in the new Lorain Catholic gym that was finished halfway through the season. He made the shot on his first try!

Mackie MacGregor singing during the Senior Follies. He really can sing. JD Szollzy is in the background playing the accordion.

I'm driving the baseline against Parma Byzantine in my last basketball game ever.

Parma Byzantine played us man-to-man in the first quarter of the sectional tournament game. I scored ten in the first half, including this running one-hander.

Sister Rita advising a very willing student at St. Mary's.

March 2006 at the annual St. Patrick's Day Mackie MacGregor Basketball Classic. I didn't actually play that day since I had a total knee replacement two months before that. Still great shooting form, even if I have gained a few pounds from the previous photo.

Mr. Rafsky trying to control that Latin I class. He never succeeded.

Coaches Havrady, Flowers, Dunning, and McComb. This was the
coaching staff our senior year. They were plotting for the next time
they would beat me up at practice.

This is my senior tennis picture. Love that hair, huh?

Shelby Boca is the blond chewing her finger. I broke up with her. Hey, when you are young and in love you are stupid. On the far right is class president and leader of "The Freaks" Bob Irelan. He's the one with the long hair. Holding the dog.

Sister Aline teaching math as only she could.

Sister Chantal. A great, funny lady who was a good sport when we (especially Conor Flanary) misbehaved in Freshman English class.

Sister Mary Neumann became Principal when Biggy Rat left. What Dale Coltaggio is doing is anybody's guess.

St. Mary's Academy Student Council Officers for 1968-69. President Terrell Small, V-P me, Treasurer Troy Dunnehy, Secretary Grace Orsini. She was and is a great friend. My one historic date with Grace was July 20, 1969. What a night to remember!

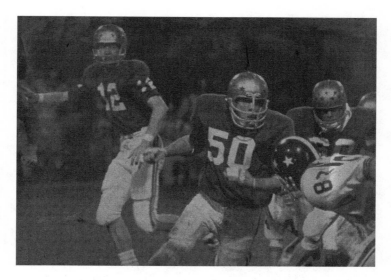

Great picture, but too bad the photographer missed the ball carrier. Will Fitzpatrick (12) has pitched the ball to Fran Dunning., who is out of the picture. I'm number 50 leading the sweep and Rod Achter is right behind me. I kicked out the corner, Achter turned up ands sealed the safety, fullback Bert Knouwer blocked EC's #87, and Dunning ran 68 yards for a touchdown. That put us ahead 30-0 against our arch-rival and heavily-favored Panthers.

"I'm open-minded and that's all there is to it!" Sister Helen Rita

Am I shooting at the wrong basket? That's me in 1969, the last year at St. Mary's Academy. Our team was really good until Fred Knillen got kicked off the team.

41

The Spartan Senior Social

By the way, we now have football helmets, shoes, school colors, and a nickname. We were now the scarlet-and-gray clad Lorain Catholic Spartans. On August 9 Coach Flowers invited all of the senior players to dinner at his house. This was supposed to be a time for us to really get together, get close, and plan our leadership for the season. Every senior was there except Will Fitzpatrick, who was at a family outing in Michigan.

We sort of milled around in Coach Flowers' backyard, drinking lemonade and socializing with each other and the coaches. We also got to see all of the brand new equipment we were going to get to wear that year. The uniforms, including the helmets, were replicas of Ohio State's uniforms. They were awesome. After watching Danny Jackson model the uniform and Coach Flowers explain it to us, we all went into his house and ate dinner. We then sat around his living room wondering what was next.

Coach Flowers spoke first. He reminded us how hard we had worked and how much each and every day playing football should mean to us. His talk was inspirational, and he told us that he wanted every senior to take a few moments and speak to everyone else present. Robbie Cavellini spoke first. He was one of our true leaders, so it made sense for him to lead things off. Tackle Jeff Brent followed Cavellini, and I spoke after Brent.

"I know football is a team sport, and that there are a lot of other guys on the field, but let's admit it, it's the seniors who run the ball club. It's our team. I think we should bind together right now and decide that we're going to go 10-0. Most of us will probably never play college ball. That means this is the last time we will ever play organized football. We've GOT to make this a great season, one that we'll remember, one we'll remember as being great. I also think we should remember how much we need each other. None of us can do it alone. We're a real team, and we've got to play like a real team to be successful."

As you might imagine, I felt that my speech was the best one.

42

The Spartan Football Retreat

The football retreat was designed to get us ready, physically, emotionally, and spiritually, to play the coming season. These days, August 11, 12, 13, were set aside by the coaches as days that were very much different than usual physical conditioning days. We were going to receive our equipment August 14, and the hitting started August 15.

We met all three days and attended services at St. Mary's Church. After Mass we went in, had breakfast, and then began meetings. We were still meeting at St. Mary's because the new school building at Lorain Catholic, including the locker rooms and the practice fields, wasn't completed yet.

Each day we had a guest speaker. The first day of the retreat the featured speaker was Big Joe Allen. He was a member of the legendary undefeated St. Mary's 1967 team. Allen had been named first-team All-Ohio and was presently playing football for Duke University. The entire coaching staff left the building, and after Allen talked to us about dedication and teamwork, he opened up the floor to let any of us talk or ask him questions. He promised to maintain secrecy but to get any ideas to the coaching staff.

JD Szollszy and I both questioned the value of silence during the retreat. You see, we had to maintain total silence. There was no talking at all while we were there, unless there was a special time like right now to speak. Allen and the rest of the players all disagreed with JD and me. They all thought that a few days of silence might actually help us focus on the tasks at hand.

The second day of the retreat we watched a movie with Vince Lombardi and Jerry Kramer, who happened to be my personal football hero. In fact, my goal was to wear number 64, which happened to be Jerry Kramer's number with the Green Bay Packers.

The third day of the retreat was probably the most inspirational. Coach Flowers gave us a talk about spirit and attitude and sportsmanship. He was one great speaker. Most of us would try to run through a wall for him if he told us to. Of course, if we didn't he might just kick the crap out of us.

43

"One Play Away"
Our Senior Football Season

Forty-two players reported for the first day of football practice for Lorain Catholic High School on August 15, 1969. It's really strange saying that we reported for action at Lorain Catholic High School, since we actually met at St. Mary's Academy. You see, Lorain Catholic High School was still not even close to being finished enough for us to dress or practice there. We were told we were going to have to use St. Mary's for the entire football season, and perhaps even some of the basketball season.

We had to report for two-a-day practices at 7:30 AM, with the day's first meetings being held in Johnston Hall at 8:30. After a short meeting we headed for Lakeview Park, where we were going to be practicing. Practice started at 8:45, and, with specialties and offensive practice, we got off the field at 11:45. We returned to St. Mary's to shower and eat lunch, and the afternoon practice sessions began at 2:05 and we were off the field at 5:30. It was a grueling schedule, but that's how you get ready for the season.

Just before we jogged onto the field before our very first practice, Coach Flowers allowed us to walk around and say something to our teammates. Robbie Cavellini and I shook hands and then hugged eat other. Robbie said, "Let's go. Good luck. We've gotta go out there and hit. It's the first day now, but before we know it, it'll be the last practice before Midview and our careers will be over." Those were words I would never forget.

After eight days of tough practices, we were ready for our first pre-season scrimmage. The Keystone High School Wildcats were going to visit Lakeview Park to scrimmage the all-new Lorain Catholic Spartans. Although the scrimmages don't count in the regular-season record, they are very valuable and very important in setting a tone for the coming season.

There are no bleachers at Lakeview Park, so everyone had to stand to watch the scrimmage. To our surprise, there were almost 500 people present to watch this very first athletic contest in the school's history. Keystone had the ball first and ran ten plays and gained very little yardage. On our very first play we ran a 17 Power and Robbie Cavellini ran 70 yards for a touchdown. On Lorain Catholic High School's very first offensive play, we went 70 yards for a touchdown.

After blocking the linebacker straight back about five yards, I heard a roar and saw Cavellini sprinting down the field. I met him in the end zone and we both just jumped up and down for a few seconds until everyone else got there. What a way to start Lorain Catholic football.

On our second series of ten plays Cavellini again broke away for a 45-yard touchdown. Later still, we reached the Keystone one-yard line. During scrimmages the coaches are out in the huddle calling the plays and telling us what to do. Coach Flowers said to Bert Knouwer, "Get us a touchdown, fullback." He then pointed at right tackle Jeff Brent and me and said, "Open a hole. Get him in there." When the ball was snapped Brent and I exploded into the Keystone defenders and Knouwer followed us into the end zone for our third touchdown of the day.

Our fourth touchdown was a sweep to the left, and I pulled, bellied back into the backfield so I could head up the field, and then began to look for someone to block. Cavellini slowed down just enough to get right behind me, and, as the safety closed in I could tell the defender wasn't looking at me at all. Rather, he was intent on tackling Cavellini. It was a very easy block, and I threw a perfect cross-body block. The defender went head-over-heels and Cavellini went 49 yards for his third touchdown of the day. For the game Cavellini carried the ball only seven times, but he gained 160 yards rushing, an incredible 22.8 yards per carry average. Bert Knouwer had a pretty good day running the ball, and even Conor Flanary gained 54 yards rushing. Quarterback Will Fitzpatrick completed a few passes, but our passing game really seemed like we had a long way to go.

Later in the second week of the season a bunch of us went to Patty Pullman's house to just hang out. We got there around 8:00, and around 9:00 a huge thunderstorm came rolling in. The sky got incredibly dark, the wind picked up, and it just poured for a few minutes. The house shook. We lost electricity for about twenty-five minutes, which was the most fun, since we were all in the basement at that point in the dark with a bunch of girls with only one candle lit. We all tried to scare the girls, but the guys ended up being scared instead.

After the storm stopped and the lights and electricity came back on, we all sat there and drank our pop and kept telling stories for a while longer. Mrs. Pullman finally yelled down the steps, "Don't you guys have a 10:00 curfew tonight?" She was asking us because we were all football players, and it was a weeknight during pre-season practice.

"Yeah, we have a10:00 curfew, but the clock says it's only 9:30." We had forgotten that the clock was plugged in, and had lost power for about twenty-five minutes during the storm. Panic quickly ensued. We sprinted up the stairs, jumped into Bert Knower's Buick Riviera and headed home. Bert was a great driver, but he had to drive really fast.

When I got home, around 10:07, my father was standing in the kitchen holding the phone. I asked him what he was doing and he told me he was calling Coach Flowers to tell him I had broken curfew. I tried to explain to my father what had happened, but he just shook his head. He said, "If your curfew is 10:00, then you need to make sure you're home by 10:00. Coach Flowers needs to know that you're not responsible enough to get home on time."

I couldn't believe that my father was going to do that, and I finally talked him out of it, but that was a clear indication to me that my father was serious about helping the coach enforce all kinds of rules.

44

Scrimmage Number 2
(Who Scheduled These Guys?)

On August 27 we traveled to nearby Amherst to scrimmage the big, bad Comets. It was a very warm morning, and there were over 1000 people at the scrimmage, which is a huge crowd for a scrimmage. Amherst was supposed to be really good, and, after our crushing performance against Keystone, I think lots of people thought we were also going to be good. I know we thought that.

After we warmed up and just moments before we started the scrimmage, Coach Flowers called us together. We weren't in a locker room, and he wanted to talk to us without everyone else hearing him. We got in even closer than normal. You don't always see Coach Flowers with that fire in his eye, but he sure had it today. He grit his teeth and set his jaw and said, "I want this ball club so bad I can taste it. When you go out there today, you've gotta hit like you've never hit before, block like you've never blocked before, tackle like you've never tackled before, and run like you've never run before. Gentlemen, all the hard work and sweat you've put into this season, all the work over the winter, the spring, the summer, all the workouts you've ever attended. Well, they all lead up to this. (He was really building now) You only get thirteen competitions a year and this is number two. Spartans, let's go out there on that field and let's hit. Let's Hit, HIT, HIT, HIT! Let's HIT! And, above all, let's come off that field winners!"

Amherst physically kicked the shit out of us. It seemed like every guy they had was 5-10 to 6-1 and every one weighed between 190 and 225. Every guy they had was just physical and muscular and mean.

Our only touchdown of the day came when Robbie Cavellini intercepted a Comet pass and weaved his way down the field for a touchdown. Other than that, we never scored. In fact, we had a tough time getting the ball back to the line of scrimmage. Fortunately for us, our defense was very strong, and we held the Amherst first-teamers to no touchdowns, even though the Comets did score on our second team defense.

We were physically sore and beat up after playing Amherst, and Coach Flowers wasn't very happy, but he really didn't go too crazy. The next day Coach Flowers surprised us all and made all of us happy. He announced that August 28 would be the last two-a-day practice. The dog days of August were over! We really needed the break. We had one more scrimmage that week, and we were losing players to soreness and injuries quickly. In the previous fourteen days we had completed twenty-one practices and two scrimmages. That had been a lot of football crammed into a short period of time. Also, at practice on August 29, we had only 27 players dressed for practice.

We actually could have kept practicing two-a-days, since school wasn't going to start anytime soon. Our new building wasn't even close to being completed, so we were going to be sitting around for another few weeks before we started school.

The night of August 29 was also a special night for another reason. Just about all of the seniors met at Jimmy Sullivan's house in south Lorain. Jimmy was a great friend to all of us, but he couldn't play football anymore because he injured his neck a year or so before. He was still "one of us," though. August 29 was Mackie MacGregor's seventeenth birthday, and, to celebrate, we all went to Cleveland to the Roxie Burlesque Show. It was my first time, and we all thoroughly enjoyed both the comics and the strippers. That's right, it was a strip tease show. We laughed our asses off at the comedians and enjoyed watching the ladies. As one of the comics said, "There's always something going on . . . . or coming off, at the Roxie."

Our little senior trip to Cleveland was supposed to get us mentally ready to play Brookside the next day. If that was the goal, it definitely failed. When I arrived at the locker room on August 30 I remember asking a couple of guys, "Do you really feel like playing today?" No one had a positive response to the question.

Brookside is usually pretty big and pretty fast, and I really blame them for us breaking the 24 game win streak last year when we lost the opener to Fremont St. Joe. The previous year we had the ball first and drove the length of the field on our first possession and scored. At that point we had won 24 regular season games in a row, and 29 games in a row overall, if you count scrimmages. We became very complacent. Brookside scored on us and they were really fired up. They held us scoreless after that, and, even though we actually tied them, 1-1, we left the field thinking we were losers. They left the field thinking they were winners, and we played like we were losers in the first half of the loss to Fremont St. Joe. We had to figure out a way to overcome that in 1969.

Brookside began with the ball, and our defense was tremendous. In their first ten-play series they actually lost seven yards. They were having trouble getting the ball back to the line of scrimmage. We took the ball over, and, just like the previous year, drove the length of the field and scored. During the drive, once we reached deep into Brookside territory, I was detected holding on a play run to the left side. Coach Flowers really chewed my butt out in the huddle, but, once we reached the one-yard line, he called upon Jeff Brent and me to again open a hole for fullback Bert Knouwer. We opened a big hole and Bert scored, giving us a one touchdown lead. The Cardinals drove right down the field, and the only way we stopped them was recovering a fumble on our own six. The rest of the scrimmage was a tough, hard-nosed, defensive contest. Second-team fullback Jules Holiday scored a touchdown for us late in the scrimmage, but it was the only other touchdown the whole day.

It should be pointed out that we were a bit short-handed against Brookside. All-world running back Robbie Cavellini didn't play and neither did two-way starter and our leading receiver Rod Achter. Cavellini had a sprained wrist, while Achter had a nasty case of infected boils on his arm. Now that is a pleasant sight.

The night of August 30 was really a first for me. After the scrimmage that day I was scheduled to work at The Lorain Journal. I wrote for the Journal's sports' department. I actually had to call up all of the coaches of the city teams and interview them concerning how that day's scrimmages had gone. When I called Coach Flowers I simply identified myself as ". . . . the Journal Sports' Department calling." I asked him how the scrimmage had gone. He hesitated and then said, "Is this some kind of a joke Francis?" He recognized my voice. When I told him, "No, Sir, I'm working for the Journal," (which, by the way, he already knew—I had to clear it with him so I could work some evenings rather late after curfew), he then told me that we had played OK, but that he didn't want anyone's name listed in the article for having done anything spectacular. I told him I understood and then hung up.

As mentioned a while ago, I had begun a relationship with the newest girl in the school, Dominique Pavlak. After writing all of my articles for the Journal that night I called her up. I had spoken to her earlier in the evening, and she told me that she would be up very late. I called her again around 11:00 PM. I should point out that my parents were out of town that whole weekend. They were spending the entire weekend at Cedar Point.

So, I called Dominique up and she told me that her father had just gotten off work and would be arriving home in a little while. Dominique was going to make dinner for her father, and she wanted to know if I would like to join him for dinner.

I arrived at Dominique's house around 11:35. She lived in a very nice house about three blocks away from the new Lorain Catholic High School. I met her father and then sat with him in the family room and watched the Cleveland Browns play an exhibition football game from the west coast. Dominique brought us a salad and a broiled T-bone steak. I sat with her father and ate and watched the game and ate, never even thinking about our midnight curfew. I figured that Coach Flowers knew that I was working that evening, and my parents were out of town, so what was the harm?

Dominique's father went to bed after the dinner, and she and I cleaned up the kitchen. After that we went out to my car. It was just before 1:00 AM. It was a beautiful summer night, the kind where you can stay out there all night without even a jacket. Dominique Pavlak and I sat on the trunk of my '61 Buick Invicta convertible and talked and talked and talked. I had only known Dominique for a few weeks, and had only started really dating her recently. That was one special night. I found out all kinds of things about Dominique Pavlak that night, not the least of which was, she really didn't want to make out very much. She was really prudish. She wouldn't let me do anything. Even her kisses were the closed-mouth kind. But she was so damn cute and funny and so, so very nice as a person. We were definitely establishing a relationship.

Around 3:30 that morning I said, for the twentieth time, "I probably ought to be going . . . ." Dominique, who was enjoying the conversation and romantic evening every bit as much as I was, finally agreed. As I drove home that night I thought about two things: how nice Dominique Pavlak was and how Coach Flowers and my parents would absolutely kill me if they ever found out how I broke curfew!

45

Preparing For A Real Battle

Our first regular-season game was scheduled for Saturday afternoon, September 6, versus Fremont St. Joseph. Remember that this was the team that had beaten us in last year's opener, thus breaking our amazing 24-game winning streak. We had not really been very successful against Fremont St. Joe, and it had a huge winning edge over St. Mary's. However, we weren't St. Mary's anymore. We were now the Spartans of Lorain Catholic, and Coach Flowers was very anxious to establish a new tradition versus the Crimson Streaks from Fremont.

By the way, the game time of Saturday afternoon at 2:00 was pretty unique, but we needed to get used to strange game times. Lorain Southview High School also opened in the fall of 1969, which meant that three public schools (Lorain Senior, Admiral King, and Southview) were going to have to share the great George Daniel Stadium in Lorain. That meant we were going to have to play at unusual times and places. In the past, if Lorain Senior or Admiral King had a home game on a Friday night, the other school had an away game that same night. That left Saturday evenings open for St. Mary's to play in the huge stadium. Southview now got the Saturday night timeslots, leaving Lorain Catholic to play some Saturday afternoons and even some Sunday afternoons.

Fremont St. Joe was coached by a savvy old guy named Coach Beier. He had been coaching there for years and years and years, and they were always really tough. They actually still ran a single-wing offense, which had been replaced just about everywhere by 1969. The scouting report for Fremont St. Joe was very detailed. We needed to learn their formations and the plays they ran from those formations. I will say this about Coach Flowers—he is one of the most prepared coaches anywhere. He takes all of the information he can about a team and really does a great job preparing a scouting report. That also means, of course, that we have to study that information a great deal. If we do a good job of learning the information, we should not have to think too much out on the field—we should just be able to react to what we already know.

On Thursday of Fremont St. Joe week I learned that I would be kicking off versus the Streaks. Our usual kicker, Conor Flanary, had a bruised thigh muscle on his kicking leg, which was aggravated every time he tried to kick. Flanary, by the way, was a very fine high school kicker. His kickoffs usually went inside the ten-yard line, and last year he was 15 out of 16 on extra point kicks. The one he missed, however, cost us the Clearview game, as we ended up tying the Clippers, 12-12.

Everyone was really excited to be playing in the very first varsity game for Lorain Catholic High School. We got to wear our brand new scarlet and gray uniforms for the first time. Here's a general set of conclusions for our performance after playing Fremont St. Joseph's: my kickoffs were an embarrassment, our defense was atrocious, Coach Flowers was furious and disgusted, and we won, 44-28. That score may sound OK to most people, but you have to remember that Coach Flowers was a defensive-minded guy. Two years ago we gave up 26 points the entire year! In the 1969 opener we gave up 28 points in one game!

Let's start with the kickoffs. I am a straight-ahead kicker, which means I don't come across the ball like every modern soccer-style kicker. I had actually sanded down the very front of the sole of my football shoes so that I had a somewhat-flat surface to kick the ball. I also had a strap that I attached to the bottom of my shoe and then around my ankle. This strap was supposed to hold my toes up to kick the ball, giving me even a better surface to make contact with the ball.

My kickoff to start the game wasn't bad, as it was a line-drive dribbler that was returned out to the St. Joe 37-yard line. Immediately after the kickoff I had to stay on the field to play defense. I hadn't thought of this . . . . what was I going to do with the strap that held my toes up? I couldn't just leave it on my shoe/ankle, because you can't run with the stupid thing attached. I loosened the strap and then just let it dangle around my foot. I played one play on defense that way and then stepped on the strap and tripped myself. I knew I couldn't just let it dangle because I would keep stepping on it and falling down. I took the strap off and threw it towards our sidelines, never to see it again. Naturally, we scored six touchdowns, which meant I kicked off seven times in the game. Every kick got worse and worse. It was truly an embarrassment, as my father reminded me after the game.

On our second possession of the game, after both teams had punted once, Robbie Cavellini exploded. We ran a "23 Trap" to perfection. St. Joe's was running an even-front defense, and we took huge splits between our linemen. I pulled and trapped the defensive tackle, and Cavellini broke through a hole for 43 yards into St. Joe territory. A few plays later the slick halfback went around the left end for 24 yards and our first touchdown.

On our next possession fullback Bert Knouwer scored on a one-yard run and we led, 14-0. St. Joe moved the length of the field to score a touchdown, cutting our lead to 14-6. We were all really disappointed when they scored, because our first-team defense had not allowed a touchdown in the entire pre-season. Knouwer scored again for us, and we were up, 22-6. Late in the first half St. Joe's executed a great drive and scored right before the half, and we led 22-14, but it was still anybody's game.

The second half was a huge offensive explosion. Neither team punted in the second half and both teams matched their first-half scoring totals, for a 44-28 Spartan victory. Cavellini gained 215 yards rushing on only 16 carries, and he scored three touchdowns and a PAT. Bert Knouwer scored two touchdowns and did a great job blocking, and Conor Flanary ran for 96 yards and scored a touchdown and a PAT. We left the field tired and drained, but we also were pretty excited about winning the first-ever game for Lorain Catholic High School.

Coach Flowers told us he wanted to meet with us as a team before we left for the day. We showered and met in the gym. The rest was unbelievable. He began in sort of quiet voice, and then he really built. He told us he was disgusted, ashamed, and angered at our performance today. He told us that never in his life, whether playing marbles, Little League baseball, basketball, or anything else, had he been more disgusted with a win. He told us we were big, fat, lazy slobs who were out of shape, and that he would do something about that in the coming weeks. He questioned our heart, guts, and desire in every way possible. We thought it was pretty cool putting up 44 points against Fremont St. Joe, but Coach Flowers sure didn't. He was really pissed.

He also told us that our curfew, instead of the usual midnight on Saturday night, would be 10:00. He did tell us that if we were going to the Clearview-Elyria Catholic game that evening in Elyria, we had to head straight home and not stop anywhere or do anything else. Curfew was 10:00, and he would be checking on us.

I went to the Clearview-EC game with junior tackle Jack Murtha, Conor Flanary, and Will Fitzpatrick. Murtha drove, and on the way home Flanary and I convinced Murtha that we had to have something to eat. Fitzpatrick really didn't want to stop, but we eventually convinced Murtha to stop at a Big Boy restaurant. We ordered our food "to go," but Fitzpatrick was still worried that Coach Flowers would find out.

Murtha dropped Fitzpatrick off at home on the east side of Lorain, and then headed west to drop me off followed by Flanary, who lived less than five minutes from my house. It was on the ride from Fitzpatrick's to my house that I hatched this awesome, practical-joke scheme.

As soon as Murtha dropped me off, I ran in the house and called Flanary's. I talked to Conor's younger brother and convinced him with my voice that I was Coach Flowers and that I was calling players to check on them for curfew violations. It was great, I absolutely convinced Flanary's younger brother that I was Coach Flowers.

As soon as I hung up from the Flanary's, I called Fitzpatrick to let him know what I was doing. Fitzpatrick, ever the choir boy, didn't want to have anything to do with this scheme, but he finally agreed to play along. I hung up the phone and waited. Sure enough, within one or two minutes Flanary called and asked me if Flowers had called. "Yeah, he called and I talked to him. He called right when I was coming into the house. He must be calling all of the seniors to see if anybody broke curfew." I know that Flanary was so worried about Coach Flowers calling that he was just about ready to pee his pants. I thought the whole thing was funny as hell, and I couldn't wait until the next day to see how it worked out.

The team met for Sunday Mass at 9:00 the next morning, followed by a workout. I know that it's Sunday, but this was a Catholic school in the 1960's, so all sorts of strange things were allowed, not the least of which was one of the great John Flowers' explosions of all time.

After Mass we dressed into workout clothes and got into our lines and started to stretch. Coach Flowers was in the Coaches' Office at the end of the gym. As we finished stretching he stormed from the Coaches' Office, where he had been privately watching the film from the previous day, and said one word, "Run."

We ran laps and we ran sprints. We did 350 jumping jacks and numerous sets of 25 pushups and sit-ups. He stepped out of the office one more time and said, "All Fours. Ten." I thought he meant that we would do all fours for ten laps around the gym. I went full speed and finished way ahead of everybody else. I stopped and stood up next to Coach Flowers when I finished my ten laps. He looked at me standing there and said, "What the hell are you doing?" I just looked at him and said, while trying to catch my breath, "I finished my ten laps." He looked at me and said, "Ten laps? Hell, I meant ten minutes." He stepped away from me and went back into the Coaches' Office, slamming the door.

Ten minutes of all fours? What, was he crazy? Nobody can do ten minutes straight of all fours. I got back down on my hands and started doing the exercise again, only this time I did it much slower than I had been doing it previously. You could hear Coach Flowers throwing stuff around the Coaches' Office. This was becoming a frightening situation.

We conditioned for almost an hour in the gym, and everyone was totally exhausted. Some guys had blisters on the palms of their hands from doing those stupid all fours for ten minutes, but the worst was yet to come. As we had already learned in previous years, watching the game films was always an adventure with Coach Flowers.

Perhaps the highlight of the entire day was the fact that the game film itself was of very poor quality. The guy taping the game missed most of the first three quarters. What we did see showed us to be rather slow and out of shape. Of course we played the game in 95 degree heat in the middle of the afternoon, and virtually all of us were playing offense and defense. By the fourth quarter we were definitely tired and dragging a bit, and those two things just didn't work for a Coach Flowers team.

Coach Flowers picked apart the film as best he could, with the film being of such poor quality. After we watched the film he stood in front of us. He paced back and forth for a few minutes before he spoke. "I have never seen a team with less enthusiasm. Where was this? (He said this as he clenched his fist and stared at it.) Hell, last year we had a 150 pound linebacker with more of this (the clenched fist) than all of you guys put together. You gotta hate. You gotta hate me and hate me and hate me, because right now I hate you. I hate you. I hate you. I hate you and you and you! You gotta hate me so that Friday night you can go out on that field and take your hate out on Clearview. I'm gonna make you hate me, because right now I hate you. You all stink. I hate you. I HATE YOU!"

He then lowered his voice to the really serious tones. "You better make up your minds to come back and hit the Clippers like you've never hit before. Knock them right out of Clearview Stadium. You gotta hate Clearview and you've gotta hate me, because right now I hate you. I'm ashamed to be associated with you. You just better come back strong next week."

When we finally reached the locker room, everyone was complaining about how hard it was. There were even guys who thought about quitting. The talk was, "He doesn't have to worry about us hating him. We already do."

My thoughts in the locker room that day centered around the practical joke I had pulled on Conor Flanary the night before. I finally asked Conor, "Hey, what do you think Flowers is going to do about you breaking curfew last night?"

I snuck a look at the only other guy who really knew what was going on, Will Fitzpatrick. He never wanted to be part of the joke, but he had at least kept quiet until now. As the story was explained to everyone else, and, as they all thought, "Wow, what's Flowers gonna do to Flanary," Flanary spoke out.

"I decided to not bring it up today. I was just gonna wait until Flowers said something. I tried to call him last night, and I had six of the seven numbers dialed to explain to him what had happened, but decided to wait."

At that point I actually got nervous. If Flanary had completed that call last night, bothered Coach Flowers at home over a prank call that I had made, I would be dead. Coach Flowers would have killed me. I broke out in a cold sweat and couldn't tell Flanary fast enough that it had been a big joke. Everyone had a good laugh about the whole incident (except Will Fitzpatrick and Flanary), but it was really at my expense as much as Flanary's. Coach Flowers would have killed me if he had found out.

46

Clearview Week and Still No School

As we entered into the second week of the regular season of football we still had not started school. Every other school has been in session for about a week, but the brand new Lorain Catholic High School is not completed. They are trying to complete the academic wings of the school so we can get started, but they've already told us we won't have the gym, locker rooms, and other extra-curricular areas finished for months. None of us are very upset that we haven't started yet. This is beginning to seem like a very, very long summer vacation.

I continued to develop a relationship with the lovely and nice Dominique Pavlak.

Monday of Clearview week was a day designed to familiarize ourselves with the Clippers and their personnel. Monday practices are also really difficult because we go full pads with mostly drills and conditioning. We did ten drills that day, and in between each drill we had some form of conditioning. We did a blocking drill followed by 75 yards of all fours and a sprint back. After another drill we did two minutes of Packer Drill, with the whistle being blown every five seconds. Drills and then conditioning. Drills and then conditioning.

When we thought we were about finished, Coach Flowers decided it was time for just conditioning. We did Packer Drill and hit 58 times. That's running in place, and then throwing your body onto the ground and getting up as fast as possible 58 times. We did seven minutes of sit-ups—I lost count at 110. We did five minutes of pushups. We did 400 yards of sprints, followed by more Packer Drill.

It was pretty tough to concentrate on Clearview's personnel after a workout like that, but here are a few highlights of the Clippers. First of all, their left inside linebacker was a guy named Rich Rhome. He was about 5-8 150, but he was very quick. I bring up his name because Rich and I were very close friends before I moved to Lorain in fifth grade. We went to grade school together and always played around. I hadn't stayed in too close of contact with him, but I was looking forward to talking to him again before and after the game Friday night.

Last year's Clearview game was one of my all-time favorites. Remember that JD Szollzy got kicked out of the game in the first quarter and I got to play both offense and defense. I actually had a couple of sacks on their senior quarterback that year, as well as one of the better blocking games I had ever played. We tied the Clippers last year, 12-12, and they had many new faces on this year's team. In their first game of the season they lost to Elyria Catholic.

On Tuesday of Clearview week we were again doing plenty of fundamental drills. Coach Flowers was working with the interior linemen on our pass blocking. After a few minutes of working on this drill he said to us, "I'm going over with the backs for a few minutes. You guys stay here and work on your stances and starts." He walked away. I was sure that he was at least thirty yards away, and I said in joking/drawl sort of voice. "Aaaawwwrrright, now we work. Mathers, let me see your stance." I was not trying to imitate or make fun of Coach Flowers. I was simply adding some fun to the practice.

Coach Flowers had not walked very far away from the group of fifteen or so linemen. He heard every word that I said, but he didn't know who said them. He quickly returned to the group. I swear there was smoke coming out of his ears and nostrils. All of the players were in sort of a semi-circle, and Coach Flowers was standing right next to me. I instinctively re-inserted my mouthpiece. He stood there and glared at us. He finally said, "All right, who's the smart aleck who said, 'Now we work, Mathers let me see your stance?'" I looked at everyone in the semi-circle. They were all staring right at me. I was NOT going to get out of this one. I raised my hand and said, as best I could with my mouthpiece in place, "I said it, Coach."

I didn't finish the statement before he hit me with a forearm right in the chest. The blow knocked me backwards, but I didn't go down. He came after me and punched me in the stomach. He was screaming at me the whole time and practice basically stopped so everyone could enjoy Coach Flowers beating the crap out of Steve Francis again. He grabbed my facemask and starting twisting my head in every direction. He slapped my helmet from one side to the other. This had to be the worst on-field beating that Coach Flowers had ever administered, and it wasn't over yet.

A few minutes later we gathered for our team offense period. We used a two-row huddle, and I was in the back row, standing straight with my hands at my back. He stepped into the huddle and the rage of a few minutes earlier reappeared on his face. He dove through the huddle to get at me again. This time he got me on the ground. He was actually on top of me like a bully, punching my face mask. He screamed at me that I should thank God that we had so few guys on the team or he would take off my helmet and beat the hell out of me. At that point I thought to myself, ". . . beat the hell out of me? What did he just do?"

Was I scared throughout that time? You're damned right I was scared. Coach John Flowers, in all his fury, is one scary fellow.

The remainder of the practice was very high-spirited. Everyone was crisp and sharp and we were beginning to get ready for the Clippers.

Remember that in last year's game JD Szollzy got kicked out of the game for fighting with Clearview's star running back, Money Goines. Supposedly, some Clearview tough guys went out looking for JD after the game. They believed that we sent JD into the game just to start a fight with Money Goines. We heard at practice that day that JD's mom got an anonymous phone call the night before that said, "Don't let your son play Friday night or we'll kill him."

We had a pep rally before every football game, and each week a couple of seniors got to speak. I specifically asked if I could speak before the Clearview game. Understand that the typical senior speech went something like this, "Well, Clearview is a really good team. We've been working really hard, and with your support we're going to go out there and beat them." A variation was something like, "We've been working really hard. Clearview is a really good team, but with your support we're going to go out there and beat them." In other words, the speeches were exactly the same only re-arranged.

I stood up in front of the school and started my speech like this, "When I was in third grade my best friend was a kid named Rich Rhome." I was going to tell the wonderful little story about Rich Rhome and how that night I was going to be blocking him on most plays. I got the first line of the speech out and the entire student body groaned and mumbled things like, "Here we go. Give Francis a mic and you can't shut him up." I did finish the speech and told the story, but I shortened it quite a bit when I heard the audience's reaction to the first line.

The night of the Clearview game was absolutely gorgeous. Very little wind, bright sky, perfect temperature. Before the specialists went out on the field, Coach Flowers told me to go out and get a few kickoffs, just in case Conor Flanary's leg didn't respond. I was surprised to get told that, especially after my terrible performance the previous week. I was also really excited about it, because going out with the specialists is always way more fun than just sitting in the locker room with Coach Havrady.

After kicking some kickoffs, I returned to the locker room. I had to pass the Clearview specialists at that end of the field. I went past an old friend of mine, Big Rick Bushkin. Bushkin is a big, heavy-set kid, but a great athlete. He's 6-4 and at least 230 pounds, but he's an outstanding football, basketball and track athlete. As I jogged past him he made his fingers into a little gun and shot me. We had played against each other numerous times in various sports. I slowed my jog so that I could actually say something to him. We talked for a second and wished each other luck. I looked over my shoulder to make sure that Coach Flowers wasn't watching me talk to the enemy, and then I finished the jog to the locker room.

Just before we returned to the field for the kickoff and the start of the game, Coach Flowers gave us one great, inspirational talk. He told us about a guy in Vietnam who continued to fight and save his friends while he was wounded. He talked about getting the adrenalin flowing, and the fact that people can do fantastic things if they forget that they are injured and just let the adrenalin take over. He reminded us that it wasn't who was bigger or faster or stronger or more experienced, or even who got the breaks, but what was important was who wanted to win the most. We took the field and we were really ready for a battle.

After exchanging punts, we started a drive on our own 38-yard line. It was very obvious that the Clippers were really watching Cavellini. They had two or three guys all over him everywhere he went. Our other halfback, Conor Flanary, picked up the slack. In fact, on the 62-yard drive, Flanary carried the ball for 47 of those yards, including the touchdown. Will Fitzpatrick's great ball-handling and faking allowed Cavellini to cruise in for the conversion, and we led the game 8-0.

Late in the first half Clearview took over after we fumbled, and they moved the length of the field to score. They also got the extra point, so the score stood at 8-8 at halftime.

We got the ball to start the second half, and on the very first play our season changed. We ran an isolation play up the middle with Cavellini following fullback Bert Knouwer. I think all eleven Clearview defenders were in on the tackle, and, when the pile unfolded, Cavellini remained on the field. He was hurt. An ambulance pulled right onto the field to take him to the hospital. As he was getting into the ambulance he picked his head up and said, "You guys better win. Win for me."

We were stunned. Our huddle broke down in tears. Our best player, leading scorer, co-captain, was gone. The ambulance took him to St. Joseph's Hospital. We still had an entire half of football to play. Coach Flowers' pre-game talk began to come true. We had to battle through the injuries. We did.

Shortly into the fourth quarter Bert Knouwer dove through a tiny hole between Jeff Brent and me for the go-ahead touchdown. We led, 14-8. Clearview drove the length of the field after our touchdown until they reached the four-yard line. On first down they reached the one. On second down their quarterback scored easily to tie the game, except they had two guys in motion on the same play. No touchdown, and they moved back to the six. They fumbled on second down, but recovered. On third down they tried a quick pitch to the left, which had been successful for them throughout the game. This time, however, Bob Knouwer, Bert's brother, stopped the play for a loss. Their fourth down desperation pass was incomplete and we took over on downs.

Just over three minutes remained in the game, and Clearview had all three of their timeouts left. We actually got one first down before they used their timeouts and stopped us. Will Fitzpatrick boomed a great punt, and the Clippers took over with only 34 seconds left in the game. We knocked a couple of their passes down, and with 0:01 left to play the Clippers had time to run one more play. Clearview ran a middle screen pass, and, after pressuring the quarterback for a second I recognized what was happening. The pass was completed, and all of the blockers were in front of the receiver. I was behind the receiver, so I had a free shot as he started to move his way down the field. It was the biggest tackle of my career.

We had beaten Clearview, 14-8, playing the entire second half without our best player and leader. We got in our cars and returned to St. Mary's to shower and change clothes. By the time we got back to school there were already students and parents and cheerleaders waiting for us. It was a great scene.

I walked up the stairs into the gym and Coach Dunning came over to me, smiled, stuck out his hand and said, "Well if it isn't Jerry Kramer himself. Nice job, Steve, real nice job." Those words meant an awful lot, especially coming from Coach Dunning, who really didn't like me very much at all.

The next day we watched the game films, and Coach Flowers hardly yelled at all. Oh, he did his usual yelling at Jack Murtha for blocking the wrong guy on certain plays, but he was actually pretty mellow. Beating Clearview can do that for a person.

We also found out that three things could happen for Cavellini. Number one, he might respond to treatments and only be out for a week or so. Number two, he could have a cast on for three weeks and then try to return. Number three, he might just have gotten injured so badly that he would need major reconstruction of his knee.

Two freshmen running backs have been brought up to try and take Cavellini's place, and Conor Flanary will now move to right halfback.

First-year player Jules Holliday will attempt to step in and play left halfback. Flanary will really have to step up and become the featured back, and fullback Bert Knouwer will also have to carry the ball more. It's pretty tough to replace a guy who was averaging over eleven yards per carry through the first two games. For that matter, it's time quarterback Will Fitzpatrick get going. The year before he threw for over a thousand yards and thirteen touchdowns, and this year we just haven't gotten untracked in the passing game. The bottom line is we will all have to accept more responsibility.

After watching the film and listening to Coach Flowers lead us in a short team meeting, he got all fired up again. He raised some emotion and ended with "Who we gonna beat?" We were supposed to respond immediately by screaming the name of our next opponent. He sort of caught us off-guard, though, and there was a second or two of hesitation by us all before we responded with a very weak and drawn out, "Gillllmmmmooouurrr." It was really bad.

Coach Flowers looked at us with evil eyes, shook his head, and said, "Aww just get the hell out of here."

47

Prepping For Gilmour Academy

Our third game is scheduled for Saturday afternoon at Gilmour Academy, a preppy, private school east of Cleveland. Gilmour is known to have great athletic teams, and their record in the past nine football seasons is 81-7-2. They run an unbalanced line and just pound the ball at people. As a defensive end against a team that runs that power sweep, it's an unselfish battle. One of my jobs, when they run all those people on the power sweep, is to take on all of the blockers, basically just give myself up and dive into the wedge of humanity. I'm not really trying to make the tackle, but I'm trying to wipe out all of the interference and the blockers. I could be trampled easily.

Perhaps most important of all is our mental approach to this game. We just absolutely cannot afford to relax after the big victory over Clearview. We have to remain focused and play with great emotion, especially since we have so many injuries. Jack Murtha has now been lost to us because of a neck injury. That means that junior guard Steven Mathers will have to play tackle, which means that JD Szollzy might have to play guard and defensive end. Danny Jackson has a pinched nerve in his shoulder, which might mean that Will Fitzpatrick might have to play defense. We hardly have enough guys to practice.

I got up a bit late on the morning of the game, which meant I had less time to cook my pre-game steak than usual. By the way, this will tell you how important my parents believed football was: Before every varsity football game I got to eat a steak. Big deal, right? Well, so had my brothers. That meant that from the time my oldest brother Bob started playing as a sophomore through this, my senior year, my parents had supplied steaks for Bob and Jack and me. We were all two years apart, so that meant that for six straight seasons we had steak before every game. We didn't have a lot of money, but my parents thought it was important for us to have that steak before the game. Of course people realize now that the steak wasn't really the best thing for us to be eating before a game, but in the 1960's, that was a huge deal.

On the 90 minute bus ride to Gilmour Academy we were all pretty nervous. This was the first game we were going into battle knowing we didn't have Robbie Cavellini. Robbie was a starter and letterman on that great 1967 St. Mary's team. Last year he led the entire northern Ohio area in total points scored. Now he was on crutches on the sidelines.

Gilmour's stadium was probably the smallest stadium we had ever played in. It only seated a few hundred people. I think there were only about three rows of seats on the visitor's side, and we always brought lots of fans.

We kicked off and they began a powerful drive right at us. JD Szollzy and I were manning one side of our defense, and we were doing a pretty decent job stopping the power sweep, but they were still gaining yardage. Their tailback, Eric Penick, was a legendary athlete. He was a junior in 1969, and he eventually went to Notre Dame and played for the Fighting Irish. He was about 6-1, 185 as a junior, and, when they pitched him the ball and he came storming at you with a bunch of blockers, including 210-pound fullback Dave Janasek, it was a scary sight.

Gilmour eventually fumbled on their first drive, and I dove on the fumble, recovering it on our 29-yard line. Something else happened on that first drive. On one of the power sweeps Janasek drove into me as I lowered my shoulder. He hit me just right, and I felt my neck and arm and shoulder go numb. I could not move my right arm. It just hung there. Fortunately, Gilmore ran a few plays away from my side, or I don't know what I would have done. The feeling started to return to my arm and I actually took my left arm and grabbed my right arm and started swinging it around. That seemed to increase the feeling in my arm. It's really a strange feeling when your arm is numb and you can't move it.

Gilmour again drove the field, but sophomore defensive back Denny McNamara intercepted Lancer pass on our ten-yard line. We were really lucky to have stopped Gilmour twice. Will Fitzpatrick led us on a great drive just before the half, and Bert Knouwer scored the touchdown for a 6-0 lead. A great Fitzpatrick fake and a pitchout to Conor Flanary got us the two-point conversion. We led 8-0 at the half.

On our second possession of the second half the usually reliable Mackie MacGregor fired a punt snap over the head of Fitzpatrick. Fitzpatrick sprinted back, picked the ball up, tried to run with it and then tried to punt it. It was blocked. Gilmour took over on our three-yard line. It took them four plays to score, but they finally did, making the score 8-6. We did stop them on the extra point however, so the third period ended with Lorain Catholic on top, 8-6.

In the middle of the fourth period Gilmour forced us to punt and took over on their own 37-yard line. They began a sustained, time-consuming drive which culminated when Janasek drove in from the three-yard line for the go-ahead touchdown. They ran a sweep for the conversion, but I closed the play down and made the biggest single tackle of my career as I stopped Penick short of the goal line.

Three and a half minutes remained and we were behind for the first time this year, 12-8. Fitzpatrick had a few nice passes in the winning drive, but he also scrambled and gained quite a bit of yardage running the ball. He hadn't really shown much of that previously, so it probably surprised Gilmour a bit. I know that it surprised us!

We reached the Gilmour 35-yard line, and, on second down and ten, Fitzpatrick heaved a pass in the general vicinity of Rod Achter and the Gilmour end zone. How Achter made the catch in the midst of the Gilmour defenders was anybody's guess, but he did, for a touchdown, and we led, 14-8.

Gilmour still had almost two minutes to try and score, but we stopped them. They tried a double pass, where a wide receiver stepped back behind the line of scrimmage and received a pass from the quarterback and then threw another pass, but they tried that to my side and I saw it happening right away, so I sprinted over and pressured the wide receiver/passer. They also tried a screen pass to my side on the last play of the game, but it wasn't set up very well and I made the tackle on that play, too. In fact, it was the second game in a row where I happened to make the tackle on a screen pass on the last play of the game.

We trudged off the field, very disappointed in our performance, but pretty happy that we were 3-0.

The next day was another Sunday and we were again in for a workout/ stretching/ film session. Coach Dunning started putting us through the workout while Coach Flowers sat in the coaches' office privately viewing the film from the Gilmour game. We knew it was going to be a bad day when we started hearing things being thrown around in the coaches' office. Finally, he stormed out of the room and screamed," These films are ridiculous! You stink! You didn't stick anybody all day!" He looked to his right and saw Gregor Armantou and Conor Flanary, neither of whom were working out due to injuries sustained in the previous day's game. Flowers looked at Armantou and said, "You didn't make a hit all day." He sort of nodded his head in Flanary's direction and said, ". . . and you. I don't know how you could've gotten hurt. You didn't hit anybody all day. You didn't make one single hit."

Flanary started to say something and Coach Flowers put his hand up, interrupted him, and said, "Aww just shut up."

After the workout came the viewing of the game film, and I wasn't really scared. I thought that overall I might have played one of my better games. I thought I did a good job overall blocking, and knew that I had done my job on defense. I wasn't supposed to make a lot of tackles. I was supposed to give up my body and wipe out blockers. The soreness in my shoulders and head indicated that I had gotten trampled quite a few times, but I was also grabbing ankles at the bottom of the pile on numerous plays, destroying the blocking scheme.

After one play in the second half, Coach Flowers silently ran it back and forth a few times without saying anything. He then said, "Where's Francis?" I raised my hand. "Up here, sir." I asked myself if I was going to be yelled at again? 'What the hell,' I thought. 'I played the best game of my career . . .'

Instead, the head coach actually said, "You know what, Francis?"

"What's that, sir," I asked.

"You and I don't get along very well. We've had our differences, and you hate my guts for a lot of reasons, but damnit, you play some ball. You've performed for us all year. I wish I had a few more players around here who hated my guts like you do. Maybe we'd have some more guys who played hard."

How strange is that? The best, nicest thing that a coach ever said to me was that I hated his guts. Well, those words coming in front of the entire team actually meant a great deal to me.

48

Lorain Catholic High School
Opens Its Doors

September 22, 1969 was our first day of school in the new building. Anyone who had attended St. Mary's Academy knew that Lorain Catholic High School could never be filled with the rich and unique history and tradition of St. Mary's, but this was a chance for us to make our own history and traditions.

The building itself is really only half-built. The completed areas of the school were the academic "PODS" and the cafeteria. The gym, locker areas, auditorium, pool, kitchen, chapel, and library were not nearly completed. That meant a couple of things: we had to bring our lunches to school every day rather than buy cafeteria food (we could buy food from the many vending machines installed in the cafeteria area), and we would continue to have to travel, after school, to St. Mary's Academy to dress for football practice, which continued to be held at Lakeview Park on the west side of Lorain.

The first day of school is always a long one for football teams. Everyone is all excited about school starting, which seems to use a lot of energy, which means that high school kids have less energy to use to practice. That whole idea seemed to be lost on one John Flowers. We were on the field for three full hours, plus thirty minutes in the gym going over the Lodi Cloverleaf scouting report, plus fifteen minutes of film study on Lodi. We didn't leave St. Mary's after practice until around 7:00 in the evening.

The first day of school also allowed me the opportunity to spend some time with Dominique. She stuck a card with my number, #64, on my locker. She was so nice.

Practice really dragged on during the week, which is always true when school started. One of the highlights of the week was the first state football rankings. We were ranked as the number four team in the state of Ohio for Class A. Even though we were 3-0, none of us felt all that excited about it. After all, the coaching staff wouldn't ever let us feel too good about ourselves.

The start of school had very little to do with the problems we were facing from The Cloverleaf Colts. They were big, fast, and also 3-0. Even more than problems from the Colts, however, were the problems faced by our team. We found out that Conor Flanary wouldn't be able to play (shoulder). That meant our only experienced back was Bert Knouwer, and he was really a blocking-back type fullback. Coach Flowers changed our offense a bit, and we decided to run an "I" formation with Bert at tailback and first-year senior player Jules Holiday at fullback. We also had a freshman back starting at wingback. In fact, of the twenty-two positions on a football field, we had ten of them being manned by players who had never played those positions before. That much inexperience causes lots of indecision, and it was obvious that, try as we might, we weren't going to be able to beat a team as good as Cloverleaf with that much inexperience.

Bert Knouwer played his ass off and carried the ball 21 times for 84 yards, but we couldn't stop Cloverleaf when we needed to, and we lost, 15-8. Will Fitzpatrick had his best game of the season, hitting eight out of eleven passes and he also scrambled for 43 more yards. Fitzpatrick also punted extremely well and even played some defense for the first time in his high school career.

We were actually leading 8-7 at the half, thanks to a 23-yard touchdown pass and conversion. Cloverleaf scored the only touchdown of the second half, at least as far as the officials were concerned. Late in the game we had a nice drive moving down the field. Bert Knouwer carried the ball into the line and gained a first down on the Cloverleaf three-yard line. However, all of a sudden, one official was waving his arms and pointing in the other direction, saying that Cloverleaf had the ball. I was at the bottom of the pile with Knouwer, and he clearly had his arm wrapped around the ball. The official stole the ball, and, eventually, the game from us. We trudged off the field losers that night, but I was personally very proud of how hard we had played against a very good team. As short-handed as we were, we had hung in there and battled.

49

When You're Young And In Love
You're Stupid

Danny Jackson had planned a big party for the Saturday night after the Friday night Cloverleaf game. Everyone was going to be there. It is very important to note that there would be no alcohol at this high school party. People may think we were a bunch of nerds, but we just didn't break training rules during the season. I think we were too scared of Coach Flowers to do anything like that.

During the day of the party I received a phone call at home. It was Bridgett Mulroney. She was, of course, my very first love, but we hadn't been together for months. She told me that she thought we should get back together and start dating again. At that time I was enjoying a great relationship with Dominique Pavlak. There was no way I could escape the feeling that I still loved Bridgett. How crazy was this? On the phone I told Bridgett that I would see her that night at the party and, "Give me a week to get rid of Dominique." There is no other explanation other than the title of this chapter, to explain what I did that day.

I took Dominique to the party and left with Bridgett. How stupid. How cruel. Dominique Pavlak had never been anything but wonderful to me. In our two or three months together we had established a bond of friendship and trust. She was absolutely great for me. Bridgett, on the other hand, had already broken my heart at least once. Why would I do something so stupid?

When you're young and in love you're stupid.

After I left the party with Bridgett, Dominique was so hurt and embarrassed that she walked all the way home, right through the heart of Lorain. From Danny Jackson's house to Dominique's house had to be three or four miles through Lorain, which is not the safest place in the whole world.

Despite this incredibly stupid and mean act, Dominique Pavlak has remained a friend for over 35 years. That says something about her. Of course she reminds me of how stupid and hurtful and mean I was every time I see her, but I guess I still deserve that.

50

"What the hell?
You almost killed me out there!"

Working for The Lorain Journal sometimes actually offered perks. I actually got to get in free to certain athletic events, as long as I was willing to write a story about the event for The Journal. Conor Flanary noticed an advertisement in the paper for a Professional Wrestling Show to be held in Lorain at the old armory. Big-time wrestling was very popular in the sixties, lost some of its luster and then came back in the eighties. It remains pretty popular even today.

Flanary asked me if I was interested in going to the event. I told him that I was not only interested, but that I thought I could get us in free. All I had to do was convince The Journal Sports' Editor that I would cover the event and write a story about it. He had no problem with that.

The event was held on a Tuesday evening, which usually meant that I would not have been able to attend. I explained to my dad that I was going to be "on assignment" from The Journal, and he agreed to let me attend.

Conor and I made sure we were there plenty early so that we could get a good seat. We didn't need to be there early at all, as there were only about 75 fans in attendance. The guy at the door was a little skeptical about someone as young as me writing for the Journal, but he eventually let both Conor and me in.

We got to see some famous wrestlers of the day, including Argentino Appollo, Chief White Owl, The Rebel, The Sheik, The Bruiser, and the reigning world tag team champions, The Hell's Angels.

There were a few things that stood out from that night:

1. The promoters carried the same popcorn machine from site to site, and the popcorn we had was so stale it had to have been popped months before.
2. Big-time wrestlers in the sixties weren't very big. Chief White Owl was probably about 6-1 and weighed about 220. He was the biggest guy there that night.
3. It's fake. I know that might come to a surprise for some people, but they really don't do all the things to each other that it looks like. That being said, the professional wrestlers of that era and any era are actually outstanding athletes who really know how to use their bodies. Back to the fake deal. Conor had to use the restroom halfway through the bouts. He went in, used the facilities, the started out the door. The Sheik, who had just finished his bout, was returning to the locker room with his opponent. One of the big deals about The Sheik was that he didn't speak English, and always had to have a translator with him. He supposedly only spoke some Middle Eastern language. As Conor was leaving the restroom The Sheik walked by, not seeing Conor. Conor heard The Sheik say to his opponent, "What the hell? You almost killed me out there." He spoke in perfect English with no accent. Conor came back to me with this incredible, stunned look on his face. "You are not going to believe what I just heard. You are not going to believe what I just heard," he kept repeating. "What," I finally asked him. He related to me that he had heard The Sheik speak English. He couldn't believe it.
4. Some of those guys are disgusting. As mentioned, they weren't very big. The reigning World Heavyweight Champions, The Hell's Angels, were about six-foot or six-one and neither weighed more than 180. They wore big, high, black riding boots and cut-off vest jackets with "Hell's Angels" on the back. They had long, greasy hair that looked like it hadn't been washed in a week. They were disgusting when they wrestled, too, as they used all sorts of nasty tricks and just kept spitting at the audience. Conor actually got hit by a 'loogie' and bragged about it for weeks.

After the show was over I got to interview Chief White Owl and The Rebel, who were pretty nice. On our way out of the Armory, as we were walking to my car, I saw The Hell's Angels walk out of a local bar with a brown paper bag. I pointed out to Conor that those guys walking right in front of us were The Hell's Angels. He insisted on talking to them, and I thought it might be fun, too. They were actually pretty nice. We reached their car, an old Chevy, just as they were getting in. They had both already opened a can of beer. When they saw two high school kids approaching them, it looked like they wanted to hide the beer, but it was too late.

We talked to them for about five minutes, and they told us they were headed for Detroit for their next event. They noticed me looking at them and the beer, and the one guy said, "Oh, this . . . . just a little road pop for the drive." By the way, they had left the Armory without taking a shower.

51

Bring Back Rich Rhome!

Oh how I yearn for the days of Rich Rhome! Remember, Rich Rhome was the old friend who played for Clearview. He was 5-9 and weighed about 150 pounds. He was quick, but so was I, and I handled him pretty well. This week is completely different. We play Tiffin Calvert High School, whose record is 4-0, and includes a 45-14 shellacking of previously-undefeated Sandusky Perkins. The Calvert Senescas (that is actually their nickname) are the biggest team we will face this year. Their roster has fifteen guys who weigh over 200 pounds. We have four, and three of them don't even play!

Calvert has some outstanding individuals, including a great running back named Dennis Smith, but he isn't really the reason I'm worried, even though he does run mostly to my side of the field. The guy who will be playing over me is named Big Joe Monaco. He's 6-4 and weighs 282. When you're that big people begin to take notice. Hell, when you're that big how can people not take notice?

On film Monaco looks quick and very tough. Sometimes he just "bull-rushes" right through guys, and other times he actually out quicks people into gaps. I hope I can just get in his way and that our backs are good enough to cut off of this sort of shield block. Speaking of our backs, we got some good news this week. Conor Flanary will be back at full strength, which means Bert Knouwer will be able to move back to fullback. Also, Robbie Cavellini had his cast removed and he's trying his hardest to walk and then, hopefully, return before the end of the season. He is one dedicated kid, and I wish I knew more people like Robbie Cavellini.

The bus ride to Tiffin from Lorain was long and laborious, and the ride home was even worse. We got shutout, 21-0. When we took the field for our pre-game warm-up I looked over and said to Conor Flanary, "I thought the scouting report said they were so big and bad. They don't look so big or bad to me." I was actually just looking at the Calvert specialists—you know, the kickers, passers, receivers, etc. Then their linemen came out to warm up. Their team seemed to fill up the entire side of the field. The noise they made during their calisthenics was impressive, and man were they big. I spotted Big Joe Monaco pretty quickly.

We kicked off, and the fourth play of the game was a quick pitch to Dennis Smith right in front of me. I beat the blocker to a spot and tackled the quick halfback for a loss. I actually had thoughts that this might be a good night for both me and the Spartans. I was wrong on both counts. Calvert kept the drive alive and reached our 29-yard line. On third and long their quarterback rolled to the right, which meant I was to drop into the left flat in pass coverage. I dropped correctly. The QB couldn't find an open receiver, so he began to scramble. He ran back to the left, which meant he was coming right at me. I moved back up towards the line of scrimmage. It was just the two of us, with no one else within ten yards. He stepped to the inside and I committed myself to that move, getting ready to make the open-field tackle. Just as I went to grab him he crossed over and cut to the outside. I reached out and grabbed nothing but air. I never touched the runner. I missed him completely, right in front of our bench and bleachers. It was the worst defensive play I ever made, and the most embarrassing.

The quarterback was finally dragged down on our four-yard line, but the first down allowed Calvert to quickly score.

In the middle of the second period Grego Armantou ran a deep pass pattern, but Will Fitzpatrick underthrew him, and the pass was intercepted. As the defensive back returned the ball down the far sidelines, I noticed that he had a wall of blockers in front of him and only Fitzpatrick to try and stop him. Fitzpatrick did a great job of fighting off blockers, and I finally caught him from behind, preventing a second Tiffin Calvert touchdown.

The Senecas moved down closer to our goal line, and, on fourth down and two, they threw a little pass over the middle for an easy touchdown. They ran the same play for the conversion, and they led, 14-0 at halftime.

At halftime I tried to review how I had played so far. I stunk. Not only did I miss that big tackle out in the open, but on offense Big Joe Monaco had just run right over me a few times.

The third quarter was scoreless, and in the middle of the fourth quarter Tiffin ran a power sweep to the other side of our defense. I saw the play developing, and it was well-blocked. I started my pursuit angle and thought I could catch the swift back. When I finally dove at him around our 20-yard line it was too late. Once again, I tackled air. Their conversion kick was good and the score was 21-0.

Fitzpatrick filled the air with passes, but when a team knows you're going to pass it makes it difficult to complete them. During the second half when we were trying to pass just about every play I was trying to block Big Joe Monaco. He was standing straight up and trying to run right over me to rush the passer. For whatever reason, I decided to punch him in the stomach. His hands were high in the air trying to block the pass and I gave him four good shots right in the belly with my right fist. After the play he grabbed me by my shoulder pads, spun me around, looked down at me and said, "Hey, watch the punching." I looked up at him and just sort of nodded. With about a minute left in the game I accidentally caused and recovered a fumble. I tried to tackle a ball-carrier and actually missed his body with mine. What I did hit, dead on, however, was the ball. It popped out and I also fell on it for a recovery.

Will Fitzpatrick completed ten out of 32 passes, with two interceptions. We gained only 79 yards passing. Conor Flanary led us in rushing with 67 yards in 14 carries, but, basically, our offense stunk. This marked the first time in his career that a John Flowers-coached team had ever been shut out. Not only that, but it was also the first time a Coach Flowers' team had ever lost two games in a row.

After the game we went into Tiffin Columbian High School and had a post-game meal with the opponents. I actually had a nice conversation with Big Joe Monaco, after I realized he wasn't going to kick my ass for the punching incident.

Since Tiffin was so far away and we didn't arrive home until after midnight, we didn't have to be dressed for our Sunday workout until 11:30. After the stretching and the workout we got to watch the game films. Everyone was really worried about how we would look, but Coach Flowers was actually kind of mild. He hardly raised his voice at all. After the film session he named ten guys he wanted to see in the coaches' office.

JD Szollzy was first, and Coach Flowers told him he would be an outside linebacker exclusively, and that he no longer had to worry about offense. Coach Flowers then called Will Fitzpatrick and me into the coaches' office together. He told me that I was being switched to right end on offense. He challenged me to learn the position this week and start the next Friday night at Cleveland Central Catholic. Coach also told Fitzpatrick to get together with me that afternoon and start learning all of the pass patterns. I was excited because I thought I was sort of being wasted as a guard. I was faster and could catch better than any of the ends we presently had. I just needed to learn the position.

Later that afternoon I got together with Will Fitzpatrick, and, after warming up for a few minutes, we ran through every pass pattern we had at least twice. We also ran some individual patterns after that, and, for the entire afternoon, I caught all but two balls thrown to me.

My first full practice as an end was a real doozy. It was one of those two hour and 50 minute John Flowers' Specials. When we do team drills the coaches try to have three players share two positions, so that guys can rotate in and out. However, since I was learning a new position, there was no rotating for me. I was in every play on both offense and defense. One thing I have found out about playing end is that it takes a lot more running than does playing guard. Lots of times guards are blocking people right in front of them, whether the play is being run to the right or to the left. Ends, on the other hand, have to block when the play is run towards them, and sprint across the field for downfield blocking when the play is run away from them. I couldn't believe how much I had to run at practice.

The next day's practice, October 7, was shorter than the previous day's. It was only two and a half hours long, but a full fifteen minutes of that practice was physical conditioning. I was again forced to play every play, and then also do all of the conditioning. I also found out some other great news that day.

Remember Big Joe Monaco? The week before I played guard and had to block against a 6-2 defense which featured that man-mountain across from me all night. This week I'm playing right end, we are playing Cleveland Central Catholic, and they play a 4-4 defense, with an outside linebacker lining up on my inside shoulder every play. His name? Big Ed Rodriquez. He's not nearly as big as Big Joe Monaco. Rodriquez is only 6-3, 270, but he's much meaner than Monaco. This hardly seems fair. CCC also features All-League fullback Bob Powell, a crunching 190-pounder, and ultra-quick quarterback Lou Lamirand. We know most of these guys personally, as we have been playing against them in football and basketball for years.

Lamirand runs the option, which is something we really haven't seen much this year. He loves to fake the pitch and keep the ball himself. We have got to contain him this week or he will run all over us and we'll be 3-3.

52

". . . . and starting at right end . . . ."

I got to start at right end against Cleveland Central Catholic, and it was lots of fun. The game ended with a very deceiving score of 18-12.

Early in the first quarter Bob Powell broke loose for a 68-yard touchdown run and we were behind, 6-0. We drove the ball to just over midfield, but were stopped. As Will Fitzpatrick lined up to punt, the Ironmen jumped offsides, giving us a first down at their 44-yard line. Coach Flowers always tried to take quick advantage of turnovers or mistakes, and he called, "Pass 17 Right end corner." That meant we were going to fake an off-tackle run to the left, and I was supposed to run a corner route away from the defense. Fitzpatrick made a great fake, and no one hit me coming off the line. I ran down about fifteen yards and then cut to the corner. There was no one near me. Fitzpatrick's pass was right on the money, I caught the ball, and ran into the endzone. The very first pass I caught as an end was a 44-yard touchdown. I handed the ball to the official and everybody jumped around and congratulated me. Sophomore running back Denny McNamara swept left end for the conversion and we led, 8-6.

In the middle of the second quarter Lou Lamirand faked to Powell and threw a beautiful pass for 58 yards and a CCC touchdown. We were behind again, 12-8.

We had a great drive down the field which was culminated by Conor Flanary making the best run of his career. Flanary swept right end and cut back beautifully against the grain for ten yards and a touchdown. He also caught the pass for the conversion, and at halftime we led, 16-12. Flanary was having probably his best game of his career, and we were both having a great time playing football.

At halftime Coach Flowers reminded us that we had to control the football to control the game. The second half was a bitter defensive struggle. I did get a little defensive action, and actually sacked Lamirand for a 13-yard loss at one point in the third period. As I tackled him, however, I landed on my right shoulder, and it went numb. It was just like at Gilmour, when I couldn't move my arm unless I took my left arm and swung my right arm around. It was sort of a scary feeling, and I just hoped that CCC wouldn't run another play to my side while I had no feeling in my arm.

Late in the third quarter we got a drive going and reached the CCC 30-yard line. A penalty and a big loss gave us a third and 27. "Diagonal Pass Left" was called, and I cut across the middle and Fitzpatrick threw the pass a bit high. I had to leap to catch the pass, and I stumbled down after I caught it, good for 18 yards. The two passes I caught were the only two passes Fitzpatrick completed for the game.

Also in the third period, I was hit the hardest I had ever been hit in a football game. Will Fitzpatrick got a great punt off and it just sailed over the head of the CCC return man. I was the first guy down the field to cover the punt, and I found myself running right next to Bob Powell, the 190-pound CCC fullback and linebacker. I looked over at him as I sprinted down the field and said, "Helluva punt, huh?" He just nodded and said, "Yeah." He then sort of veered toward me and wound up and hit me with a vicious forearm shiver right to the side of the head and knocked me up and off my feet. I landed and just rolled over with an instant headache. Pow! It was an awesome hit, and clean enough to not draw a penalty. I just should have been ready.

Another reason the CCC game was fun was because of the attitude of Conor (The Crow) Flanary and me. We had just decided that we were going to have a good time. When I changed positions from guard to end, I also changed positions in the huddle, and I now stood next to Flanary. That meant we were going to keep up a steady stream of dialogue, and there are few people funnier than Conor Flanary. He had a great game and I kept telling him, "Damn, Crow, you be sweet tonight." Flanary had started calling me "Bingo," so we had comments on just about every play.

Every once in awhile someone in the huddle (usually Fitzpatrick) would tell us to shut the hell up, but we were really having fun.

Late in the game, after we had totally controlled the ball but couldn't score, CCC took over deep in their own territory. Junior linebacker Calvin Stack sacked their quarterback, who ended up fumbling the ball into the endzone, which was recovered by one of their lineman for a safety. We got two points and led the game, 18-12. After the safety Central Catholic had to kick off, and they actually tried an on-side kick from their own 20-yard line. Tackle Jeff Brent alertly recovered the ball, and we had possession.

The officials were discussing things with Will Fitzpatrick, and Flanary and I took control of the huddle. Brent lined up in the huddle right in front of Flanary and me, and we got around him and started singing "For He's A Jolly Good Fellow." Flanary actually stepped in front of Brent and got down on one knee and started bowing to him. Mackie MacGregor finally got mad and yelled at us. "Shut up, damnit, and get in the goddamn huddle."

Rod Achter, who hardly ever said anything, actually spoke up, "C'mon, you guys, we didn't win yet." Everybody else just glared at us. We should've known better and just shut up, but we were having too much fun. I actually stepped in front of the huddle, where Fitzpatrick usually stood to call the plays, and said, "All right you guys, here's what we're going to do. We're going to run a tackle-eligible. Brent, since you're already the hero tonight, we'll let you catch this one. Get out there a long way and Fitzpatrick will get you the ball." Brent and Flanary cracked up, but everybody else was really tired of our little fun time. My parting shot to the huddle, before I got back to where I was supposed to be, was simply, "You guys are too damned serious." I guess we were lucky that Fitzpatrick was meeting with the refs, because he never would have let the huddle get that crazy.

Flanary was a workhorse for us and gained 102 yards rushing on 18 carries. Fullback Bert Knouwer was really instrumental in our second half ball control, as he gained over 50 yards in the half and finished with 67 yards in 14 carries. As mentioned, Fitzpatrick only completed two passes for 62 yards, but he did show some great scrambling ability and actually gained 56 yards rushing.

In the locker room after the game everyone was feeling pretty good. It seemed like it had been a long time since we could enjoy a victory. The victory was also the 20th straight North Central Conference win, dating all the way back to the second game in 1965.

Also in the locker room after the game, Coach Flowers told me to make an appointment to see the team physician about my shoulder/arm injury. He had noticed that I got hurt on the sack, even though I didn't leave the game.

The next day at the film session I began to notice something that I had only been slightly aware of the previous night. The entire game the Ironmen only ran six plays to my side of the field. It wasn't "my" side of the field; it was also Mackie MacGregor and Calvin Stack's side, too. I do recall being somewhat bored on defense as the game went on about a lack of action, but it really came out while watching the film. Mackie MacGregor's older brother was an assistant coach for CCC, and he later explained that they thought we had one side of our defense which was much stronger than the other, and they actually planned to run as few plays as possible to our side of the field. As I said, that became blatantly clear as we watched the film

The cameraman who shot the game should be shot himself. These were the worst films ever. Most of the time he got only half of the line, and he never did actually follow the ball. My touchdown reception wasn't on the film at all, and, on the other reception, he got Fitzpatrick throwing the ball but never moved the camera to the guy catching the ball. Basically, it was a worthless film as far as I was concerned. They only ran six plays to our side and neither of my receptions was on it. Great.

The team physician was actually a chiropractor, and after talking to me and giving me a few tests determined that I had a pinched nerve in my neck, not my shoulder or arm. Of course, the nerve, when pinched in my neck, caused me to lose feeling all the way down my arm. He made it seem like a rather serious injury and made me go through a series of stretching exercises, electric shock treatment, penetrating sound wave treatment, and an ultra-wave nerve treatment before taking x-rays.

Tackle Jeff Brent went with me to the doctor, and he was given much of the same treatment. We were told to not engage in any contact until further notice. We both went to Coach Flowers' house to tell him what the doctor had said. He just nodded and said, "Well, if you're going to take a blow, this is the week to do it, because after this week comes the big push."

I looked at him and said, "But Coach, I don't want to take a blow."

"Yeah, well, I realize that, but we'll follow the doctor's orders. If he says you stay out, you stay out."

53

All-Time Record Temperature For October 13

The temperature reached 82 degrees on October 13, which was an all-time high for Lorain, Ohio. The practice scheduled for October 13 was pretty much nothing but fundamentals and conditioning. Every player dressed in full gear for the practice except Jeff Brent, Robbie Cavellini, and me. When we reached Lakeview Park Coach Flowers saw the three of us and said, "You guys can't hit, right? But you can run, can't you? I want you to run like hell out there today. You gotta push yourself to improve and you gotta stay in shape."

After the quickness and agility exercises, the team started in on the individual position drills. Since Cavellini couldn't even run yet, it was up to Jeff Brent and me to run. We started off jogging together, but the big tackle soon developed leg cramps and had to stop and stretch numerous times. My original goal was two miles, but I soon passed that. I ran three and a half miles, and, when I finished this the team conditioning was set to begin. We started with 300 yard sprints, followed by all fours and more sprints. We jogged, sprinted, and ended with Packer Drill. I was more tired on a day when I didn't even wear pads than I ever was at a regular practice.

I also had another appointment with Dr. Gigliotti that night. He worked me and stretched me and then relaxed me. He also explained to me what the problem actually was. I had a loose joint where my shoulder met my neck. When I got hit a certain way a nerve would be entrapped in that joint, and, when it closed around the joint I would lose all the feeling in my arm. He told me that it was quite serious, and that if it happened again I would have to stop playing football. I decided then and there that it wouldn't happen again, if you know what I mean.

The next day was also very warm, but we didn't wear full pads out to practice. We left our shoulder pads in the gym, which meant there wouldn't be any hitting during the practice. I'm sure Coach Flowers realized how sore and beat up most of the guys were now that it was the middle of the season. We spent our time going over the scouting report trying to learn all we could about the Hawken Academy Hawks, our opponent for the next Saturday afternoon.

Hawken was a big, physical team with a record of 2-3. However, they had a great offense and liked to outscore teams. This would be a big challenge for our defense, because our offense wasn't very good. In fact, since the Fremont St. Joe game, when we still had Cavellini and scored 44 points, we had scored only 54 points in the other five games combined. That's just not good enough, especially when our defense had given up 68 points in those same five games.

Hawken's squad was very large, especially two of their backs. Their fullback was 6-2 and weighed 220, and one of their halfbacks was 6-1, 195. We were going to have our hands full again on Saturday.

Wednesday's practice was really high-spirited. The weather had cooled off a bit, and we still didn't wear full practice gear. In fact, everyone was even more pumped up at practice on Wednesday because we got to wear our brand new team sweats. We had never had team sweats before, and the red sweatpants and the practice jerseys looked awesome together, and, as I said, everyone had lots more spirit.

Our Wednesday practice was sharp, especially the pass offense, as I was settling in to the new position quite well, and Will Fitzpatrick was beginning to get more comfortable passing to me. We actually got to watch a film of the Hawken team, and, as I have already said, they were huge. Mackie MacGregor had the line of the day when he said to all of us after watching the film, "You know the old saying, the bigger they are the harder they hit." That's really funny coming from our biggest guy, isn't it?

Conor Flanary and I had decided during the last game that things were way too serious, so we really started to have some fun at practice, in the locker room, and even at school.

Speaking of school, things were moving right along. It was interesting every day listening to the construction as the rest of the school was being built. We never stopped hearing pounding, sawing, drilling, etc., as the construction crews tried to finish more and more areas of the building.

On the next Saturday we traveled to Hawken Academy east of Cleveland for another Saturday afternoon game. This was real football weather: bright sky, a brisk wind from the northwest, and about 45 degrees. We arrived at Hawken around 12:20, and the specialists were to take the field at 1:20. Coach Flowers told Rod Achter and me to be sure and go out with the specialists and catch some passes, as much to get used to the wind and the field conditions as anything.

I had a horrible pre-game. I had never had any problem catching the ball with my hands, but on this day the ball felt like it weighed ten pounds, and it kept bouncing off of my shoulder pads. I couldn't catch anything. I was even misjudging some passes that Will Fitzpatrick threw. The other thing that bothered me about the pre-game was the fact that I broke a pretty good sweat, and then the cold wind started chilling me whenever I stood around. I guess I needed to keep moving.

I just didn't think my "psyche" was right on that day, and Conor Flanary must have been thinking the same thing. We received the opening kickoff, and it sort of skittered off of the kicker's foot down around our 20-yard line. It was right in front of Flanary. Instead of picking the ball up, though, he just let it roll and stop. A kickoff is a free ball, and Hawken sprinted down the field and fell on the ball. That was a major, major screw-up by Flanary. What was he thinking?

Only a great goal line stand prevented Hawken from scoring, but we spent most of the first quarter deep in our territory. Will Fitzpatrick got off a couple of great punts to help us out, but we were still fighting a field position battle. Late in the first quarter Hawken faced a third and long situation from our 43-yard line. Their quarterback faded to throw, and junior linebacker Calvin Stack sacked him and knocked the ball loose. I was the second player there, and I tried to pick the ball up. I missed it the first time, and actually fell to the ground, but there was a wild scramble for the ball, and, when I got back up and got into the scramble a second time, I wasn't going to be denied. I scooped the ball up at the Hawken 45-yard line and raced towards the goal line. I ran all the way for the touchdown, and we led, 6-0. Bert Knouwer ran the extra point in and we led, 8-0.

On the series immediately after the touchdown, Hawken ran an option to my side of the field. I faked like I was going to go after the quarterback, then turned and went after the pitch man. I arrived at just about the same time as the ball, and I knocked it away from the halfback, but Hawken recovered and kept possession.

In the second quarter Fitzpatrick attempted a pass into the right flat, where it was alertly picked off and returned 49 yards for a Hawken touchdown. Their two-point conversion was also good, so at halftime the score was 8-8.

Hawken's school is quite far from the field, so at halftime we actually just got back into our bus, which was parked right next to the tiny stadium. Coach Flowers came onto the bus and was fuming. He told us that if we didn't come back and win this game he would quit as our coach and we would have to play the rest of the season without a head coach. He told us that we were going to stop Hawken, get the ball, and jam it down their throats. We weren't going to pass or run anything fancy. We were just going to run right at them.

Sure enough, we stopped Hawken on their first drive and we took over on our own 31-yard line. Fullback Bert Knouwer was the workhorse, and we ran right at Hawken. The longest gain we had was seven yards in the drive, a drive which used fourteen plays and gained 60 yards. When we reached the Hawks' 13-yard line, we ran another play to our left side. Knouwer reached the 9-yard line. Since I was the right end and the play was run to the left, I went across the field to try and get a downfield block. I didn't block anybody, but right near the end of the play a Hawken player knocked me down and I fell into the back of the legs of another Hawken player. The official only saw me hit the Hawken player from behind, and he called clipping on me, which was a fifteen-yard penalty. On third down our drive was stopped when Fitzpatrick threw an interception.

After one first down we again stopped Hawken and started another time-consuming drive. The fourth quarter started and we were bogged down on the Hawken twelve-yard line. Fitzpatrick called "60 Diagonal Pass Left," which meant I was the primary receiver on a slant pass across the middle. I was concerned with first down yardage first, and a touchdown second. I got both. The pass was thrown a little high, and I had to leap to make the catch, and before I hit the ground a Hawken player tried to tackle me. He just sort of knocked me off balance, and I put my hand down, righted myself, and dove into the end zone. Bert Knouwer ran for the conversion points, and we led, 16-8.

Late in the game Danny Jackson intercepted a Hawken pass and raced 48 yards down the sidelines for a touchdown, completing the scoring in a 22-8 Spartan victory. In the locker room after the game it seemed like a lot of pressure was gone. As I considered how the game had gone, I began to get worried. Early in the game I had moved prematurely on the snap count, and I was also charged with offensive pass interference in the second quarter on a pass that was underthrown and would have been intercepted if I hadn't interfered. Not only that, but in that same second quarter I was detected clipping when Fitzpatrick scrambled and took off running. That call was a terrible call. I had cut across the field, and, when Fitzpatrick took off I peeled back to help block for him. He set up a linebacker and I made a great low block that was definitely not clipping. Coach Flowers even yelled at the ref and yelled out to me that it was a bad call. Adding up the two clips, the offsides, and the pass interference, I had cost my team 50 yards in penalties. I couldn't wait for the films the next day to receive a royal reaming from Coach Flowers.

As Coach Flowers had said a week earlier, the "other" games were finished now, and we were ready for "The Big Push," which meant we were playing league leader Parma Byzantine next week, followed by arch-rival Elyria Catholic, and, finally, Midview, which was one of only two teams who had beaten us the previous season.

54

No Time For Heroes

The headline in the Sunday Journal for our game against Hawken read, "Lorain Catholic Rally Clips Hawken, 22-8." The "kicker," which is the smaller headline above the major headline, said, "Star Stephen Francis 'Almost' Goat." Great. That's just what Coach Flowers likes—picking out one player and saying something special about him. The 'Almost Goat' comment was referring to the 50 yards in penalties charged to me, specifically the one clipping penalty down near the goal line during the third quarter.

Coach Flowers never liked to give too much credit to an individual, and he had read the morning paper. I expected the tongue-lashing that came my way during the film session. Coach Flowers found every single mistake I made, and never once said anything nice like, "Hey, way to be there to pick up that fumble." Or, "That was a great catch and run on the winning touchdown." Of course he might have said something nice if either of my big plays were on the film, but, once again, the photographer missed my two best plays, but he sure caught every penalty and mistake I made.

Bert Knouwer, by the way, had a career day against Hawken. If his body was as big as his heart, he'd be an All-American. He was one tough kid, and he never complained about anything. He just kept playing hard. Against Hawken he carried the football a school-record 29 times for 144 yards. Most of the carries were straight ahead into the teeth of the defense, but his effort in the game was actually inspiring. Play after play he carried defenders forward to gain more yards.

On Monday after Hawken everyone was fired up. Robbie Cavellini was going to try to play against Byzantine. He wouldn't be 100%, of course, but

Robbie Cavellini at 75% was better than most guys at 100%. Besides that, his return was about as inspiring as the way Bert Knouwer ran against Hawken.

It's normally a good idea to try and get spirit flowing and increasing as the week goes along, and, since we didn't play Byzantine until Sunday afternoon, we might be peaking a little early, but what the heck, coaches love spirited practices, and even the Monday fundamental day was spirited. I think the seniors can see the light at the end of the tunnel, and many of us are really ready to complete the season, even though I am having the time of my life catching passes, scoring touchdowns, and playing both ways.

Byzantine is 6-1, and 2-0 in the North Central Conference, so this will be their championship game. We are 5-2, and only 1-0 in the NCC, so we have to beat Byzantine and Elyria Catholic in order to win the league championship. Of the seven games Byzantine played, Coach Flowers had copies of six of the films. They were obtained from the opposing coaches. The one tape we didn't have was Elyria Catholic, and we would never ask the hated Panthers for anything.

Byzantine looked really good on film. They were big and powerful. Their quarterback was a great athlete who really liked to run the ball. He was an outstanding runner, but not that great of a passer. He was also a great leader, and he had brought them back from behind numerous times. Remember that this team has already beaten big, bad Elyria Catholic by the unusual score of 8-3.

Byzantine's defense was actually pretty simple. They ran a six-man line with two linebackers. All six linemen were big and mean and they tried to sit in there and smack you around and stop you on the line of scrimmage. That included jamming offensive ends every single play, which makes it very difficult to get off the line and get into a pass pattern. Their defense sort of reminds me of Amherst, the physical team we had scrimmaged in the preseason. Remember, the team that completely stopped our offense?

We also received some bad news on Monday of Byzantine week. Outside linebacker Calvin Stack, who had been playing right next to me for a few weeks now, had a ruptured clavicle and was lost for the season. Stack was really coming into his own as a great defensive player, and we would really miss him.

As far as school goes, the senior guys have befriended one of the construction workers. A middle-aged guy named John always seems to be around when we weren't doing anything, so he has kept us up to date with the construction of the building. He told me that we were, ". . . weeks away . . ." from the gym and locker rooms being ready. That probably means we will have to travel all the way to St. Mary's Academy for the start of the basketball season.

Our school schedule this year is very unique. We have 21 periods in the day. That's right, 21. Each period, or "POD," is only 20 minutes long. Some classes meet two pods, or forty minutes a day, and some classes meet three pods, or sixty minutes. One of the classes I am taking is Journalism I, which meets PODS 15 and 16. The teacher is a new teacher, Mr. Hacnik. He doesn't really like me. You see, I have been writing for The Lorain Journal for about three and a half years, and I really think I know more about journalism than he does. I made the mistake of telling him that. Guess what? Teachers don't really like to be told things like that, even if they are true. One day in class I was sitting near the front corner of the room, and I really had to pass gas. I let out one fart silently, and felt pretty good. The second fart echoed off of the desk seat. It was loud. The moment it came out, Mr. Hacnik pointed to me and said, "How To Win Friends and Influence People by Steve Francis." I believe that was as embarrassed as I have been in a long while.

We are beginning to work on publishing a high school newspaper for Lorain Catholic High School. I look forward to working on that staff as the sports' editor.

Robbie Cavellini is getting stronger every day. He definitely didn't have his smooth moves back yet, but he is strong enough to start against Byzantine at both right halfback and safety. The importance of Sunday's game was not lost on anyone. St. Mary's had won the last three North Central Conference championships, and we were protecting a 20-game league win streak. In addition to that, Coach Flowers had never lost a league game in his two-and-a-half years as a coach in the league.

55

You Know The Old Saying . . . .

When we got to Lakeview Park for practice I noticed that junior tackle Steven Mathews only had one sock. Our practice shoes were old, canvas, high tops, which were uncomfortable if you had on two pairs of socks on each foot, and I can't even imagine what they would feel like if you were barefoot. Anyway, when everyone was ready for practice Coach Flowers always had a little talk for us and then we jogged out to the field. I was watching this unfold, so I got really close to Mathews as he approached Coach Flowers. Coach Flowers absolutely hates it when you are unprepared for practice, and, if you have an equipment malfunction before practice he really goes crazy. As we were jogging to the field after Coach Flowers' talk, Mathews jogged up next to Coach Flowers and said, "Uh, Coach."

"Yeah Steve, what's up?"

"I, uh, only have one sock today."

"You know the old saying, Steve."

"Uh, no Coach, what is it?"

"Tough shit," replied Coach Flowers as he picked up speed on his jog to the field.

I thought I was going to lose it. I started laughing and couldn't wait to tell everybody who wasn't right there to hear the exchange. "You know the old saying. Tough shit." That is absolutely classic Coach Flowers.

We also have a few freshmen playing with the varsity now. One of them is a talented-but-not-too-smart running back named Dennis White. He makes mistake after mistake after mistake, and Coach Flowers is constantly yelling at him to remember the plays, the snap count, etc. After Tuesday's Byzantine practice we were jogging off the field and White said to me, "Hey Steve. I had a good practice today. I didn't make one offensive mistake today." Not so funny, huh? Well, you see, White didn't play offense that day. He only played defense. I told you he wasn't too smart.

Sometimes I think Coach Flowers should have been a doctor. Late in the Byzantine week we had arrived back at school after practice, and he said to Steve Mathews, "How's that leg, Steve?"

Mathews mumbled, "Uh, pretty good, Coach."

Coach Flowers looked at him and said, "What do you mean pretty good? It's real good, isn't it?"

Mathews looked at him and in all seriousness said, "Uh, yeah Coach. That's what I meant. It's real good."

The healing powers of Coach John Flowers!

56

"I Wonder Who Won Homecoming Queen."

The Byzantine game was only our second home game, and we asked if we could wear our scarlet pants and white jerseys. They should look really good on television, as the Byzantine-Lorain Catholic game was tabbed as the high school Game of the Week on a Cleveland television station which showed high school replays on the following Wednesday. We were all excited about seeing ourselves on TV. The Byzantine game was also our Homecoming game, even though most of us didn't understand how you could have Homecoming festivities in the very first year of a school. Think about it . . . . who's going to come home? We don't have any alumni, since we are the very first senior class.

Byzantine's uniforms were a replica of the Dallas Cowboys', and, when we took the field to warm up it sounded like we were going to be playing the Cowboys. I had never heard a high school team warm up louder than Parma Byzantine. They had lots of guys and lots of loud, deep voices. It sounded like they were mature men. As we warmed up we tried to be as loud, but it seemed that the louder we got the higher our voices got. Byzantine definitely "won" the warm up.

We received the opening kickoff and pretty much went nowhere. Fitzpatrick got off a good punt and the Buccaneers started on their own 32-yard line. They promptly went 68 yards for a touchdown. Most of the damage was done by their quarterback on straight QB sneaks or quarterback draws. Their game plan against our 4-4 defense was to ignore our defensive tackles on the sneaks and just release the center and both guards on our two inside linebackers. They had us outnumbered 3-2 when they did this. The quarterback just got up to the line and took the ball and ran straight ahead. They had taken big splits on the line and our defensive tackles

were trailing the play almost immediately. On the quarterback draw the
QB would take the snap, drop back three steps, and then run straight
ahead. Their guards blocked out on our defensive tackles and their tackles
released on our linebackers. We had no answer for these two simple plays,
and they ran them time and time and time again and gained significant
yardage every time.

The Buccaneers mounted another drive in the second quarter, and at
halftime they led, 16-0. At halftime we had no clue how to either move the
ball or stop the Bucs. The coaches were trying to devise a change in strategy
while we all sat there quietly. I thought it was too quiet. I caught Conor
Flanary's eye and he stood up and came over to me. I think he thought I
was going to be serious about some deep strategy for the second half, but
I looked up at him with a very straight face as he leaned over to me and
I said, "I wonder who won Homecoming Queen." We had to work pretty
hard to stifle ourselves from laughing.

By the way, my cousin, Amy Chudinski won Homecoming Queen and
they announced that at halftime of the game.

Conor Flanary really boomed a kickoff to start the second half (he was
more relaxed after my halftime comment) and the Byzantine return man
slipped and fell at the one-yard line. We thought we were still in the game,
and our spirits soared. We had been handcuffed the entire first half with
horrible field position, and we had only attempted two passes. We held
Byzantine on their first drive of the second half, and, after a weak punt,
we took over on their 32-yard line.

That field position allowed us to pass when we wanted to, and we wanted
to right away. Flanary caught two passes on the drive, and Grego Armantou
also made a big catch. Bert Knouwer blasted over from the one to make
the score 16-6, and Flanary made a spectacular catch for the conversion,
and it was 16-8 and a brand new ballgame.

The fourth quarter started and it was still 16-8. We had the ball around
midfield, and Fitzpatrick got sacked for an eight-yard loss. On third and
eighteen we ran the diagonal pass again, and Fitzpatrick drilled a pass right
to me. I caught the ball, turned up the field, and ran into two Byzantine
defensive backs. We had a great collision, and I thought I fell forward
enough for the first down. The officials measured, and we were just short.
On fourth and one Bert Knouwer slammed into the middle of the Byzantine
line and gained a full yard, which would have given us a first down with
the momentum. One of the side judges came running in to spot the ball
from Knouwer's run, and we couldn't believe where he put it down. We
were about a foot short before the play, Knouwer gained at least a yard,
and when they brought the chains in again we were still short a couple of
inches. Incredible. That was a game-changer.

On the very first play after the controversial spot, the Buccaneers ran a power sweep right at me. I made one step too many to the outside, tried to take the blockers while standing up, and the tailback cut inside of me and then quickly to the sideline, where he outraced our secondary for 45 yards and the clinching touchdown. If I had just closed down tighter and taken the blockers on harder, we might have been able to stop the play.

Byzantine added another touchdown on the last play of the game, and we ended up losing, 30-8. That is a very deceiving score, as the game was much closer than that.

The locker room was the most sentimental fifteen minutes of my entire life. Everyone was silent and upset. It was terrible.

The Homecoming Dance and party made things a little better, but all of the players were still in a funky mood. We had never experienced losing a North Central Conference game. Of course, we had never experienced a Homecoming Dance on a Sunday evening, either.

Now that school was in full swing, Will Fitzpatrick and I resurrected something that Fran Dunning and I had done the previous year. We started a football pool. We took ten NFL or college football games, printed them on a sheet, and sold the sheets for twenty-five cents a piece. We always had a tiebreaker (total points in one of the games, for example) and we guaranteed a 10 to 1 payoff for the winner, meaning the winner each week got two dollars and fifty cents on a twenty-five cent bet. That may not sound like much money, but we sold over fifty of the sheets on some weeks, which meant Fitzpatrick and I were making five bucks each. Again, that may not sound like much money, but remember that in the fall of 1969 a movie ticket cost $1 and a McDonald's hamburger cost 35 cents. Five bucks a week a piece was good money for as little work as we had to do.

We just went around early in the week and sold the pool tickets, oftentimes to underclassmen who knew they probably had little chance to win. We kept the winners on the up-and-up, since we did have principles. By the way, I would type or print one page of the sheets (I could get six of the pools on one piece of paper) and then one of the priests who taught at Lorain Catholic (Father William Snyder) would print ten or so copies of the original. I would then cut them up and begin to sell them. Even many of the teachers liked to play.

I've been told since then that this enterprise was probably very illegal, but it was small-time and quite profitable. The whole idea came from Fran Dunning the previous year, and we made even more money because we started the pool earlier in the school year.

57

EC Week! Nothing Like It!

This was it, the most important week of the season, and a week when coaches generally don't have to say even one word of motivation. Everyone points to this week, and, as chronicled in other years, this week even gets the non-athletes fired up.

It had been four years since we had lost to Elyria Catholic. My oldest brother Bobby was the captain of the team in 1965, when they beat the Panthers and started this mini-streak. The 1966 game was that memorable 8-6 game where St. Mary's never gained a first down and still won the game. The 1967 game was a resounding 34-6 Irish victory spearheaded by Mick Dunning and my brother Jack. Last year, 1968, saw us get off to that great start and lead 15-0 before EC had even run a play. We were huge underdogs in 1968, but we led 30-0 at halftime on our way to the 30-6 win. This was the big year, though, since it was the first year for Lorain Catholic and our senior year. The senior year is the year that everyone remembers, so we just had to keep the streak alive.

In all four of those previous games the North Central Conference championship was at stake, and the Fighting Irish of St. Mary's prevailed each year. This year Parma Byzantine has already won the league, so this game is simply for bragging rights and pride. Right from Monday morning announcements our Principal, Sister Mary Newmann, was warning students to stay away from Elyria Catholic and be sure to not get involved in any of the vandalism that had marked this rivalry in the past. She really wanted to stay away from a repeat of the previous year when the students from EC drove past our school and were basically attacked by our student body.

Since we played Byzantine on a Sunday afternoon and we had to get ready for EC, we didn't have the usual full-team film session. We got to watch the film in Coach Dunning's office during our study halls. Byzantine just beat us up. They were clearly better than us.

We did get the scouting report on Elyria Catholic, and they are very big once again, but not as big as they sometimes are. They run a very versatile offense, with two running backs, a split end, a tight end, and a flanker. Their receivers are big, outstanding athletes, standing 6-2, 6-4, and 6-5. Their quarterback, Paul Mascenik, was in the same class at St. Vincent's School with Rich Rhome from Clearview. I had gone to school with those guys for almost six years, and I still kept in touch with them. Heck, I had gone to Mascenik's tenth birthday party.

The flanker is Dale "Flash" Kaminski, a speedy athlete who can do almost anything. The split end is 6-4 Mark Straka, probably the best overall athlete in Lorain County. The tight end is 6-5 Mike Kearns. All three receivers are excellent basketball players, and Mascenik knows that pretty much all he has to do is float the ball up in the air and one of those guys will come down with it. EC also has a couple of excellent running backs.

At Monday's practice it almost appeared that Coach Flowers was discouraged. I didn't think that he was nearly as fired up as he usual.

On Tuesday we received some of the best news of the season. Both Conor Flanary and Calvin Stack will be able to play against EC. We found out that Flanary had actually played the entire Byzantine game with a broken hand. In fact, he had the darn thing in a cast on Monday, but showed up that day with the cast off and ready to play. Conor's father actually had to sign a waiver of responsibility for the doctor to remove the cast and allow Conor to play.

Stack's story is altogether different. He had suffered a separated shoulder two weeks before, and the doctor put his arm in a sling and told him his season was over. Now, less than two weeks later, he was miraculously healed. Stack told me that he went to the doctor's office and told this old doctor, "You better put my arm in a cast. He asked me why. I told him that if he didn't put it in a cast I was going to go out a play football, since my arm didn't hurt anymore. I took my arm and swung it around aver my shoulder and head in a big loop like I wasn't supposed to be able to do. That old doctor looked amazed. He checked me out, and here I am back at practice."

Stack has been one of the big surprises this year, and has really turned into an excellent outside linebacker, generally teaming with Mackie MacGregor and me on one side of our defensive line. He's made me look good on lots of occasions this year. It was really good to have him back.

On Wednesday of EC week we figured we would have a short practice, since Coach Flowers had to drive to Cleveland to be in the studio for the 6:30 taping of the high school football show. As mentioned earlier, a station was featuring the Byzantine-Lorain Catholic game, and we were all excited to see ourselves on TV. We were sort of right. Practice for some of the players ended when Coach Flowers left around 5:30. For the rest of us, it was just beginning.

Practice was going along fine until it came time for the "Team-up" portion of the practice. We were running plays at the second-teamers as they showed us Elyria Catholic's 5-3 alignment. The "Red Shirts," as they are called at LC, chose today to play defense like the Pittsburgh Steelers. It was actually only supposed to be ¾'s speed, and the Red Shirts usually roll with the blocks and try to not get hurt. Senior Dan (The Cat) White was leading the Red Shirts, and they got more and more fired up. They were all over the place making big hits and stopping us time and time again.

Perhaps the worst part of the scrimmage was the fact that the coaches were calling our plays, and they refused to run any passes or any plays to the outside. The Red Shirts soon figured this out, and they stacked the middle of the defense with fourteen or fifteen guys at times, stuffing us on every play. I have no idea why the coaches allowed this to go on, but it was incredibly discouraging, and all it did was make us mad.

After every play the first unit would huddle up and try to fire each other up by yelling and smacking helmets. I actually said very little the entire practice, as I think this mind-game was not helping us at all. When Coach Flowers had seen enough, he led the Red Shirts off of the field and they all left. The starters were the only guys left, along with Assistant Coach Dunning. This was the second-to-last week of the season, and the coaches chose to hit us with just about the biggest, toughest physical conditioning session of the season.

We did wind sprints, quarter mile laps, pushups, sit-ups, Packer Drill, etc. After twenty solid minutes of this torture, twenty minutes where we had not stopped even once to catch our breath, Coach Dunning blew a whistle and called us together. We huddled around him, thinking that practice was over. He talked to us and told us how disappointed Coach Flowers was in the season, and how beating EC would make things much better. After a few minutes of talking, he blew the whistle again and told us to get back to the conditioning. He ran us ragged for another session of conditioning. He blew the whistle again and said, "OK, let's end strong with ten forty-yarders."

Ten forty-yard sprints are plenty tough, but on this day we had to sprint the forty yards and then return to our lines running backwards. That is really difficult, and more than one guy fell over backwards as he tried to return to the original line. Fifty straight minutes of conditioning is really tough, and that's what we finished when Coach Dunning called us together one more time. This time he tried to fire us up, and someone asked if we could redeem ourselves the next day and scrimmage the Red Shirts again. Just about everybody was jumping up and down and getting fired up except Conor Flanary and me. I looked across the group of players as everyone was yelling, and Flanary caught my eye and just rolled his, as if to say, "This is pretty ridiculous, don't you think?" I did think that, of course, so I just nodded at him.

As we jogged off the practice field in the dark, I heard Flanary say, to no one in particular but with a scared, whiny voice, "Please don't make us play them again, Coach. We'll get killed." I was just about the only person laughing.

By the time we got back to the locker room, just about all of the Red Shirts had gone. The starters pretty much kicked the other guys out immediately so we could have the area to ourselves. We were shocked when Coach Flowers walked in. It got quiet right away, and I mean right away. He had showered and changed clothes and was getting ready to leave for Cleveland for the television program. We just looked at him, wondering what he was going to do or say. He realized how down we already were, and he tried to start pumping us up again, saying only positive things. Robbie Cavellini actually apologized to Coach Flowers about our performances on the field that day at practice.

"Sorry, hell, don't be sorry," the coach said. "Just go out and beat the hell out of them when you get your chance tomorrow."

I rushed home after showering, ate, and sat in front of the television. This was exciting, as we were about to see ourselves on TV for the first time, and, even though we had lost the game, we expected at least some nice things to be said.

It was a bad television program. Coach Flowers was in a very strange mood and barely said anything. His answers to the reporter's question were short and curt. Byzantine Coach Dave DiCarlo was very gracious in victory, mentioning how tough and disciplined Flowers'-coached teams were. In the entire show, Coach Flowers mentioned two player's names: Will Fitzpatrick and Mackie MacGregor. That's it. He never added anything to the play-by-play recap of the game. He just sat there sulking.

One of the few comments he made really showed the mood he was in. Byzantine tried a long pass on first down at one point in the game, and it was incomplete. The Byzantine Coach said, "We should know better than to try and trick a John Flowers-coached team with a play like that."

Coach Flowers said, almost under his breath, but clearly audible on the television, "Maybe you should have run another quarterback draw." That comment was a reference to the fact that Byzantine had run all those sneaks and QB draws. Their quarterback ran for well over 200 yards in the game, and we never really adjusted or stopped him. All in all, the television program was very disappointing.

The Thursday practice of EC week was a strange practice. You could tell throughout the first hour-and-a-half that some guys were holding back. Some of the starters were just chomping at the bit to get back at the Red Shirts for the day before.

Before we got to the team offense, we ran our dummy passing drill. The backs and ends run full speed, while the line goes half-speed, with no real pass rush. There isn't supposed to be any contact in the secondary, but the very first pass we called changed that rule right away. I caught a quick pass and turned up the field. After we caught a pass we were supposed to sprint up the field at least ten yards. The frosh team had finished its season the week before, and was now practicing with us. One of the highly-touted frosh defensive backs sprinted up and hit me as hard as he could. I have pretty good balance, and he didn't knock me down, but he knocked me back a few yards. It was a great hit, and one I was definitely not ready for. I almost threw the ball at the kid, but I decided there was a better way to handle it.

I caught the next pass near the sideline and turned up the field. A different frosh DB came up to make the hit, but this time I was ready. I picked up some quick speed and veered right at the defensive back. Just before contact I lowered my shoulder and then brought my forearm up and delivered the hardest hit I ever had in football. I absolutely leveled him and ran right over him. Everybody sort of gasped and then started getting fired up. It was an awesome hit.

The practice continued and we still hadn't scrimmaged. It was getting dark, and I really didn't see how we were going to scrimmage. I found out a few minutes later. We actually had quite a few people watching practice that night. I don't know if Coach Flowers had asked them to come, but when we were ready to scrimmage, the observers pulled their cars around, aimed at the field, and turned their lights on. We were scrimmaging by the lights of several cars just off the practice field.

The scrimmage was a big success as far as the starters were concerned. We ran any play we wanted for a big gain. Of course, we also used our entire playbook, which meant that the Red Shirts couldn't put every player inside of the tackles. We trapped, ran wide, and even completed some passes in the dark.

We were set to play EC on Saturday night at George Daniel Stadium. Friday of EC Week was Halloween. We had a short, light practice, and then we all rushed home to eat and return by 7:00 for the annual snake dance, bonfire, and pep rally, which was also going to be followed this year by a Halloween Dance. As mentioned numerous times before, EC Week was not just for the players, but the entire student body got fired up.

The players on the football team got to ride on a big truck, and the entire student body trailed behind, holding hands in a long, single file.

The cheerleaders were right behind the players' truck, leading the rest of the students. The snake dance left the campus of Lorain Catholic and went out into the neighborhood near the school before returning to the back parking lot. A huge pile of wood and cardboard had been assembled, and by the time we returned after the snake dance, there was a huge fire roaring.

School Director Father Thomas Boone and Athletic Director Jim Englund each spoke to the crowd. Team captains Robbie Cavellini and Bert Knouwer both gave good speeches (Bert predicted a 20-0 Spartan victory), and then it was time for Coach Flowers. His speech was short and to-the-point. He reminded us that no matter what had happened in any of the previous games, tomorrow night was all that mattered. The success of our entire season would be determined by around 10:00 the next night.

After the pep rally, most of the student went in to the school for the annual Halloween Dance. The players weren't going to go to the Dance this year, since we would be playing the next night and we had a 10:00 curfew. Everyone was just standing around in the parking lot, when Coach Dunning called the seniors together and invited us to his parent's house for cider and doughnuts. I need to point out that in previous years the Dunning house was a place where players gathered all the time. Fran Dunning had not only been our captain the previous year, but he was really one of our best friends, and we practically lived at his parent's house out in Avon Lake.

Coach Dunning explained that he thought the seniors should stick together the night before the EC game. I really didn't have any plans until just before the seniors were leaving for Coach Dunning's house. Sometimes things just happen. One of the JV cheerleaders, Lynette Franconi, was standing outside the school when I went to get my coat from my locker. There were lots of kids hanging around, most of them going in to the Halloween Dance. Anyway, Lynette was standing there when I went by and she said, "Hey, Stud, where are you going?" She was always talking like that and sort-of flirting.

I don't know why or how it happened, but I quickly shot back, "I'm going to Lakeview to make out with you. Let's go." I began to walk to my car.

Lakeview Park, as mentioned, was the classic teenage parking spot. I was heading to my car with thoughts of going to Coach Dunning's house when Lynette Franconi caught up with me and surprised the hell out of me. She put her arm through mine and said, "Let's go." She didn't want to go to Coach Dunning's house, and, suddenly, neither did I.

As I drove past the door of the school, Bridgett Mulroney was standing there staring at my car. The rest of the evening was fun and interesting, at least as fun as it could be for a virginal Catholic kid in 1969. In other words, it really wasn't all that much fun.

58

A Lousy Day For Anything

The Saturday of the EC game was a lousy day for football. It was a lousy day for anything. It was cold, but that wasn't the problem. It rained. It rained some more. It rained all day. Lots of football players like to play in the rain, and sometimes it's pretty fun. It wasn't fun at all on the day we played EC in 1969.

When we arrived at George Daniel Stadium it was raining harder than it had all day. Sheets of rain were coming down sideways. When we went out for specialties, I couldn't believe how much water was out there. The track surrounding the field was a lake, and we had to wade through it just to get to the soaked field. Coach Flowers had reminded me before we went out that if I was going to catch a pass tonight to go ahead and use my body to catch the ball. He told me that if I tried to catch the ball with just my fingers the ball would squirt through. We didn't have gloves like they do now, and, when I went to catch the first pass in the warm-ups, it went right through my fingers, just like Coach Flowers had told me. I picked the ball up and tried to throw it back to the center, but it already felt like a shot put. The ball was already soaked and very, very heavy.

We had a very short specialty period and Coach Flowers got disgusted with the rain and sent us back to the locker room.

I trudged back into the locker room, and the guys who didn't go out for specialties wanted to know how it was out there. I told Jeff Brent, "It's beautiful out there. It's a beautiful night for football." He looked at me like I was nuts, which I was at that point.

The rest of the pre-game arm-up was OK, until we went to run our team offense. The rain came down harder. It was difficult to even see, it was coming down so hard. We returned to the locker room one last time, and we were very sluggish. It was hard to be mentally ready to play in that slop.

One of Coach Flowers' great ideas was a tradition he started when he first arrived at St. Mary's a few years before. When the captains went to the center of the field for the coin toss versus Elyria Catholic, the remaining seniors got to go along. The captains meet the officials and other captains at midfield, and the remaining seniors stand on the forty yard-line with hands behind their backs. It's an awesome tradition. This year's coin flip was special for another reason. One of our captains, Robbie Cavellini, was a very close personal friend to one of the Panther's captains, Joe Ruvoli. Cavellini and Ruvoli were friends, neighbors, and had played on the same grade school team at St. John's. In fact, they were the captains at St. John's when they were eighth-graders. They were very nearly best of friends, and when it came time to pick a high school, Cavellini came to Lorain while Ruvoli went to Elyria.

Ruvoli called "Tails," and the coin landed "Heads." As instructed earlier, Bert Knouwer chose to defend the south goal, which meant we were taking the wind rather than the ball. Not many teams are willing to give up possession of the ball, but Coach Flowers figured that with the very strong wind and rain, having the best field position might be the key to the entire game.

Conor Flanary booted a pretty good kickoff, and the Panthers returned it to their own 32-yard line. On the game's very first play Panther QB Paul Mascenik tried to hand the ball off to fullback Mike Crist. Crist is a very hard runner, but this time he ran without the ball. Defensive end JD Szollzy recovered the fumble, and everyone must have immediately thought back to last year's game where we got every break early in the game and capitalized.

We ran two plays into the middle of the EC line and gained only four yards. I was sure Coach Flowers would call a pass on third and six, but we ran the ball again and lost two yards. On fourth and eight we again ran a dive and didn't gain the first down. From there the Panthers drove 74 yards for the game's first touchdown. Junior halfback Doug Gerber ran the final twenty yards, and Crist blasted over for the conversion, and EC led, 8-0.

Only some great punting by Will Fitzpatrick kept us from losing the field position battle worse than we were. In the middle of the second quarter JD Szollzy got hurt. He was playing left defensive end. The next defensive end was Brad Knouwer, Bert's junior brother. Brad could only play right defensive end, which meant I had to switch sides, since I was a senior and was expected to be able to do that. I was definitely not comfortable playing the left side. The difference in which arm makes the first contact and which arm has to remain free to contain changed when I changed sides. It seemed like EC was running every play off tackle to our left side. We were stopping them, but never for less than a five or six yard gain. They were moving right down the field. When they reached our 15-yard line we got lucky and they fumbled and Bert Knouwer recovered for us.

We couldn't move the football, so we had to punt into the very strong wind and rain. This time Fitzpatrick's punt was pretty much coming back to us by the time it landed. Elyria Catholic just let it go, and by the time I could stop its backward movement it had traveled only out to our 34-yard line.

The Panthers reached our five-yard line, and, just before the half was over, Joe Ruvoli kicked a 22-yard field goal to give them an 11-0 lead. I rushed hard from my defensive end position and actually got a fingertip on the field goal, but I didn't deflect it enough to knock it off line.

In the locker room, Coach Flowers was upset that we weren't going anywhere with the football. We tried to make some changes in our blocking, but I really didn't think that was going to help. Due to the weather conditions neither team could pass very well and without a passing attack the bigger and stronger Panthers just crowded the line and waited for us to try and run the football.

The Panthers had just about moved the ball at will, and we didn't have an answer for them. In fact, we never even discussed what EC had done offensively in the first half. At the start of the second quarter, just before I had to change sides in the defense, the Panthers had taken their flanker, Big Mark Straka, and moved him to a second tight end position. This meant that they had four big linemen on the right side of their line. We, on the other hand, had only three defensive players there. Our defensive tackle played on the outside eye of the guard, outside linebacker Bert Knouwer played on the inside eye of the original tight end, the third player from the center, and I had to play on the outside shoulder of the widest lineman, who happened to be the second tight end, the fourth player on that side of the line. It wasn't really an unbalanced line, because they still had a guard, tackle, and split end to the other side, but they did have four guys on our side of the line. Since Bert was on the inside of the third player and I was on the outside of the fourth player, there was a natural hole between us, and EC exploited that area. The original tight end turned Bert to the inside, the new tight end turned me to the outside, and bingo, there was a pretty gaping hole for them to run. In defense of Coach Flowers and the other coaches, we never really brought this up and told them about it at halftime, and the days of great communication from the coaches in the press box to down on the field hadn't been created yet.

We did get some offense in the third quarter, and actually reached the Panther 28-yard line, but on fourth down Fitzpatrick scrambled and kept fading back before he was sacked at the EC 46, an 18-yard loss. The huge loss was part my fault. I was supposed to be the primary receiver, and, as I came off the line, Mark Straka knocked me down. I tried to get up and he knocked me down again, and this time he sort of layed on top of me. I couldn't get out for the pass and Fitzpatrick ended up with the huge sack. Fitzpatrick literally had no one to throw the ball to.

The closest I came to catching a ball came early in the fourth quarter when Fitzpatrick's pass was too high. I leaped and got a finger on it, but really had no chance to catch it. As I landed from my leap a Panther DB, Mark St. Marie, blasted me. It was the hardest I had been hit the entire season, except for the Bob Powell upside-the-head forearm.

EC scored on a short pass over the middle in the fourth quarter, and after the conversion kick we were down, 18-0. This was embarrassing. On the final play of the game, for the second week in a row, our opponents scored. They never attempted the extra point since all of their fans ran out on to the field. Elyria Catholic 24, Lorain Catholic 0. I had chased the running back down the field, so I at least had a chance to congratulate some of the Panther players after the game as I fought my way through the crowd of fans on the field.

Mark Straka shook my hand and said, "It's about time we beat you guys, isn't it? Yeah, it sure is about time."

Since I had stayed on the field and congratulated some of the EC guys, I was the last guy to enter the locker room. It was like a morgue. Coach Flowers talked to us very quietly and told us to head back to St. Mary's to shower and change. As we waited to leave the parking lot, the guys in Knouwer's car, Flanary, Rod Achter, Szollzy, Cavellini, and Mackie MacGregor and I, discussed the season, the team, and that night's game. Most of us were on the verge of tears, since we were the first class in quite awhile to lose to EC.

We talked about how we weren't nearly as bad as our 5-4 record, but that the injuries we had sustained throughout the season really prevented us from becoming the well-oiled offensive machine we were used to. We all agreed that the loss of Cavellini had hurt the most, and that with a healthy Robbie our running game and passing game would have been better. Remember, too, that Cavellini was a great defensive player, and had started as a sophomore on the legendary 1967 team. I also pointed out that the previous year Cavellini and Fitzpatrick were both relative unknowns, and that we had surprised a lot of people with our offense.

Another factor in our 5-4 record had to be our schedule. Three teams we had played the previous year, St. Stan's (47-18 win) St. John Cantius (52-0 win) and Xenia Woodrow Wilson (34-6 win) had been replaced by Tiffin Calvert (21-0 loss), Cloverleaf (15-8 loss), and Gilmour Academy

(14-12 win). Our schedule this year had been much, much tougher. To compare Tiffin Calvert or Cloverleaf with St. John Cantius or St. Stan's was ridiculous.

When we had all showered back at St. Mary's, Coach Flowers said he wanted to talk to us. The locker room had been totally silent after the game. Coach Flowers smiled and mentioned that Rod Achter was always the last guy out of the locker room. Tonight, however, Will Fitzpatrick was the last guy out. Fitzpatrick had really taken the loss hard. We had all had tough seasons, but Fitzpatrick felt like he was responsible for us losing four games. He was really down.

Finally, we were all assembled in the gym. Here comes a royal tongue-lashing, we all thought. Instead, Coach Flowers was pretty mellow. He controlled his temper and never raised his voice. He sat on a chair in front of us and said, simply, "Why?" He wanted to know why we were 5-4 after working so hard for a full year. Just like in the car, he wanted anyone and everyone to explain what had happened. Just like in the car, I voiced my theory. We had too many injuries to ever really become a smooth-operating football machine. Without much depth, it was very difficult to hang in there with the tough schedule we had played. Every team needs an easy game now and then, and we hadn't played an easy game yet.

When we finished the meeting, the last thing Coach Flowers said was, "I'll be damned if I'm gonna be 5-5. This week we're gonna hit in practice, we're gonna scrimmage, and we're gonna play football. We're gonna hit hard this week in practice, and the survivors are gonna play against Midview."

59

Midview Week—
The Last Football Game Ever

At our Sunday meeting we watched films of the previous day's debacle. This time, however, Coach Flowers was sort of mellow as he ran the film. He usually runs each play back and forth at least five times, watching and criticizing numerous players. This time he ran each play twice, hardly raised his voice, and we just went on. The film itself, of course, was of terrible quality, as it was raining so hard that you could hardly see the field. I'm surprised the photographer even took any film at all.

At this point it's easy to say, "You can't cry over spilled milk. Bring on Midview!"

I went over Bridgett's house after dinner, and she wanted to know what Lynette Franconi was doing in my car after the pep rally on Friday. I told her the truth, at least part of the truth. "I gave her a ride home," was my answer, and that was actually true. I did, after all, eventually give Lynette Franconi a ride home.

Bridgett just looked at me and shook her head. I had a feeling that I hadn't heard the end of this.

Our final game of the season was against Midview High School, which is located in Grafton, Ohio. Midview was a member of the Lakeland Conference, and, if you remember, was one of only two teams to have beaten us in the 1968 season. We destroyed them, 52-6 in 1967, but the year before they came into the game with a 3-6 record but really fired up to get revenge from the previous year. They upset us, 30-23. The school is located just south of Elyria, and actually pretty close to Elyria Catholic

High School. The Middies were again 3-6, but they were very dangerous, as they had kept the Run-and-Shoot offense they had unveiled against us the previous year. Their quarterback is a great athlete who scored two touchdowns against us the previous year. This year he had thrown for over 800 yards, and that included missing two-and-a-half games with an injury. They were definitely going to test our pass defense.

In the 1968 game we had just won the conference championship by destroying EC, 30-8, and we had a terrible mental letdown against Midview. It was a very cold night, we were scheduled to go out to dinner as a team after the game, and it didn't seem like anyone really wanted to play. This year we would be looking for revenge.

Monday's practice was full of conditioning and fundamentals, as well as a long scrimmage. I really question the conditioning during the last week of practice. Will conditioning actually play any part in the game Saturday? It's not like it's going to be 90 degrees in November. Incidentally, the final game will be played at Clearview High School, but is listed as a home game for us.

Tuesday's practice was the best practice all year. We played "nutcracker." I don't know who invented the drill, but Jerry Kramer wrote about it in his classic book "Instant Replay." Here's how we played it: We placed rubber cones in a rectangle about five yards by ten yards. We had a center, a lineman on each side of the center, a quarterback, and a runner. There were three defensive players close to the line, and one defensive back behind them. A coach stood behind the defense and pointed which way he wanted the ball run. The quarterback called the signals, took the snap, and handed the ball to the running back, who tried to reach the far end of the pit and score a "touchdown."

This was great fun, and I kept jumping in to the blocking line. There were lots of big hits that day, and everyone was all fired up as the practice went along. Maybe the best thing of all about Tuesday's practice was the fact that Robbie Cavellini ran with the same speed, confidence, and shiftiness he had possessed at the beginning of the season. With a healthy Robbie Cavellini, there is no way Midview had a chance Saturday night.

We had another great practice on Wednesday, and the first-teamers got to play defense in the Nutcracker Drill. The previous day all we did was block and run, but on Wednesday we got to really turn up the heat and hit people. The Nutcracker drill is really designed for defensive tackles and inside linebackers, and, being a defensive end, I barely got to play, only getting in about five plays in the entire drill. Three of those plays I had to play in a down lineman position and Mackie MacGregor was blocking me, so it wasn't all that much fun for me.

As mentioned, Midview is going to run the Run-and-Shoot offense, which they had unveiled for the very first time in last year's 30-23 upset of

St. Mary's. This year they added a motion man on every play, which meant they would have three receivers on one side of the formation on basically every play. The motion man could also become an extra blocker if they chose to run a quick sweep or an option. This is a complex offense which will take lots of concentration to stop.

An interesting defensive personnel move this week is the insertion of Robbie Cavellini as a defensive end. I guess the coaches thought that the guys in the secondary were doing okay, and maybe we needed a little more quickness up front on the defensive line. The defensive ends this week will be in pass coverage on quite a few plays, especially on swing passes to the motion man. Cavellini will start at one defensive end, and I will start at the other, and with both of us being pretty quick athletes, the coaches figure to be able to cover the swing passes pretty easily.

Coach Flowers never mentioned it, but it appears that he is trying to start as many seniors as possible this week. Only a few underclassmen will start Saturday night, including Calvin Stack, Jack Murtha, Steve Mathews, and sophomore defensive back Danny McNamara. All of the other starting positions will be handled by seniors.

After practice on Wednesday we watched films of the previous year's St. Mary's-Midview game. They say you don't really realize how good something is until you don't have it any more. I think last year's films proved that. Fran Dunning was really a great runner, and Robbie Cavellini was awesome in that game, too. Both guys rushed for over 125 yards, and some of their runs were tremendous. One play in particular amazed all of us. Fran Dunning made a run of about 30 yards, and he never stopped hitting guys, spinning, bouncing away, cutting, and churning his legs. We ran it back about ten times, and on one of those we actually counted the number of guys who had a shot to tackle him. Nine guys hit him or tried to tackle him on one play. He was finally dragged down on the Midview 24-yard line. Dunning wasn't really that big or powerful (5-8, 160), but he had great balance, slashing moves, and great desire. I really didn't remember Dunning being that good, but, as Coach Flowers always says, "Films don't lie."

When we finally got over watching the great offensive moves by Dunning and Cavellini, we got down to the business of watching Midview's offense. This year's Midview team was not as versatile as the year before. At that time Bob Mahl played one of the slotbacks, and they had a great quarterback and a bruising fullback. Those guys graduated. Now they had Bob Mahl at quarterback and a fast slotback named Bob Keller. Their offense wasn't really all that developed yet, but that didn't mean they weren't dangerous as hell.

On Thursday at practice I almost got into it with a coach who was yelling at me during a drill. We were running a defensive end/outside linebacker drill against a group of freshmen and sophomores. We had four guys: two defensive ends and two outside linebackers. They had all eleven guys. When they ran plays in our direction, they could very easily just cut into an area where we didn't have any players. The drill was totally unrealistic because they kept running into an area where we would have had defensive tackles and inside linebackers, not to mention a safety. Coach Havrady kept yelling at me, "C'mon, can't you even stop the freshmen?" I decided after about ten minutes of this that I had had enough. I looked at him, started to open my mouth, and just stopped. I decided that it wouldn't make much sense to create a scene on the second-to-last day of practice.

The seniors all got together after practice and decided that we would all stick together the next two nights. We decided to go to a movie together on Friday evening and then go to a party at Conor Flanary's after the game on Saturday. I don't recall who brought it up, but we decided that we would ask Coach Flowers if he wanted to go to the movie with us. Coach Flowers has been a huge influence on each and every one of us, albeit in different ways. When we asked him about the movie after practice he agreed to go with us.

Before practice started on Friday, Robbie Cavellini came to me and said, "I told you it would go fast. It seems like only yesterday that we shook hands before the first practice, and here we are, our last practice together." I'm not going to kid you tears welled up in my eyes. I remembered Robbie talking to me on August 15, before we took the field for the very first time, and now here we were, ending our careers together.

On Friday after practice we decided that we would go to the movie in downtown Lorain at the Tivoli theatre. The movie was "Marlowe," starring James Garner. Every senior was there, and we all sat together in the middle of the theatre. Coach Flowers sat near the back, but he bought a bunch of boxes of popcorn for us to share. It's little things like that that people remember. On the way out of the theatre he thanked us for asking him to come along. The evening was sort of a sentimental time, as we realized that we weren't going to be together, all together, many more times in our lives.

On the day of my last game I actually got to sleep in. After getting up and reading the Cleveland Plain Dealer I took a little walk out in my backyard. I realized that this would probably be the last time that I would ever lace on football gear.

I spent the afternoon in the house watching the Iowa-Indiana football game, except for the half hour or so that I shot baskets outside. Whenever I get down or in any kind of a strange mood, I find that shooting baskets can really improve my mood. I love basketball even more than football, but I needed to concentrate for a few more hours on football. When I returned to the house I actually fell asleep, and was awakened by my mom just in time to eat my pre-game steak.

The locker room was noisier than most pre-game locker rooms usually are. I got dressed next to Robbie Cavellini, and he caught my eye and said, "This is it, our last one together." I glanced at him and said, "We've been through a lot together. Let's go out winners, Robbie." We looked at each other, then down at the floor, then back at each other. Then, simultaneously, we grabbed each other and hugged, very firmly, with honest emotion and sentiment. We couldn't believe that it was almost over, all the hard work, sweat, tears, blood, and effort that we had put in side-by-side, and for what? For this: friendship, brotherhood, teamwork. We were close, very close. I guess that's what high school football is—thirty-five or forty guys putting out and sucking up the tough times for a few great moments like this.

It's hard to understand how we could share so much and be so close, and, unless you've ever experienced something like this, you probably don't really understand. After we finished the hug we just looked at each other. We didn't really want this to be the end.

After we were all dressed, we had one more meeting in the gym, where the Red Shirts walked through the Midview offense and defense. Finally, we put on our cleats and walked out the back door as a team for the final time. Just outside the door, on the side of the building, is a large figure of The Blessed Virgin Mary. Before every game since Coach Flowers had been in Lorain, the entire team, coaches, managers, everyone, bowed their heads and said our pre-game prayer:

> Oh God and St. Sebastian,
> We go to play our game,
> But whether we win or lose,
> Pray no disgrace to St. Mary's name.
> We pray keep safe from injury,
> All your Irish true,
> And in our struggle for victory,
> We offer this game to you.

I don't know about anyone else, but my entire body was filled with goose bumps. That was just one more emotional moment that evening.

The pre-game calisthenics were not the loudest or most spirited we ever had, and I think the seniors were more in a business-like mood. We knew what we had to get done. I was thinking about Bob Mahl and Bob Keller and how I needed to play my position and help our team stop them. They were both explosive and ready to play, overcoming earlier injuries.

We returned to the locker room for the final pre-game talk. We were using the upstairs locker room at Clearview for the game, so we had to trudge up the stairs to the smallish locker room. Coach Flowers reminded us of how hard we had worked and how we only got a few opportunities to play this great game of football. He was really building emotion, and to culminate the fiery part of the talk he reached out and grabbed a player to emphasize physical play. The player was Danny Jackson, and Coach Flowers started swinging him around like a rag doll. Jackson had cleats on, so he had no grip whatsoever on the floor, and Coach Flowers was using this lack of stability to the utmost. It was almost funny watching Coach Flowers swing Jackson around, but, at the same time, it really got us mentally and emotionally ready. We took the field for the final time.

Sophomore back Danny McNamara returned the opening kickoff out to our 39-yard line. On the game's first play Coach Flowers called for a long pass to Robbie Cavellini. Cavellini went racing down the right sideline, and Fitzpatrick, after a great fake, lofted the ball out to him. The pass was a bit short, and Cavellini had to come back for the ball, but he was so far behind the Midview defense that he had time to come back, catch the ball, and turn and start running again. He went 61 yards for a touchdown on the game's very first play. Fitzpatrick made another great fake on the conversion and then passed the ball to McNamara for the two points, and we led, 8-0, just 27 seconds into the game.

The rest of the first quarter was a bit of a standoff, as the Middies moved the ball fairly well by passing it but couldn't establish a really great drive because of a serious lack of a running game. Midview's best drive of the first half ended on our ten-yard line, and we then started to really move the ball. Bert Knouwer and Cavellini were having great nights running the ball, and Midview knew they had to respect Fitzpatrick's passing. It was almost like we were back at the beginning of the season, when we had both a great rushing attack and a dangerous passing attack. It took us 16 plays, but we capped the 90-yard drive with a McNamara six-yard run. Cavellini added the conversion run, and we led, 16-0.

Late in the first period Grego Armantou had sustained a leg injury. After our second touchdown we were preparing to kickoff, and we had only ten guys out on the field. Coach Flowers yelled to Coach Dunning, "Who's the next sub on the kickoff team?" Coach Dunning answered him, "Stephen Francis." Coach Flowers said, "What?" I knew I was the next guy, and I was standing right next to Coach Flowers. He remembered and I remembered the day two years earlier when, as a sophomore, I had gotten out of my lane and given up the touchdown against Our Lady of Lourdes. He had hit me 22 times as he ran that play back on the film, and he also swore that, "You will never be on the kickoff team again as long as I'm the coach." It was one of the most memorable moments of the 1967 season, so it was easy to recall for both of us. He remembered those words and so did I, and yet, here I was standing next to him, ready to enter the field and take my place on the kickoff team. I had a wry smile on my face inside of my helmet. I bit down hard on my mouthpiece.

Coach Flowers turned and looked at me. "You're in. Remember to stay in your lane." I nodded at him and the smile came through for both of us. I started out on the field and he quickly grabbed me and spun me around. He looked me right in the eye and said, "Don't let them return the damn thing all the way." I smiled and said, "Yes sir."

My position on the kickoff team was the third player from the west sideline. I lined up and sprinted down the field. Conor Flanary's kick was very high and speedy Bob Keller caught it at the twelve. He sprinted straight up the field for about ten yards, took two steps toward the west sideline, and then cut hard to the east. He found an opening and burst through it.

I saw what was happening and changed my pursuit angle immediately. I started sprinting towards our 20-yard line, a long way away, but at the angle I thought I might need to catch Keller. By the time he crossed midfield he was in the open. I had a pretty good angle on him, but he was just too fast. I chased him from about the 35-yard line until I dove at the ten. I actually got a piece of his shoe and he started to stumble, but he made it into the end zone. They missed the conversion, and the score stood at 16-6.

As I returned to our sidelines after the conversion try, I saw Coach Flowers standing at about the thirty-yard line with his hands on hips, just shaking his head and looking for me. There was no possible way he was going to blame me for this one. The returner had run to the other side of the field, and I had almost caught him. He was looking at me and I started to say, "That wasn't my fault. He ran to the other side." Coach Flowers just put his hand up to stop me from saying anything and said, "Let's just keep playing football."

Our next drive covered 63 yards in eleven plays, with Cavellini scoring from the one to make the score 22-6. For the conversion, Coach Flowers called "Pass 34," which meant Fitzpatrick would fake a quick dive to Cavellini and then stand up and throw a quick pass to me in the flat area. Fitzpatrick's fake was great, and I ran a good pattern, staying inside the defensive back and still in the end zone. Fitzpatrick stood tall in the pocket and delivered the pass in the perfect spot. He had to throw it over a defensive end, past a linebacker, and in front of a defensive back. It had to be delivered low and to the outside. The pass was perfect, but the catch sucked. I had to dive for the ball, but it was right where I should have caught it. It went right through my arms.

We led at halftime, 22-6. The first half wasn't really a very well-played half. Both teams had several penalties, and it was undoubtedly the dirtiest game I had ever played in. It seemed like there were two or three late hits on every play. The linemen for both teams were punching, shoving, kicking, spearing on every play. You know what? That was really fun, and guys on our team like Mackie MacGregor and JD Szollzy loved to play that way. They seemed to be in the middle of many of the late hits.

In the locker room at halftime Coach Flowers had little to say about things, but he did scold me a bit for dropping the conversion pass. He knew that Will Fitzpatrick had thrown the ball into the only area he could, and he knew that I should have caught the ball. Being an ex-quarterback himself, he was a little protective of his QBs, which was fine.

When we reached the field for the start of the second half I went around and talked to every senior one last time. JD Szollzy and Mackie MacGregor were really ready to play. They were like little kids in a candy store. I couldn't believe how much fun they were having playing dirty football.

The third quarter was becoming a defensive struggle when Fitzpatrick boomed a punt over the head of Bob Keller. I was the first guy down to cover the punt, and it was just Keller and me around the Middie 35-yard line. He let the ball bounce and bounce and just about stop before he tried to pick it up. As he was trying to pick the ball up I dove right into him and landed on the ball, both causing and recovering the fumble. Mackie MacGregor started to "high five" me in the huddle and I said, "Why the hell would he try something stupid like that? Who does he think I am, some derelict?"

We quickly drove for our fourth touchdown of the evening, with Cavellini scoring from the one for a 28-6 lead. Midview now had to start passing just about every play. It was clear that quarterback Bob Mahl's earlier injury had forced the Midview coaches to tell him to not run with the ball. Even when he had a wide open place to scramble, he stayed in the pocket and passed the ball. Midview drove to our eleven before we stopped them and took over the ball.

We began another great drive until we reached the Midview 46-yard line. On third and twelve, "Pass 24" was called. I was supposed to run seven yards downfield and then cut across the field. I knew that seven yards wouldn't be enough for a first down, so I ran a bit deeper. Fitzpatrick read my pattern beautifully and snapped a quick throw right to me. Once I caught the ball I headed straight up the field. I sensed the Midview safety coming up to hit me, so I lowered my shoulder and ran right into him. He tackled me, but as soon as I hit the ground I was back up, looking for the first down marker. We had gained 15 yards and a first down.

From the Midview 31 we had no trouble moving down the field for our final touchdown of the year. Cavellini capped a brilliant comeback performance with his fourth touchdown of the night. Danny McNamara caught a pass from Fitzpatrick for the final conversion, and we led, 36-6.

Midview now was going to fill the air with passes, and we were ready. Once we realized that Bob Mahl was not going to be a threat to run, it was easy to drop lots of guys back into coverage. Our defensive ends this week (Cavellini and I) were actually extra defensive backs. In the middle of the fourth quarter Midview had moved to our 35-yard line. Almost unbelievably, in the huddle before the next play I told everybody, "You know what? I'm going to intercept the next pass."

I dropped into my zone but I realized that no one was there, so I headed more towards the middle of the field. I just sensed where Bob Mahl was going to throw the ball, and he never saw me. I jumped in front of the Midview receiver and intercepted the pass. As soon as I landed the Midview receiver grabbed me and just sort of hung on. I couldn't get away from him, but he couldn't drag me down either. I spun around into the secondary and heard one of my teammates yell, "Steve, Steve, here." He wanted me to lateral the football so he could start to run. I thought for a split second (that's all the time I had) and decided to go ahead and lateral the ball. As I went to pitch it back another Midview tackler arrived and hit my arm, sending the ball about ten feet into the air. Fortunately, Danny McNamara was close enough to recover the ball and we took possession.

Our offensive unit came on the field, along with Danny Jackson, who happened to be an offensive end. He tapped me on the shoulder and told me he was in for me. "Uh-oh," I thought, "Coach Flowers wants to see me right now."

When I reached the sidelines he called me right over. He put his arm around my shoulders like he was consoling me, when, in actuality, he was scolding. I guess the talk could have been a lot worse, but he reminded me to be a smarter football player and that the lateral was really stupid. As usual, he was right. As I stepped away from him he also saw that I was discouraged, and he stepped towards me and said, "Get your head up, Steve. You've had a helluva year." Once again, as usual, he was right.

One play later Coach Flowers sent me back into the game. He told me the play to run, which was a long pass to me. He was hoping to score one final touchdown, but, really, he was just trying to give me another chance to make a play. I ran the pattern as fast as I could and probably went too deep, because by the time I turned, Will Fitzpatrick was facing heavy pressure and his throw was short and wide. I came back for the ball and dove for it, but it bounced about two yards short of me. That was the last play I ever got to play.

The final score was 36-6, and we had the consolation to at least say that we went out winners. Our final record of 6-4 was a huge disappointment for us and for the coaching staff.

The locker room was filled with spirit after the game, and I really didn't want to take off my equipment. All the seniors just kept milling around, talking and sharing the moment. None of us will ever forget those minutes.

When we finally arrived back to St. Mary's to shower and change, Coach Flowers came into the locker room and congratulated every senior. He also asked us if we would stop in the coaches' office before we left for the evening.

Usually a fast dresser, I was actually the last guy out of the locker room that night. By the time I came out of the locker room, only Will Fitzpatrick and Robbie Cavellini were left in line to talk to the coaches. I was the last player to talk to Coach Flowers. He asked me if I wanted to play college football. I hadn't really thought about it very much, but I told him right away that I definitely did. He told me that he might be able to get me some scholarship money from a small school. He also told me that I had been one of the biggest and most pleasant surprises on this year's team. He told me that I had done a great job. He thanked me. I thanked him for everything. He stood up. We shook hands. I walked out, and that was it for my high school football career. It was over.

The rest of the night was spent at Conor Flanary's house for an all-night, end-of-the-season party. All the seniors were there as well as some underclassmen, and it was quite a party. Flanary and Mackie MacGregor had saved programs from every game, and we picked out "All-Opponent Team," comprised of the best players we had played against all season. We also picked our "All-Name Team," which was comprised of players with the weirdest names from the opposing teams. We actually had beer to drink, which was a first for some of us. Other guys acted like they had done it before, but, since I hadn't, it was a unique experience. We had pizza and pumpkin pie to eat, which, when you combine those with the beer, created a rather unique combination. Everyone stayed up all night, and we finished the evening by attending 5:30 AM Mass at St. Mary's. At Mass I must not have been too drunk, because I can remember thanking God for giving me the opportunity to play the season and have the great times I did with these other guys.

60

A Disappointing Banquet

The first annual Lorain Catholic High School Football Banquet was held November 18. It was not a very nice banquet. School Director Father Thomas Boone spoke, as did Athletic Director Jim Englund. No one listened to Father Boone's talk (we were all still mad at him for not bringing The Fighting Irish and Green and Gold to LC), but Coach Englund had some interesting things to say. He told us that he thought we established a good work ethic for teams in the future. What he meant, of course, was that we showed how hard you had to work, even if you don't win every game.

When Coach Flowers got up to speak, it almost sounded like he was upset about something, or, at least, bitterly disappointed in our senior class. He was not upbeat at all, and he created a very strange mood. His attitude towards our class actually encouraged some of my classmates to harbor some resentment towards Coach Flowers for years. Fortunately, those feelings are all gone as far as I know. He did mention me in one simple sentence, and said that I had a relatively serious injury and never complained and never missed a game.

The awards presented at the banquet were very few, but they were well-deserved. Bert Knouwer was awarded Most Valuable Back and the Spartan Man-of-the-Year Award. The Man-of-the-Year Award is supposed to go to the player who worked the hardest and had done the most for the program. Bert really deserved this. Jeff Brent was selected by the coaches as Most Valuable Lineman, which was also very deserved. Jeff was a solid lineman for us for three years. Only three guys made All-NCC: Mackie MacGregor, Danny Jackson, and Danny McNamara. We all thought this was very strange. First of all, there were only four teams in the North Central

Conference this year, which meant we should have had five or six players on the 24-man All-League roster. Most of the time, coaches nominate players on their teams who are veterans. That would have left out Jackson and the sophomore McNamara, both of who were playing their first year of varsity football. We also found out later that Coach Flowers had not even nominated Mackie MacGregor. When the All-League team had no center nominated, a coach from another school nominated Mackie. That's really strange.

After the banquet the seniors got together and were pretty upset. We thought that Jeff Brent, Bert Knouwer, Will Fitzpatrick, Conor Flanary, and I should have all been nominated or at least considered. Again, a number of guys sort of felt betrayed by Coach Flowers for not being pushed harder for All-League.

A week later The Lorain Times, a small newspaper trying to compete with The Lorain Journal, selected their first All-City team. The list included players from Lorain High, Admiral King, Southview, Lorain Catholic, and Clearview. Mackie MacGregor, Bert Knouwer and I were all named first-team All-City. That was very exciting when I read it in the newspaper.

One final thought about the season: the injury to Robbie Cavellini really ruined our season. If you include the three scrimmages and the ten games, we were 5-0-1 when he played at full-strength. We were 3-4 when he was hurt or playing at half-speed. One guy can make a big difference. I guess it's time to turn my thoughts to basketball.

61

The First Spartan Co-Captains

Unlike some guys who want to take time off after one season before heading into another, I was looking forward to basketball so much that I reported on Monday after school to St. Mary's Johnston Hall for the start of basketball practice. We had to practice at St. Mary's because the gym at Lorain Catholic hadn't been completed yet. In fact, one of the first things Coach Englund told us was that we were going to be playing our first seven or eight, or even nine games on the road, since we didn't have a gym to play in. The school had decided that we would not play any games at St. Mary's, but we would use it as a practice facility. Perhaps the reason for this is that St. Mary's floor is 75 feet long, which is nine feet shorter than the traditional and recommended high school length of 84 feet. The new Lorain Catholic gym was going to be 94 feet, which is the length of most college gyms, and lots, lots longer than any other high school gym we had ever played in. Regardless, we were going to practice at St. Mary's and wait until the LC gym was ready to play a home game.

Practice had already started a week or so earlier, so Will Fitzpatrick, Jack Murtha, and I had some catching up to do as far as getting into "basketball shape." Believe me, we were already in great physical condition from the football conditioning we had experienced with Coach John Flowers.

Right away I could see that we were going to be very small. We didn't have anyone over 6-2, and we really only had one varsity player that tall. That didn't count a classmate of mine who was coming out for basketball for the first time since our freshmen year. Dave Prosalak was a kid that nobody ever even heard talk. He just went about his business of being a good student, but here he was out for varsity basketball. Perhaps I should mention that Dave was six-feet-seven inches tall. As far as I could remember, St. Mary's/Lorain Catholic had never had a player that tall before. Unfortunately, when we started doing drills I could see why Dave had not played basketball in the past few years. He was really, really slow. I mean he was really slow. He could barely keep up in the drills when any running at all was involved. It's really too bad, because he had a pretty nice touch as a shooter, but he would never be able to get a shot off in a varsity game because he was so slow.

One other thing that I noticed right away was that Joey Laszoff had really worked hard on his game and was going to be a premier player. Remember that Laszoff had actually started the season at the point guard position as a sophomore, and he started about half of the games the previous year, so he also had some experience going for him. He and I were the only two lettermen back from last year's great team. Since there were only two seniors out for basketball (Fitzpatrick and me after Prosalak was cut) Coach Englund decided that we wouldn't have a vote, but that he would appoint the two of us co-captains. To be a captain for Coach Englund was very special, as he often had private conversations about the team and the season with the captain(s). It was very special to me to be named co-captain, and I took the position very seriously, as did Fitzpatrick.

Basketball practice is almost always more fun than football practice. Football practice is often times work, since the fundamentals of football can be practiced against a dummy or a blocking sled, and football requires so much more conditioning. In basketball, you can condition right in the drills, especially if you are doing full-court drills, which we often did.

62

The Jocks Versus The Freaks

Once the football season ended, the atmosphere in the school itself seemed to change. The tough guys like JD Szollzy and Robbie Cavellini didn't have to worry as much about facing Coach Flowers on a daily basis, even though he had been named the Dean of Students at Lorain Catholic High School. The school had taken on a social/political attitude that was splitting the students into two groups: "The Jocks," and "The Freaks," at least that's what we called them.

"The Jocks" were really led by the senior football players, guys like JD Szollzy, Robbie Cavellini, Conor Flanary, and Mackie MacGregor. They were all very conservative politically, which meant, in 1969-70, that they supported the United States in the Vietnam War. "The Freaks," led by Class President Bob Irelan and Joe Wendell, opposed the war and weren't afraid to say so. The Freaks also had longer hair than the jocks, which isn't saying much for two reasons: The Jocks wore very short hair by choice, and The Freaks couldn't wear very long hair because of school rules. The rule said that hair couldn't be over your eyes or ears. That's pretty short. The way some of The Freaks got around this was by combing the longer hair back over their ears, so that it technically didn't cover their ears. You could see some of these guys leave the building and immediately shake their heads, causing the hair to flop down over their ears and eyes.

The girls in the class, even the ones who dated The Jocks, seemed to like The Freaks more, for whatever reason. In fact, this split had occurred in other classes in other ways. Remember the mention of the Class of 1969's NFP's (Non-Football Players)? Their split was less political than ours, but it still existed.

In the spring of 1969 we held class elections for the next school year. I had been the Vice-President of the Student Council for the school year 1968-69, so it was a natural step for me to assume the leadership role as President of Student Council for my senior year. I would have had to run for the position and been elected, but I thought it was still pretty much a given that I would win. However, a really good friend, Dan (The Cat) White, came to me and asked me if there was any way I would consider not running for Student Council President. He was my friend and he really, really wanted to be the President. I didn't really care that much so I actually accepted his suggestion and ran for re-election as Vice-President. I lost in a landslide to fellow senior Maggie Gonzales. In fact, in that election year, a slate of jocks ran together, including Mackie MacGregor, Conor Flanary, and Will Fitzpatrick. All four lost in the senior class election. Bob Irelan was elected President of the senior class, and the other three positions were held by girls. We couldn't believe it. The Jocks had been voted out by The Freaks and the girls. The point is this: we may have been very close as a group, but we were seriously outnumbered when it came to politics.

I need to explain the use of the word "we" in the previous sentence. My best friends were The Jocks. They were the guys I hung around with for the most part. However, I was also a tennis player, and the number one tennis player in the school was Joe Wendell, one of the leaders of The Freaks. He was also a very good friend, so I was as close to someone caught in the middle as anyone. I had friends who were both Jocks and Freaks.

The girls would back The Freaks in a political contest, but they still liked The Jocks more and they dated more Jocks (even if they wouldn't necessarily vote for them).

63

Good, Clean, Wholesome Fun

On the Friday after the football season ended, a bunch of my friends were going to go to Gore Orphanage in Vermilion, Ohio. The Legend of Gore Orphanage goes like this: If you travel down into the Vermilion River Valley late at night when there is a full moon, you can, if you get very quiet, hear the screams of the children who died in a terrible fire at an orphanage in the valley. Hardly any of us had ever gone there, but someone got directions and we decided to go.

As we headed down the winding, single-lane road, it became very spooky. The road was so narrow that the branches of the huge trees on either side of the road actually met above the road, making things even darker than they appeared. When we reached the bottom of the valley, the five or six cars slowed down. Someone got out and looked across this rickety, wooden, one-lane bridge. Somebody walked across the bridge and sort of tested it to see whether it was strong enough to hold cars driving across it. We decided that it would be better if we just walked across the bridge rather than drive. Everyone got out of their cars, and started walking across this bridge to an open area on the other side. It was really spooky, and the girls were holding on to whomever they could.

When all of us got across the bridge, someone reminded us to be very quiet and we could hear the screaming children. With Conor Flanary and Mackie MacGregor both present, it took a few minutes to actually get people quiet. Those two guys kept saying hilarious things and kept people laughing. Finally, it got quiet. Oh my God! You could clearly hear a high-pitched sound that really did sound like a child screaming. We all freaked out and started running back to the cars.

The following Sunday Bert Knouwer, Patsy Conrad and I drove down to the bottom of the road where we had been the previous Friday evening. Everything seemed so much different in the middle of an afternoon as opposed to late one Friday night. We walked across the bridge and walked down a roadway about seventy-five yards. We found the fence and the foundation of the building that had been the orphanage. It was very old and crumbled, but it was also very clear that it had existed. The road went right past the old orphanage and further down the river valley. When we walked away we talked about whether we were more scared now that we had found the ruins of the actual orphanage, or less scared now that we seen the grounds during the light of day.

Just for an historical note: There really was an orphanage on the spot where we had been standing and the orphanage did, indeed, burn to the ground in the early years of the 20th century. No one seems to know if anyone was actually killed in the fire, but the screaming noises can be explained. Just a little ways down the valley away from the orphanage, the Ohio Department of Transportation built a bridge carrying Route 2 over the Vermilion River Valley. The bridge is several hundred feet high, and when the wind blows beneath the bridge a high-pitched sound is carried north right into the area where the orphanage had been.

That may explain the sounds you hear when you go to the bottom of Gore Orphanage Road, but on a late Friday night in 1969 I think I heard babies screaming!

The very next Friday night a bunch of us got together and went to a cemetery in Amherst, Ohio, a town about five miles from Lorain. This cemetery was in the middle of the town, and it was a huge cemetery. It's very important to point out that in 1969 Amherst was a very conservative community, so conservative, in fact, that no African-Americans lived there. The town was all white.

So, about a dozen of us traveled to Amherst to walk through this cemetery. We had heard that you could hear people moaning and crying late at night. We pulled into the cemetery and got out of the cars. There were a few people missing from the group that had walked around Gore Orphanage the previous Friday, but nobody thought anything about that at the time. We were about to be in for the shock and fright of our lives.

JD Szollzy, Robbie Cavellini, and Jimmy Sullivan knew of our plans to go to the cemetery that night, and they were there waiting for us. They had parked somewhere else, and they were hiding behind some tombs and gravesites. They were also all dressed in black outfits.

The guys and girls walked through the cemetery about fifty yards, and then we stopped and listened. Once again, Conor Flanary and Mackie MacGregor were cracking jokes throughout the walk, and, when we finally got them to be quiet, everyone started listening carefully. All of a sudden we heard these screams and yells and saw three guys in black sprinting at us. Everyone, including me, freaked out. We screamed, turned around, and started running back to our cars. It was so scary it was ridiculous, but it was also damn-near riotous. One of the girls in the group fell down and just layed there crying and screaming. She actually peed her pants! When Cavellini and Szollzy caught up with her and told her to settle down (after chasing the rest of us back to our cars!), she got up and walked back with those guys to where we were parked.

When we realized what had happened, all the guys tried to act macho and say they weren't scared, but that was a bunch of crap: everybody was scared just about shitless. We all did have a good laugh afterwards, but then another incident completed the night.

We had to take Szollzy, Cavellini, and Sullivan back to their car, and, when we did, we were suddenly surrounded by Amherst policemen and Lorain County sheriff deputies. We had four cars now, and there were four police cars. The law enforcement officers actually approached our cars with their guns drawn. Once again, we were scared just about shitless. They made us get out of our cars, and they carefully checked our cars for weapons, drugs, alcohol, etc. It was a scary scene. They actually told us that they heard we had something called a "zip-gun" with us. They thought we were coming to Amherst for a big fight with Amherst kids. We were just looking for a little no-harm-high-school-kids'-fun, and, instead, we got rousted by law enforcement officers.

One other person who wasn't present that Friday evening was Bridgett Mulroney, who was still my girlfriend at the time. I later found out that she went to a party in Elyria with Barb Shine. Bridgett was totally honest with me, and she said she had been drinking and smoking, and even making out with a kid from Midview that she had met. I was crazy with envy, and acted like a little kid, pouting about everything she had told me.

At school the next week we had this big fight, and she told me she was breaking up with me again. She told me that I was being too possessive and that she wanted to experience the world and meet new people, blah, blah, blah. I was crushed again, especially since I had been the one who had exploded when she told me about attending the party in Elyria. I was the one who had reacted so poorly, and now she was breaking up with me. Of course, she really didn't have to go to that party in Elyria. This was horrible, again! When you are young and in love you are stupid!

I had given Bridgett a beautiful emerald ring for her last birthday, and when we had this fight at school she took the ring off and threw it across the cafeteria. How could she do such a thing?

64

The Spartans Take The Floor

After three weeks of basketball practice the Spartans of Lorain Catholic were ready to play our first game. It had been a strange three weeks of practice. I had started the previous year as the point guard, but, since we were so small and I could jump better than just about anyone on the team, Coach Englund asked me if I would mind trying to play forward. Even though I was only 5-10, I welcomed the challenge of playing forward. I figured, what the hell, the team needs me to play there, since we had Joey Laszoff and another pretty good guard in Tommy Buell. Those two guys were going to start in the backcourt, and the three football players, Jack Murtha, and Will Fitzpatrick, and I were going to start on the front line. That lineup meant that we were going to be really small: 6-2, 5-10, 6-1, 5-9, and 5-10. That had to be the smallest team that Coach Englund had ever started in all of his years as a coach. We were pretty quick though, and we hoped to be successful with pressure defense and enough scoring from fast breaks and Joey Laszoff.

Our first game was at South Amherst High School on November 26, 1969. South Amherst was a small school on the edge of Lorain County, and it frequently had some pretty good athletes. This was one of those years. I made a basket early in the game, one in the second quarter, and one in the fourth quarter. I also made two free throws, but I missed six free throws. That's right, I was 2-8 from the free throw line. I also fouled out late in the game when we were trying to come back from behind. The South Amherst gym was really tiny, and the host Cavaliers used their home-court advantage to its full benefit, as they beat us, 95-81. I couldn't believe that we gave up 95 points in one game. The gym was one that if you took just a few dribbles over half-court you were laying the ball up.

We had four guys in double figures, including Joey Laszoff (I knew he was going to be really good) who scored 26. He actually made eleven baskets, some of them from long range. Remember that there was no three-point line in 1969, so all of his shots, no matter how far away from the basket, counted only two points.

When I got home after the game my father was waiting for me. We talked about my performance and the team's and he pretty much layed it on the line for me: I had let my team down, especially fouling out. Even before that, I had not shown enough leadership as the captain. He was a pretty harsh critic, no doubt about it.

Ten days later we traveled to Sandusky Perkins for a match-up with the Pirates. Perkins always had great athletes, and they had given us one of our better games the year before when we beat them, 70-67. They had graduated a few guys from that team, but they also had plenty of returners. We had spent lots and lots of time on defense since the South Amherst game, and I was confident that we would play better against Perkins.

Once again, I started at forward, but this time next to 6-1 junior Dirk Coltaggio. Will Fitzpatrick was going to come off the bench against the Pirates. When the public address announcer announced the starting line-ups, we went out to center court and shook hands with a player from Perkins. The guy I shook hands with, #21, shook hands with me, looked me in the eye, and said, "We're gonna kick your ass." By the time I said, "What?" he had let go and was heading back to his side of the court. A moment later Joey Laszoff came over to me and said, "Did your guy say, 'We're gonna kick your ass' to you?"

"Yeah, he did," I said.

"You think they will?" asked Laszoff.

"Probably," I responded.

I may as well not even have played the game. I was useless. I played basically the whole game and played decent defense, but on offense I was totally lost. I took one shot and missed it. I was 0-3 from the free throw line. I had no rebounds and no assists. Talk about a liability for a team. I was worthless, and we lost the game, 48-46. Had I done anything at all to help my team, we might have won the game. Laszoff scored twelve, and sophomore post player JR Kesen came off the bench to score eleven.

On the bus on the way back after the game, I walked to the front of the bus and asked Coach Englund if I could talk to him. I was the captain of this team and I had just played the worst game of my career. Something had to give. After thinking about it for awhile, I told Coach Englund that I needed to be moved back to point guard. I wasn't tall enough to play forward, and my strength was my passing and leading the team. I told him that if I didn't get moved back to the point I might as well quit, since I wasn't helping the team at all as a forward.

Those were strong words coming from a high school kid, and I was really sticking my neck out. After all, Coach Englund could have simply said, "Yeah, well, maybe you should quit to help this team." He could have said, "I'm the coach and I will tell you where to play." Instead, he told me that he would think about it over the weekend.

On Monday at practice we began preparing for our first league game, at Parma Byzantine. Coach Englund always had a meeting before practice on Monday to basically announce the starting lineup for the next game. I was announced as the starting point guard. Joey Laszoff would be the other guard, and the three post players would be Coltaggio, Kesen, and Fitzpatrick. That lineup at least gave us a chance to rebound with other teams, as we were now 6-1, 6-2, and 6-1 in the post.

Parma Byzantine was coming into the basketball season with the momentum from their great football season. Most of the basketball players were also football players, so I knew most of them personally. Their best player was a forward named Mike Telep, but they also had their football quarterback, Mike Toth, who had destroyed us in the football game.

We played hard and led at halftime by two points and at the end of three quarters by one point, 39-38. We really believed we were robbed by the officials, as we shot nine foul shots in the game to Byzantine's 25. The Buccaneers outscored us, 18-13, in the fourth quarter to pull out a 56-52 victory. We were now 0-3, and we were starting to lose close games. I made five baskets in the game, scored ten points, and felt much more comfortable at point guard. Laszoff scored 24 to lead us, but we needed to figure out a way to get our first victory.

The night after we lost to Byzantine we had to travel to Clearview for a big battle with the Clippers. We always had great games against Clearview, regardless of the sport. Clearview was huge, with 6-5 Rick Bushkin, 6-4 Jerry Mahaffey, and 6-5 Ed Skvarna leading the way. We knew we were going to have to battle hard on the boards to stay in the game, and we gave a great team effort. We were up by one at halftime, but got crushed, 18-8 in the third quarter, so we were down 39-30 heading into the final stanza. We put on a furious rally and scored 27 points in the fourth quarter, but came up short, 58-57. We once again thought we had been screwed over by the officials, as we shot 18 free throws and the Clippers shot twice as many, making 24 out of 36. They shot 18 more free throws in a high school game than we did. There's something wrong with that stat. Of course, they were so much bigger than us that we had to foul more just to get position for rebounds, etc. In the fourth quarter alone we shot four free throws and they shot twelve. It's pretty hard to win when the opponents shoot twice as many free throws for the game and three times as many in the deciding fourth quarter. In fact, we made seven more baskets in the game than Clearview did, but they made fifteen more free throws than we did.

At this point, we are 0-4, and we had lost the last three games by a total of seven points. When were good things going to happen to us?

One good thing happened to me after the Clearview game. I had a date with Mary Wendell, Joe Wendell's sister who was a junior. She was hot, hot, hot. I had planned this out very well. I parked my 1961 Buick Invicta in front of the school, and gave Mary the keys, so she could just meet me in the car. She got a ride back from the game at Clearview with someone else, and then just got in my car, started the engine, and turned on the heater. After the game we returned to Lorain Catholic (Clearview is only about four miles away), got off the bus, and then dispersed to our cars. I got in my car, which was already running and warm, threw my gym bag in the back, reached over, and gave Mary Wendell, one of the hottest girls in the school, a great big, slow, wet kiss. I had seen someone in a movie do that, and I decided that I would try it some day. I hadn't even said, "Hello," but I didn't think I needed to introduce myself. I just leaned over, reached out, pulled her close, and gave her a great big kiss. It was awesome. It was also the last kiss I got from Mary Wendell that night or any other night. Hey, so it didn't really work that well for establishing a relationship, but it was cool when I did it.

Our next game was at Cleveland Central Catholic. This was one game I really thought we could win if we just played our regular game. The Ironmen were struggling just like us, and they didn't really have much size or scoring power. We did it! We were down, 40-32, at the end of the third period, but we put on a ferocious rally to outscore the Ironmen, 16-5 in the fourth quarter to win the game, 48-45. We were all very excited to finally win a game, especially a close game where we had to fight and scrape all the way. I made three baskets and all three of my free throws for nine points to help the team. Everyone was so excited to finally win a game, and we hoped to keep it going.

Avon was the next game, and we again battled hard throughout the game. We were down 47-46 going into the final quarter, but we just couldn't pull it out, losing 63-59. I scored in double figures for the second time, hitting five baskets for ten points. Once again, we lost the game at the free throw line, as we shot thirteen free throws and Avon shot 32. We scored three more baskets than they did, but we were outscored 19-9 at the free throw line.

A week later we traveled to Rocky River to play a new opponent on the schedule. We had never played the Pirates before, in basketball or just about anything else. Rocky River is a rich suburb on the west side of Cleveland, and it frequently had excellent athletic teams, including basketball.

Early in the game Joey Laszoff picked up his second foul, so he had to sit down for awhile. I decided that I would have to pick up the scoring slack a little bit once he left the game. I scored eight points in the first half, and, when he continued in foul trouble in the third quarter, I kept shooting. Also playing great in the third quarter was Dirk Coltaggio, as he scored nine points in the third quarter alone. We were up seven points at the half and seven going into the fourth quarter when we knew we would get Laszoff back. We held the seven point lead throughout most of the fourth quarter, too, and with 2:34 to play in the game I was dribbling the ball up the floor against the Pirate press. I was bumped three times from the right and finally heard the whistle blow. I stopped, went to give the official the ball and headed for the free throw line, where I was sure I would be shooting a one-and-one. Instead, the official pointed at me and said, "I've got an offensive foul on number 23 with the elbow." I looked at him and said, "What? You've got to be kidding me." The opposing player had been bumping me the entire length of the court and he was going to call the foul on me? I knew I couldn't say anything else, or I would get a technical foul, so I headed towards the bench, since that was my fifth foul.

As I got near the bench I saw my father, his face livid with anger, screaming at the referee. That was really the only time I ever saw him do that, but he was really fired up. All of the Lorain Catholic fans were all over the ref. They couldn't believe the call. We were ahead at the time, 57-50. We made one more basket in the game, and, with just seconds to play, Rocky River scored to make the score 59-58, with us still in the lead. There were three seconds to play, and Rocky River called an immediate timeout. We had the ball underneath the basket, and all we had to do was throw it in after the timeout. Will Fitzpatrick took the ball out of bounds and looked for someone to throw it to. Guard Tom Beull faked one way and cut the other and Fitzpatrick threw the ball where he thought Beull would be. The only person there was a Rocky River Pirate who caught the ball and calmly made a shot that gave them the win, 60-59. Talk about devastated, Will Fitzpatrick went in the locker room and up-ended the entire table with the cups of pop. Pop went flying everywhere. We couldn't believe that we had lost this game. This was clearly the toughest loss to take the entire season so far. The only time Rocky River led in the game was the final score.

Every year during the holiday season Coach Englund invites the alumni to come back and scrimmage against the varsity. Every year the varsity destroys the alumni, basically because the varsity is organized and well-conditioned and the alumni play run-and-gun offense and very little defense. Over Christmas break this year we scrimmaged the alumni. We got crushed. Let's face it, the recent alumni from St. Mary's were really excellent players, and most of them hadn't gotten out of shape yet. The really killed us on the boards, and I think Coach Englund changed the entire idea of an alumni scrimmage after 1969-70.

Our next game was supposed to be against Hudson Western Reserve Academy, but the day it was supposed to be played it snowed like hell and the game was postponed. Instead, we didn't play another game until Saturday night, January 10, when we traveled to Fremont St. Joe. We hardly ever played St. Joe in basketball, but we opened the season with them in football every year. We didn't know what to expect when we entered their gym, which wasn't much bigger than Johnston Hall.

We warmed up right in front of the St. Joe student section, and they were really boisterous. They were so close to the court that even during warm-ups we could reach out and touch them. Our warm-up included a short period where we just got into two small groups and passed the ball around. I threw some behind-the-back passes, and I also spun the ball on my finger before passing the ball to a teammate by bouncing it off of my head. The St. Joe students were all over me. They really thought I was showboating, which I probably was, but it was so much fun getting a response.

St. Joe played us tough, and they led at the end of every quarter, including 57-49 after three quarters. We exploded in the final quarter behind Joey Laszoff, and outscored the hosts, 18-7 in the final quarter to win the game, 67-64. Laszoff scored 24 points in the game, including fourteen in the last quarter alone. I scored eight and dished out eight assists, playing one of my better overall games of the season, but it was Joey Laszoff who really led us to this win. It was really great beating the Crimson Streaks in both football and basketball in one school year, and it made the long bus-ride back from Fremont much shorter.

65

"Hey, I want to talk to you!"
Jocks versus Freaks Part Two

One of the absolute coolest things about Lorain Catholic High School when it opened was the study hall arrangement. I have already mentioned the cafeteria, called the Commons, with its wall of vending machines and round tables throughout. During the school day that area was called the "Open" Study Hall. There was a teacher assigned to the area, but all he/she did was take attendance. Students were allowed to walk around the Commons, use the vending machines, talk to one another, or even play cards. The "Closed" Study Hall was in the brand new library. If a student wanted to study in quiet, he/she would check in at the library, where the atmosphere was silent. There were even small, enclosed desk areas in the library called "study carols," where students could go to be alone and concentrate. Do I even need to say that I spent most of my study hall time in the "Open" Study Hall in the Commons? My class schedule during my senior year was pretty easy, and I spent the first forty minutes and the last forty minutes each day in study hall, usually in the open study hall in the Commons.

January 12, 1970 was a beautiful winter day with snow falling outside for most of the day. The flakes of snow were the large, soft kind that stuck on your nose and made the trees and everything look beautiful. I was sitting in the Commons during the last period of the day. My feet were up on the window sill and I was simply watching the snow fall. I was just relaxing, being a cool senior.

Suddenly, a young lady was standing right next to me. She was short, about 5-2, with long blond hair. I had never spoken to her before. She was a junior and a first-year student at Lorain Catholic, having transferred from one of the private Catholic girls' schools in Cleveland. Her name was Shelby Boca, and she seemed upset or at least determined about something.

"Hey, I want to talk to you," she said firmly.

I sort of cocked my head in her direction and said, as coolly as I could, "So talk."

"I think what's going on around here is ridiculous. This school is so split it's stupid. This whole jocks and freaks thing is terrible, and it's got to change."

I again sort of half looked at her and said, "I agree."

She started to say something else but stopped and said, "You do?"

"Yeah," I said, getting ready to use one of the signature lines of the 1960's, "I think everybody ought to just do their own thing." How ridiculous is that?

She looked at me and said, "Do you really believe that?"

"Yeah," I said with a shrug. "Don't you?"

"Well, yeah, but . . . ." She just looked at me rather suspiciously, and I'm pretty sure that she didn't believe that I believed what I had just said. "Well, I'm having a party at my house after the game Friday night. Why don't you invite your jock friends and I will invite my friends, and we'll all start to get along."

I shook my head and said, "I don't know who you are and I don't know where you live, but I don't think that's a very good idea."

"Why not," she asked.

"Well, you know JD and Robbie don't get along with a lot of the Freaks, and if they're there, something might happen. They might just kick their asses. Not only that, but they might just trash your house."

"You just said that everybody ought to get along. Let's do this and change those stupid attitudes," she said.

Again, I just sort of shrugged my shoulders. "OK, it's on. Where do you live?"

I also asked her for her phone number and she wrote it down on a little slip of paper.

I called up Shelby Boca that evening to tell her that I had talked to some people and they were in for the party. I also found out how nice she was. Her father had passed away a few years earlier, and she was the youngest child in the family. She lived with her mother in a very nice, basically brand new house about a block and half away from Lorain Catholic High School. The next day in school I gave her a note, and she returned the note with an answer, and she invited me over to her house to meet her mom. That night I went to Shelby Boca's house and met Mrs. Boca. Shelby's mom was one of the most vibrant, wonderful people I have ever met. She laughed a lot and it was very clear that she really enjoyed life. I thought that my relationship with Shelby might go someplace, and I was glad to see that her mother not only liked me, but was the kind of person we could both hang around with.

Wednesday night I took Shelby out for a Yala's pizza, and we just sort of sat around and talked. I found out that she was a very liberal-thinking person and was sincere in her belief that the students at a small school like Lorain Catholic should be able to get along. The party situation was finalized on Thursday and it seemed that quite a few people from the Classes of '70 and '71 would be there.

One other thing that was happening that week . . . . The Lorain Catholic Spartans got to practice in the new gym. Coach Englund got to make the first basket in the gym, and it certainly would have been embarrassing if he missed the shot with everyone watching. I couldn't believe how long the floor looked. As previously mentioned, the floor was 94 feet long, and it seemed even longer than that. When we ran sprints on that floor end-to-end, it was forever. The 75-foot floor at St. Mary's was a lot easier to run across.

The rest of the gym was pretty cool. The bleachers opposite the scorer's table were twelve rows high, and they held all of the home students and all of the visitors fans. The scorer's table side also had plenty of bleachers; in addition, that side had an upper deck, with another eight rows of bleachers. The gym had seating for over 1600 fans, which was way more than twice as big as Johnston Hall, St. Mary's old gym. The locker rooms were state-of-the-art, with lockers that actually opened and closed and showers that ran hot water that you could actually adjust. Golly, were we going to be spoiled?

The very first game hosted by Lorain Catholic would be a league games versus arch-rival Elyria Catholic. There was a scheduled dedication ceremony after the game in the Commons with dignitaries like the Bishop of Cleveland and several local politicians. As a co-captain, Coach Englund made it very clear that I was to attend the dedication reception, at least for a little while. I wanted to head right over to Shelby Boca's for the party, but I had other responsibilities.

One of the strangest things ever occurred right before the game. As the players got up during the third period of the junior varsity game to go and get dressed for the varsity game I was handed a note. It was from Bridgett Mulroney, and it was filled with good luck wishes and was concluded by the words, "I love you." What the hell was that all about? I figured that she knew how much I really loved her, and she was just trying to get my mind ready to play against EC, so I sort of blew off the whole idea of those words. I had a game to play.

Just before the tip-off of the varsity game, Co-Captain Will Fitzpatrick and I went to center court where we were presented with an American flag. It was presented by a local veterans' group, and the flag had actually flown above the United States Capitol Building in Washington, DC. We held the flag while the crowd joined in the singing of our national anthem. It was really kind of a cool thing to get to do, but I was really ready to play basketball.

Earlier in the week Coach Englund had been trying to decide what defense to play against the Panthers, and, if we were going to play man-to-man, who would guard whom? I told him that I could harass Dale "The Flash" Kaminski from end line to end line, and that I was very confident that I could stop him. Will Fitzpatrick said the same thing, with the same amount of confidence, about guarding EC's best player, Mark Straka, the same 6-4 athlete who had hurt us in the football loss. The other Panther starters, by the way, were also football players: Doug Gerber (touchdown on the last play of the game), Mark St. Marie (safety who blasted me after I tried to make a catch), and Mike Kearns (6-5 tight end who caught a touchdown pass against us). Needless to say, Will Fitzpatrick and I were pretty familiar with these guys, as we had played against them since CYO football and basketball in grade school.

The Panthers entered the game with an outstanding record, and I'm sure they were supremely confident that they would crush us, since our record was, well, less than outstanding.

We started off the game, played before a standing-room-only crowd in our new gym, pretty well, even though we were having a tough time stopping Straka. Fitzpatrick was doing his best, but Straka was bigger and stronger, and Fitzpatrick got into foul trouble early. We were down, 18-12, at the end of the first quarter, but in the second quarter everything began to click for the Spartans. Led by eight points each from Joey Laszoff and substitute post player George Brent, we actually stormed back to lead at the half, 32-26. I know that the Panthers had to be stunned, as we were not supposed to be this close to them.

At halftime we were so pumped up it was tough to relax. I was offered a large bottle of this new sport drink, something called Gatorade. I drank two whole bottles of the stuff while I sat in the locker room, and when we went out for the second half I felt like I weighed ten pounds more than before. I know that it was supposed to give me energy, but it certainly didn't seem to be doing its job, as I felt nothing but bloated. In the first half I had held Flash Kaminski to four points, while Straka had already scored fifteen.

In the third quarter EC just kept dumping the ball inside to Straka, and he either scored a basket or went to the free throw line. He hit six out of seven free throws in the quarter, as well as two more baskets, and

EC stormed back ahead in the game, 46-41. We were still in the game, though, if we could just figure out a way to stop the Panthers and score some ourselves. It wasn't to be, as the hated Panthers outscored us 19-10 in the final quarter for a 65-51 victory. We scored 32 points in the first half and only 19 in the second half, while EC outscored us in the second half by twenty points, 39-19. The best team won. Straka set the scoring record for the brand new gym by pumping in 37 points. We just had no answer for him. Flash Kaminski did get free for some points in the second half and ended with eleven.

We were all pretty crushed when we got to the locker room, but I was ready to hurry and shower and dress so I could get to the dedication reception and then to the party at Shelby Boca's. I was a perfect gentleman in meeting the dignitaries in the Commons after the game, but, after making a few rounds and shaking some hands, I asked Coach Englund if it was OK to leave.

When I got to Shelby's house just a few minutes later, there were cars parked all over the place. She lived in a very, very nice neighborhood, and there were cars parked on both sides of the street, up and down the block. There was also an empty space in her driveway, which I took.

I rang the doorbell, and Mrs. Boca welcomed me. I could hear the music from the basement, but I couldn't hear much "people noise," you know, people talking, laughing, etc. I immediately got worried. Mrs. Boca told me that everyone was downstairs, and I headed down the steps. When I reached the bottom of the steps, I noticed two things: first, you could cut the tension in the air with a knife. There was just an air of impending doom. Second, when I reached the bottom of the steps, on my left stood the Freaks and some girls, and on my right were the Jocks and some other girls. Bob Irelan, Joe Wendell, and the Freaks had on their long overcoats. Robbie Cavellini, JD Szollzy and the Jocks had on their black leather coats. I said "Hi" to everyone and gave Shelby a sort-of half-hug.

"How's it going?" I asked.

"Everything's fine," she said.

"Excuse me for saying, but it doesn't really look like everything's fine."

Just as I said that, I heard the opening of a can. I looked over and Bob Irelan had a can of beer. At almost the same time, JD Szollzy opened a can of his own. Shelby Boca's basement had a finished side (furniture, TV, stereo, bar, etc.) and an unfinished side (washer and dryer, etc.). The Freaks were on the unfinished side, while the Jocks were in the finished area. The area beneath the stairway was open, so you could see from one side to the other. After hearing the cans open, Bob Irelan and JD Szollzy looked through the open stairway and said to each other, "What do got there?" One guy said, "PBR" (Pabst Blue Ribbon), and the other guy said, "Bud."

They asked each other how much they had, and each guy had about four beers. All of a sudden, there was, as they say, a common bond of interest. It's sad to give credit to alcohol for anything, but it seemed to be a peace-maker. People began to share, and people began to see that everyone wasn't so different after all.

By the way, it's important to understand that I was neither offered any beer nor did I ask for any. I took the athletic code of conduct/training rules very seriously, and so did everyone else. Everybody knew that Will Fitzpatrick and I were playing basketball and that we would never consider drinking or breaking training rules while we were in season. After the season . . . . that was another story.

The last three people at the party were Will Fitzpatrick, Shelby Boca, and I. I was driving that night, so I had to take Fitzpatrick home. The three of us were in the finished side of the basement, and it was rather late. Fitzpatrick actually fell asleep, and Shelby and I started making out. It was really the first time we had done anything other than a quick kiss and hug. As opportunistic as I usually am, I just couldn't get myself to do much with my best friend sleeping five feet away. That was, from beginning to end, one strange party. It did seem to bring classes of people together, and it definitely brought me closer to Shelby Boca. What a great young lady. I hadn't even thought about Bridgett Mulroney in a week, and that was great.

The next week we were scheduled to play host to a rematch with Sandusky Perkins. They had defeated us, 48-46, when we had played them very early in the season, but this time I thought we would get them. We lost the stupid game at the free throw line. We ended up 11-25 from the line, and I was a dismal 2-7. Perkins hit 19-28. We actually made more baskets than they did, 18-17, but they won the game, 53-47. The worst thing about the Perkins game was the fact that Co-Captain Will Fitzpatrick suffered a very serious ankle injury. The injury actually knocked him out for the rest of the season. It was one of those 'sprains that are worse than a break.' I was now the only senior on the squad.

The next night we traveled all the way to Gilmour Academy to play the Lancers. We got crushed, 75-58.

I continued to develop my relationship with Shelby Boca, and she continued to amaze me. She was so smart and funny and liberal. I had never really met anyone like her. She was also nice, friendly, and passionate about life. Perhaps the very best thing about Shelby Boca was the way she smelled. I don't know if it was her shampoo or what, but she smelled wonderful. I could see this relationship going somewhere.

66

The New Tradition of "The Pit"

The big thing that happened at school that week occurred during lunch. We had our usual thirteen guys sitting around the round table called "The Pit." If you didn't want something from your lunch, you simply tossed it into "The Pit," and everyone else sort of dove for it. I was always accused of never putting anything into "The Pit" and always being the first one to grab stuff. That week was "Let's Get Francis Week," and they certainly did.

First, someone bought a small bag of potato chips. The bag of chips sat on the edge of the table for quite a few minutes, and I began to think that they might be potential for being tossed into "The Pit." Sure enough, near the end of lunch the bag of chips were tossed into the middle. I dove for them and so did everyone else. They actually let me grab the bag, and then everyone else just pounded fists down on top of my hand and the bag of chips, which is when they became a bag of crumbs instead of chips.

As if that wasn't enough, the next day someone had a small coconut cream pie and he took one bite out of it. He decided he didn't like coconut, so he tossed it into the middle. I again reach for it, and, again, as I grabbed it everyone just pounded down onto my hand. The coconut cream pie squished up between my fingers, all over the table.

Two days later, another coconut cream pie played into the best prank of all. About ten minutes from the end of the lunch period, Robbie Cavellini stood up on a chair and yelled, "Hey! Quiet!" Everyone in the cafeteria got quiet, because this was, after all, Robbie Cavellini. He looked down from the chair and motioned to someone to hand him the cream pie. "I have here a coconut cream pie," he shouted. "How much money would you give me to smash this pie in Stephen Francis' face?"

Kids from all over the cafeteria started shouting amounts of money, and Cavellini hopped down from the chair and said to everyone else at the table, "Well, go collect the money." All the other senior football players went around the cafeteria and collected money from the other students. They returned to the table and dumped the money. There was $17.85 on the table." I had just been sitting there for the entire time, and I said, "You're not really going to do that, right?" Cavellini looked at me and said, "Of course I'm gonna do it. I can't disappoint all these kids, can I?" He looked at the other guys and said, "Grab him and stand him up."

They were on top of me in a second. I tried to get away, but Mackie MacGregor and Bert Knouwer had my arms behind my back. I realized it was useless to struggle. I was standing there in the middle of the Commons/Cafeteria, and Cavellini yelled, "Drum roll." A few kids started pounding on the tables, and Cavellini yelled even louder, "I said drum roll." Now virtually ever student in the cafeteria was pounding on the table in front of him/her. Cavellini then put his hand up with one finger. Everyone yelled, "One." He put up two fingers and everyone yelled, "Two," and, finally, "Three," at which point he took the cream pie and smashed it in my face, using his hand to spread it around. I had a coconut cream pie all over me.

There was a thunderous applause as I headed to the rest room to wipe off the pie.

That afternoon we hosted Western Reserve Academy in a make-up game from one which had been postponed from a month or so earlier. We were up at halftime, but eventually fell in a low-scoring game, 46-36. The Pioneers were very, very tall, and we had trouble rebounding and getting any offense going against them.

On January 30 we played host to Cleveland Central Catholic, a team we knew we could beat, since we had already defeated them once. We played our best game of the season and put four guys in double figures and scoring the most we had since the first game of the season. We won, 70-51. I scored eight points and established the school record for assists in one game with 13. Sophomore Tim Tomko played his first varsity game and scored eleven points, as did junior Tom Beull. Sophomore center JR Kesen scored twelve, and Joey Laszoff was as great as usual, hitting for 26 points. It was awesome scoring that many points in a game, as we had been held down to 36 points in the previous game.

We continued our hot play the very next night when we hosted Columbia. Seventy points one night and 63 the next, as we handled Columbia, 63-49. We were beginning to play much better as a team, and we seemed to be peaking as the season headed into February.

The first week of February also brought about tryouts for the first annual Festival of One Acts. Every class was going to have the opportunity to present a one-act play, directed by someone in the class. I was chosen to direct the Senior Class production, and there was one thing that I knew I wanted to do: have a very small cast. All of the plays that we were going to present that year were written by famous playwright Eugene O'Neill. I started looking through the scripts that were available and I chose "Thirst," which is a one-act play about three people on a lifeboat after being shipwrecked. The three people were an officer from the original crew, a female dancer, and a Cuban sailor. I knew that I could pass for a Cuban sailor, so all I had to do was come up with an officer and a dancer. My best friend, Will Fitzpatrick, agreed to be the officer, and he convinced me to ask Dominique Pavlak to play the dancer. I thought that she would probably not want to work with me in the play after how horribly I had treated her in the fall of that year, but she agreed to join us in the little venture. Will's dad owned an old rowboat that could pass for a lifeboat, so all we were going to have to do for a set was bring the boat in, put it on stage, somehow sort of anchor it so it didn't rock too much, and then close the center curtain to the edge of the boat. We had about two months to rehearse, and Will and I figured that any time spent with Dominique would be fun, so we began to get ready.

The next basketball game we were supposed to play was the rematch with Elyria Catholic at the EC Coliseum. The previous year we had broken their undefeated home win streak, and we knew that they would be ready for us this time, especially since we actually led them by six points at halftime in the first game. One of the coolest things for a young athlete is traveling to opposing schools' gyms and seeing how hostile the crowd can get. Actually, in walking around the Coliseum before the game, we discovered posters with our pictures on them. Needless to say, the posters weren't very complimentary, but it was still cool to see your own picture as the centerpiece of a nasty, spirit-building poster. I actually took one poster with my picture on it off the wall and stuck it in my gym bag when I first arrived at the gym.

The first quarter was up and down the court, and we had everyone contributing. I scored six points in the first quarter, and we were only down, 20-18, at the end of one. EC moved out to a four point lead at halftime, but in the third quarter Joey Laszoff exploded for five baskets, and at the end of three quarters, the score was tied, 52-52. We were playing our best game of the season when we needed to, and the final quarter was going to be the deciding one.

The Panthers, behind old nemesis Mark Straka, exploded for 24 points in the last quarter while holding us to ten, so the final score was 76-62.

I ended with ten points, sophomore center JR Kesen had 18, and Joey Laszoff was held to 15. It was actually a fun game in front of a huge crowd, and the Panthers at least knew they were in a game.

67

The National Love Weekly

We had only two regular-season games to play, but before we finished the season it was time for a little mischief. Will Fitzpatrick and I thought there were far too many serious high school romances going on around the school. Of course I had been involved in the Bridgett-Dominique-Bridgett-Mary-Bridgett-Shelby situation, and there were even more of those kinds of things. The situations that really bothered Will and me were the ones where things had just gotten too serious. To see high school kids arguing about phone calls and telling each other that they were in love in the hallways of a Catholic high school was a bit ridiculous. Of course a girlfriend throwing an emerald ring across the cafeteria was different. Wasn't it?

Will and I had seen enough. Lorain Catholic High School had a student bulletin board just down the hall from the office. Students were allowed to pin any kind of message or announcement on the board for the entire student body to see. The announcements were supposed to be checked and approved by someone in the office, but Will and I weren't interested in that.

We wrote a scandal sheet, with comments about couples in the school. Was this dangerous? Sure, but we hoped to stay anonymous. In the first issue of The National Love Weekly we had articles about Bert Knouwer going to the movies with a girl no one knew (he was dating someone else who everyone DID know), an article about JD Szollzy and his girlfriend, and even a love quiz, which asked questions about "dates" that people had been on. We carefully printed the scandal sheet and pinned it on the student bulletin board. The response was absolutely crazy. There were so many people mad that someone was commenting on the seriousness of high school romances that it was unbelievable. Numerous students wrote nasty responses and pinned them next to The National Love Weekly. At that point, no one knew who had actually written the underground newspaper.

The following week we came out with a double issue, two full pages of scandal. There was an article about senior Jimmy Sullivan dating a divorced lady (he was), and Conor Flanary dating another girl in the senior class (he wasn't). There was even a totally false article about Joey Laszoff dating a girl from Lorain High School. In order to make the second issue better, Will and I thought we needed to print numerous copies, since the original could be taken down from the bulletin board by an irate reader. We needed access to a copy machine, which wasn't the easiest thing to garner in 1970. The priest who had printed the football pool sheets, Father Snyder, was the first person we asked, and he readily agreed to join in the fun.

When the second issue of The National Love Weekly hit the bulletin board the response was greater than the first. There were people accusing all sorts of others of being the scandal-monger. Will Fitzpatrick and I just played along and acted as disgusted with the scandal information as anyone.

Finally, one day during last period, I received a note to go to the office. When I got there Will was already sitting there. He looked at me with a very serious look on his face. I said, "What's up?" He just frowned and said, "What do you think?"

We were called into Sister Mary Neumann's office and told to sit down. She closed the door. I hadn't been in the Principal's Office in years. In fact, that was the very first time I was in the Principal's Office at the new school, and we were several months into the school year, which I thought was pretty good.

Sister Mary Neumann walked around her desk and reached down and picked up a copy of The National Love Weekly. "Are you two responsible for this?" She was holding it in her hand and sort of waving it at us.

I looked at Will, back at Sister Mary Neumann, and said, "Yes, Sister, we're responsible for that, but we really didn't mean any harm. We just thought that there were too many romances around here that were getting too serious and too much like a soap opera and . . . ." I was talking really fast, and the principal just put her hand up to make me stop.

"I got it," she said. "This has got to stop. If you ever do anything like this again, you will be expelled from this school. Do I make myself perfectly clear?"

Will and I both nodded. "Yes Sister," we both said.

"There's one more thing," she said. "This is printed on paper from one of our copy machines. I know this because of the mark on the back of the paper. I want to know who copied this for you."

There was a very serious silence in the room. I sort of cleared my throat and said, "Sister, you can do anything you want to me, but I am not going to tell you who copied that for us. Will doesn't even know who did it, so he's off the hook anyway, but I am not going to tell you who copied that. No way."

She looked at me and realized right away that I was set in my decision. "OK, now you two get out of here and don't attempt anything else like this the rest of the year." We walked out of the office and realized we had dodged a bullet. Heck, I think that was the first time Will Fitzpatrick had ever been in trouble in school, and I was the cause. Too bad I didn't feel sorry for him!

68

Elbow Tipping And The End Of The Season

Aweek later we headed across town to the other new school in Lorain that year, Southview High School. Southview was coached by George Simonovich, who actually had been the coach at St. Mary's before Coach Englund returned. Southview featured the leading scorer in the entire area, a junior named Hank Chawansky, who was averaging over 26 points a game. That was just another challenge for me.

Through the course of the year I had perfected an illegal defensive move that was virtually undetectable by the officials. It's called elbow-tipping. When a player shoots the ball the defensive player frequently puts his hand up near the face of the shooter, trying to disturb the rhythm of the shot. Sometimes players reach out and actually hit the elbow of the shooter, and, if you hit it hard enough, it's virtually guaranteed that the shot will be off-line. I had combined the two moves. You see, sometimes officials can see when a defensive player swats at an elbow, and they call a foul. Officials are much more lenient when a defensive player tries to put his hand in the face of the shooter, as long as you don't touch the shooter. I worked very hard at putting my open hand up into the face of the shooter, but, on my way towards the shooter's face, I would hit his elbow straight up into the air, usually with my thumb. When I tipped a guy's elbow, he couldn't make the shot. Further, if I tipped his elbow enough times early in the game, I didn't need to tip it later in the game. All I had to do was get close and he started flinching. That was the game plan against Hank Chawansky.

The local papers were really playing up the game because it featured the two best junior players in the area, Joey Laszoff and Hank Chawansky. They were also the two leading scorers in the area, and the papers and radio stations were calling this a showdown between the two. We knew going into the game that Laszoff and Chawansky wouldn't be guarding each other, since I was going to be all over Chawansky, tipping his elbow at every chance.

Hank Chawansky shot twelve shots in the first half, and I tipped his elbow on seven of them. He made two baskets. He got away on a fast break for his first basket and on the second basket I tipped his elbow straight up and he banked in a shot from the top of the key. That's right! He banked one in off the glass from the top of the key. Pure luck. I needed to tip his elbow just a little off to the side, not straight up. He was complaining bitterly to the officials that I was fouling him, but I had perfected the elbow-tipping move so well that the officials couldn't see it, and you can't call what you can't see.

The officials did call one foul on me, which occurred on a baseline drive by Chawansky in the third quarter. He made one of his two free throws that time, and he also hit two baskets in the quarter. Hank was so frustrated that early in the fourth quarter he fouled out, scoring his season-low fourteen points. Laszoff scored 24, and the papers the next day indicated that Laszoff had won the battle, but I had guarded Chawansky. We also had two other guys in double figures, and we won the basketball game, 69-65, holding on after we led by eleven going into the final period.

In the last few weeks of the season I had two sprained ankles, both of which occurred because of the new floor at the Lorain Catholic gym. The floor was very "tight." The brand new varnish was almost sticky, and if you tried to slide your feet along the floor you almost stuck. I was a very aggressive defensive player and really moved my feet, and twice in one week my feet stuck on the floor and I rolled both ankles. I was also a football player, and I wasn't about to let a sprained ankle stop me from playing. I just hobbled to the trainer's room and had the trainer tape my ankles. I also got the thermo treatment, which meant they submerged my feet to just above the ankles in buckets of ice water. Talk about pain! This treatment was supposed to flush out any swelling in the ankle joints by basically freezing the joints for about ten minutes and then taking my feet out and moving my ankles as much as possible, getting blood rushing in to the frozen area. The technique actually works, but it is incredibly painful while you are going through it. After just a minute or so it feels like there are needles being shoved into your foot. By the time you take your feet out of the ice-filled bucket, you pretty much can't feel anything in your foot. The danger of the treatment, of course, is that some people with poor circulation could actually get frostbite.

I went through the thermo treatment each day for almost a week, and there is no question that it does its job—the swelling was removed from my ankles. Of course that doesn't mean they weren't still weak and sprained, but at least the swelling was gone. The trainer ended up using an entire roll of tape on each ankle just for support, and I kept playing, never missing even a practice.

During a late-season practice when I had both ankles taped, I was playing defense and my foot again stuck to the floor. I was going full speed sideways, and I went down again clutching my ankle. Coach Englund just yelled, "Get up, Francis," as I stayed down on the floor, writhing with pain. I hobbled to my feet and told him I needed to see the trainer again. "What is it now?" he asked. I just told him I had to see the trainer. I went to the side of the court and sat down while practice continued. The trainer arrived and I took my shoe off and then pulled my sock down. The tape which had been supporting my ankle had split. I had torn through an entire roll of tape on my ankle. The trainer told me that if I hadn't had my ankle taped it surely would have broken. I just told him to re-apply some more tape so I could go back and practice.

By the time I returned to the floor my sock was pretty much bulging out from the amount of tape that was supposed to be supporting my ankle.

In our last regular-season game we hosted Parma Byzantine. The Buccaneers had defeated us by four points the first time we played them, and we were confident that as well as we were playing late in the season we could get them in the second game. We were wrong. We fell behind early when we just couldn't make a shot, and, despite playing them even in the final three quarters, we lost, 61-54. Joey Laszoff had one of his better games, as he racked up 28 points, including 19 in the second half. We couldn't seem to stop Byzantine, however, and they made eight out of nine free throws in the fourth quarter when we were trying to come back. It was a tough way to end the regular season, and it was especially tough when we saw the sectional draw: we had to play Byzantine a third time in the first game of the sectionals.

As we started to prepare for a third battle with Byzantine, both of my ankles were very sore, but I wasn't about to let that stop me from playing in what could be my final high school basketball game. I continued to practice through the pain. Early in the week of preparation for the sectional game something happened at practice that really affected us. Not only did I have two sprained ankles, but Joey Laszoff also suffered a serious sprain. The funny thing about his sprain was the reaction of Coach Englund, and it tells something about the value of each of us.

Remember that when I went down for the third time, and it really made no difference that it was the first, second, or third time for me, Coach Englund responded by yelling, "Get up, Francis." When Laszoff went down, Coach Englund rushed out onto the floor right over to Laszoff and tried to see if he was okay. In fact, he stayed down with him for a few minutes, and then told us to shoot free throws and then practice was over. So, with one guy it's "Get up," and with the other guy, the star player, it's "Practice is over."

I really never thought much about the difference in treatment, since I was a football player/athlete, and I was simply going to play through any injury. I guess it would have been nice if Coach Englund had stopped practice and worried a little more about me, but that's just the way it was. He knew I was tough and could take a beating and getting yelled at. After all, I had played football for Coach John Flowers.

69

The Final Game

The sectional was played at North Ridgeville High School, the same site as the previous year's sectional which we had won. North Ridgeville had a very nice large gym, and we were really excited about playing the game. We figured that we had lost two close games to Byzantine, and it was time for us to turn the tables. Unfortunately, we were going to have to play without a healthy Joey Laszoff, as he was still nursing the sprained ankle.

Byzantine started the game in a man-to-man defense, and I just had great confidence in beating the guy guarding me. I knew, just like the Rocky River game when Laszoff was in foul trouble, that I would have to do a little more offensively to help the team. I made two baskets and six-of-six from the free throw line in the first quarter alone to lead us with ten points. I was penetrating against their man-to-man and there was no way they were going to stop me. I either drove shot and scored, got fouled, or dumped it to sophomore post man JR Kesen who scored.

When the second quarter started I thought that this might be my all-time record for points in a game, which stood at a measly 14, which I had scored on numerous occasions. Unfortunately for me, Byzantine changed defenses to a 2-1-2 zone at the start of the quarter, which effectively took away my penetrating drives. I was never really known as an outside shooting threat, and, with Laszoff hobbling, we struggled to score against the Byzantine zone.

Despite a big comeback in the fourth quarter, we fell for the third time that season to Byzantine, 60-52. All three games were close, but they were just a little better than us. I ended the game with twelve points, eight assists, four rebounds and four steals, which was, overall, one of the best games I played in my career. I sat in the locker room in my uniform for a long time. I didn't want to take it off. My high school career in basketball was over. My favorite sport was finished. Will Fitzpatrick, my best friend and the only other senior on the team who had been hurt halfway through the season, came over to me in the locker room. He knew how much the end meant to me. We just sort of looked at each other and shook hands. All of the underclassmen were showered and dressed before I was ready to go. Coach Englund came into the locker room and tried to hurry me along, but he also knew that this last game was very important to me.

Unlike football, where lifelong friendships had developed amongst the seniors, the basketball season was different. I only had one real friend on the team, Fitzpatrick, and he had gotten hurt. I also knew that Coach Englund and every one of the underclass-men on that basketball team, that 5-13 squad, was already looking forward to the next season when they would have just about everyone returning.

At the basketball banquet a week later, Joey Laszoff was named Most Valuable Player, as well he should have been. He had averaged over twenty points a game for the season, and was one of the top players in the area. I was awarded the very first Spartan Shirt Award, given to the outstanding defensive player on the team. Coach Englund always referred to me in the paper as "hard-nosed," which he jokingly explained at the banquet meant "... this guy can't shoot, but he does play tough defense." I ended the season averaging eight points a game and set the standard for assists in a season as well as steals and recoveries. The assist record of 113 stood for a few years before being demolished by a player on one of Coach Englund's many outstanding teams. Joey Laszoff was First Team All-North Central Conference, and I was named Honorable Mention All-NCC.

70

My First College Visit

Just after the basketball season ended Mackie MacGregor and I visited The Defiance College in Defiance, Ohio. I knew some people at DC already, including my tennis doubles' partner from the two previous years, Phil O'Keefe. My oldest brother's best friend from high school, Mike Gerald, was also a student at the small, liberal arts college. Mackie was visiting DC as a football recruit, and I was going there as a basketball/tennis recruit, or at least I thought so.

Our visit was pretty interesting, and I got to meet the athletic director and former basketball coach. I didn't get to meet the present basketball coach, who was also the tennis coach, because he was still in the midst of a college basketball season. We both liked the place, even though it was pretty small.

On the way home from Defiance it started to snow pretty heavily. Mackie decided that we should stop and call his mom and tell her that we were on the way home, but that it might take awhile longer since we were going to have to drive slower due to the snow. We stopped in a little town on Route 6 in northwest Ohio named McClure. There was a combination gas station-ice cream parlor on the corner of Route 6 right in the middle of McClure.

Mackie and I entered the place and I told him that I would buy him a milkshake. He went to the counter and asked the lady if there was a phone booth in town. She told him that there was a phone booth just outside the store and around the corner. Mackie went outside and returned a few minutes later. I was eating my pineapple milkshake when he stepped in and motioned me to come with him. I handed him his chocolate shake and followed him into the snow.

We got to the phone booth and Mackie opened the door and just pointed at the phone. There were no dials on the phone! This was 1970, mind you. There was a crank on the side of the phone. We had no idea how to use the phone, and we just started laughing. We returned to the ice cream parlor/gas station and asked them what to do. They looked at us like we were strangers from outer space.

"Just turn the crank three times and wait for Mabel and then tell her what you want," she said. We couldn't believe this. We almost did feel like strangers from another planet. Planet Earth in the 20th century!

We returned to the phone booth and turned the crank three times and waited. Sure enough, Mabel answered and asked us how she could help us. When Mackie explained what he wanted, Mabel spent a minute or so getting things going, and, sure enough, Mackie was talking to his mom.

After the phone call we returned to the ice cream shop to finish our milkshakes. We were laughing about the phone adventure when some locals asked us what we were laughing about. We hesitated to tell them, but when we did they were almost offended that we would be laughing about the McClure Phone Company. They explained to us that there were only three or four operators and they rotated shifts. Everyone was on a party line in McClure, and, you could often ask the operator if someone was home and she would know. The operators were known to just say to people, "Oh, don't try to call the Smiths. They're not home." The three or four operators knew everyone in town and they knew everyone's business in town.

Just as a post script, both Mackie and I went to Defiance College and graduated. He took a semester off before enrolling, so he graduated in 1975, while I graduated in 1974. Mackie MacGregor had an outstanding college career at DC, starting at center all four years, while I played tennis all fours years and qualified for the NAIA National Tournament twice. I also tried out for basketball and got cut. We didn't let The McClure Phone Company scare us off!

71

The Senior-Faculty Game

A wonderful tradition that Coach Englund brought from St. Mary's was the annual Senior-Faculty Game, pitting senior guys against faculty members in a hard-fought basketball game. The senior basketball players weren't allowed to play, but the other senior athletes took on members of the faculty. Coach Flowers was a great basketball player, as was Coach Englund. When they combined with Coach McComb, Coach Havrady, Mr. Clay, Mr. Muth, and others, they could be pretty formidable.

In 1970 girls' interscholastic athletics hadn't really gotten started, so the girls played intramural basketball. I coached a senior teamed named The Rappers. The girls' intramural championship was played just before the senior-faculty game. My team won the championship easily, and then Will Fitzpatrick and I were supposed to coach the senior guys against the faculty.

We put a team out on the floor that included Robbie Cavellini, Conor Flanary, JD Szollzy, and our secret weapon, Dave Prosalak, the six-seven kid who had been cut from the varsity team. It was a hard-fought game, but the faculty prevailed, as Coach Englund hit some free throws down the stretch to help them hold on for the win. Overall, it was a great evening of entertainment, and helped get Will Fitzpatrick and me excited about coaching as careers.

72

"Turn The Page, Will"

J ust before the tennis season began the school presented the "Festival of One-Act Plays." Remember that I was directing the senior production of Eugene O'Neill's "Thirst," with Dominique Pavlak, Will Fitzpatrick, and me in the three roles. We actually got the scripts and were supposed to start rehearsing back in February, but the big problem with casting your friends in the roles came when we were supposed to be rehearsing.

We didn't have very many rehearsals, and when we did rehearse we did lots of gossiping and just talking. In other words, when it was time for the presentation no one really knew his/her lines. I had by far the fewest lines, so I was the closest to knowing my lines. I pretty much sat at the end of the lifeboat looking out into the water. Will and Dominique had the vast majority of the lines, and they weren't going to be able to learn them. Our solution seemed brilliant. Both of them would have the script for the play in the bottom of the boat. No one could see the scripts except them, and they could easily look down and use them whenever possible.

The play started OK, but then it started dragging a bit. No, it dragged a lot. The brand new theater at Lorain Catholic wasn't really very large, seating around 300. It had a wide, thrust stage, which meant the 300 seats were in curved rows very close to the stage. At one point in our production there was a very distinct lull, with silence on the stage. No one knew whose line it was, and, at a very opportune time when everyone else in the theater was silent, Will's dad said in a voice loud enough for everyone, including those of us on the stage, to hear, "Turn the page, Will."

Everyone in the place started laughing. Will turned bright red (you could really see it with his blond hair and fair complexion), Dominique sort of coughed-laughed, and I just turned away from the audience so they wouldn't see me laughing, but they could definitely tell I was laughing, since my body was shaking. We barely got through the rest of the show, but, in the end, we were fine.

73

When You Are Young and In Love You Are Stupid
Part Two

I had been dating Shelby Boca for over three months. She was so awesome and nice and hot. Man did she smell good! We had such a great time together. We probably would have had an even better time than we did if I wasn't so . . . . let's say backward, inhibited, and, especially, inexperienced. Late in April I got a note during study hall from Bridgett Mulroney saying that she wanted to talk to me. I only had a second after school because we had a tennis match, so I called her that evening.

I asked her what was up and she told me that she thought we should start going out again. I didn't know what to say, so I didn't really say anything. She said, "Well?" I said the only thing I thought was appropriate when you are young and in love and stupid.

"Give me a week to get rid of Shelby."

That spring I broke up with Shelby Boca. We talked and I made up some stupid excuse about seeing other people or I wasn't good enough for her or some other bullshit line. If breaking up with Dominique Pavlak had been the dumbest thing I had done in my short life until then, breaking up with Shelby Boca topped that for stupidity. The bottom line was I broke up with Shelby Boca to go back with Bridgett Mulroney. I was young, in love, and stupid. Twice in one year I had broken up with great young ladies to go back to Bridgett. That's not to say that she wasn't wonderful—I was, after all, in love with her.

About ten years later I was sitting at a Defiance College Men's Basketball game with some guys I had gone to college with when, into the DC gym, walked Shelby Boca. I couldn't believe it. I said to the guys I was with, "See that blonde that just walked in? I used to date her in high school. I haven't seen her in ten years. Boy did she smell good!"

They were like, "Yeah right, you dated her. What's she doing here? If you dated her, why don't you go talk to her?"

"I will," I said. I immediately went down from the top of the bleachers and talked to Shelby Boca. It was great seeing her again, and we renewed old friendships. Shelby is married to a lawyer and they still live in Defiance, Ohio.

74

Bringing People Together
The Senior Retreat

In April of our senior year the senior class officers joined forces with the Student Council and school religious leaders to organize and sponsor the first annual Senior Retreat. Members of the senior class were going to be locked in the school together for an entire weekend, giving us a chance to get closer to each other, and closer to God (this was, after all, a Catholic school).

Some college-aged kids trained in this sort of weekend were actually in charge. We all went home from school on Friday and returned by 5:00 with sleeping bags, cots, etc., as well as food, snacks, etc. for the weekend. A short religious service in the Chapel started the weekend and was followed by music, games, self-disclosure, etc. We talked about our Catholic education and how it had influenced our lives. Does any of this do any good? I don't know, but retreats like this one had been going on for a long time and they have continued to go on since then. They are often called "lock-ins" now, and they are usually less religious than in 1970.

There is no question that the highlight of the weekend was Saturday night when all of the couples in the class sort of met in the foreign language classrooms. It was dark when we got there, but it seemed that every couple sort of found its own area. Bridgett and I ended up in the corner of the French classroom, which was very appropriate considering what we were doing.

By the way, there were a few seniors who either chose not to attend or had a good excuse (they were working, etc.) Mackie MacGregor and JD Szollzy were two of the few who didn't attend the retreat, other than coming by late at night and peering in the windows and making faces at us on the inside. One other thing we got to do during the weekend was play on the school's new trampoline. It was a huge, rectangular tramp, and most of us had never been on a trampoline before. We were totally fearless though, so it didn't take long for us to get pretty good on the trampoline. At least no one was killed that weekend on the silly thing.

The weekend finished with a full Mass on Sunday. Everyone was totally drained from staying up virtually all night both nights. I don't know if it actually brought us closer together as a class, but there were plenty of my fellow classmates who believed that it did, so I guess it was time well spent.

75

The Politics of the Spring of 1970

Something else happened in the spring of 1970. The United States crossed the border of Cambodia during the Vietnam War and all hell broke loose on college campuses throughout the country. By far the most famous riot occurred at Kent State University on May 1-4. Students burned down the ROTC building and Governor James Rhodes sent the National Guard onto campus. Right around lunchtime on May 4, and no one has ever really explained why or how it actually happened, the National Guard troops opened fire on the protestors, killing four young people.

One of the students killed was from Lorain, and I knew him. Bill Schroeder had been a great athlete at Lorain High School, and he was actually a member of the ROTC at Kent State. He was merely walking by when he was hit by a stray bullet. My oldest brother Bob was also a student at Kent State at the time, and when we heard the news of the riot and shooting, I became very concerned. Even though my brother wasn't part of the riot, he was still a student at Kent State, which meant he was a part of history.

Speaking of history, every senior in the State of Ohio is required to take a government course. Our course was called POD (Problems of Democracy) and was taught by Coach Englund. We spent lots of time on current events, and you can imagine the classroom discussions following May 4. People's true colors came out, and the Jocks-Freaks split returned. Coach Englund was an outstanding teacher (one of the three best I ever had in high school, college, or graduate school), and he was always willing to allow class discussions about political events. The Kent State situation was living history, and we discussed it, on-and-off, for days. There were two very clear sides to this issue, and they came out in every class discussion.

The Freaks really thought the whole idea of National Guard troops on a college campus was repulsive. The Jocks said things like, "Hey, if the National Guard told the kids to disperse, then they should have dispersed." I was more torn than that, since I knew one of the dead students and my brother was actually there. The best thing I can say about the situation is that it really forced to people to think about things that were more important than our next tennis match or the Physical Science quiz the next day.

76

An Undefeated Tennis Season and
A Chance To Qualify For State

Mr. Mike Parrish had taken over the tennis team the previous spring at St. Mary's with absolutely no experience in either coaching or playing tennis. We ended up with a 13-0 record, the last undefeated team in the school's history. Two players had graduated from that team, but we still had five starters back, and we anticipated a good season. The best thing about Coach Parrish's first year was that we had broken him in the right way. We convinced him that we needed ice cream or something else to eat before every match. We hoped to continue that in the spring of my senior year.

Joe Wendell returned as an outstanding player, and he moved into the number one singles position. I was perfectly content to play number two singles, even though I think I could have beaten him. He did beat me the previous summer in the Lorain City Tournament, so I guess he deserved to start the season at number one. I never challenged him, because I never really wanted to play number one. I also played number two doubles with Terry O'Keefe, the younger brother of the guy I had played doubles with the two previous years, Philip O'Keefe, who was now playing college tennis at Defiance College.

Once tennis got going it seemed like the spring just flew by. The tennis team continued to win match after match, and I was personally undefeated throughout the season. I continued to ask Coach Parrish for something to eat/drink before every match, and he came through just about every time, and we got off to a great start.

We played Lorain Senior High School in our last regular season tennis match. Our team was 11-0 at the time, and I was personally 21-0 going in to the match. I had sat out one doubles' match earlier in the year to give a younger player a chance to play. My doubles' partner, sophomore Terry O'Keefe, was really developing into a fine player. O'Keefe also went to Defiance College and he eventually had a great college career.

As the final match unfolded, Terry and I both won our singles' matches, but we lost the other three singles' matches, putting us behind, 3-2. It takes four points out of seven to win a match, and Terry's singles' match took a long time. By the time we were ready to start playing our number two doubles' match, our number one doubles' team was already well on its way to losing, which meant we were going to lose our first match of the year as a team. Early in the first set of our #2 doubles' match we lost that #1 doubles' match, which meant we had lost the match as a team. Terry was really upset. He knew that our team's undefeated season was over. However, I had plenty to play for. I was undefeated as an individual, and I wasn't going to let a sophomore lose my final regular-season match. On one of the change-overs I actually grabbed him and shook him and said, "Listen, damnit, I know we lost the team match, but that doesn't mean that you and I have to lose our match. Let's play to win and end the season together undefeated." He responded well, and we pulled the match out, giving me a perfect 23-0 record for the regular-season.

In Ohio in 1970 there was only one division in high school tennis. We were one of the smallest schools in the state that actually sponsored a tennis team, so we were at a distinct disadvantage. One of the very best things that Coach Parrish did, and I told him to try to do this, was to get me placed in the district quarterfinal bracket with the number four seed, whoever that might be. When I saw the district draw sheet, the number one seed was Dale Watts from Rocky River, number two Jimmy Rakestraw from Elyria, number three Joe Wendell from our school, and number four some kid from Westlake. I was in the same quarterfinal bracket with the kid from Westlake.

The District Tournament was held on the campus of Oberlin College, and only two players from our district were going to qualify for the State Tournament. I won my first round match easily, but I really struggled in my second round match. I noticed that the kid from Westlake who was seeded and would be my next round opponent, was watching me play. He was really watching both of us play, as he knew he was to play the winner in the next round. I actually saw him walk away laughing, because I'm sure he thought he would easily win the next round.

In the quarterfinals I played one of the better matches I had played all season, and I upset the number four seed, 6-2, 7-5, which moved me into the elite of the tournament, the semifinals. I was one win away from qualifying for state.

The semifinals were held the next day, a Saturday, at Oberlin College. I was matched up in the semi's with Dale Watts, a tall, red-haired lefthander from Rocky River who was seeded number one. On the court right next to us were number two seed Jimmy Rakestraw from Elyria and number four seed Joe Wendell from Lorain Catholic. We were the smallest school in the tournament and we were the only school with two players left, and I was the only unseeded player left.

I really struggled early in the match with Watts' left-handed blasts. He was hitting the ball deep to one side and then short to the other. He had a vicious underspin backhand, and I couldn't handle it at all. He quickly won the first set, 6-1. During the changeover after the first set, Coach Frank Hicks from Admiral King walked around the fence and said softly to me, "Hit it to the T. Outlast him. Hit it to the T." I looked out at him and had a curious look on my face. Why was a coach from another school helping me? First of all, it was illegal for a coach to talk to a player. Of course, he wasn't my coach, so it wasn't illegal in that regard.

Coach Hicks, despite his argument with Coach Englund a few years before that, was the man who ran the summer tennis program in the City of Lorain. He gave lessons to hundreds of kids over the years and had actually worked with me a bit. He also ran all of the local tournaments, so I had worked with him during those times, too. He cared about Lorain kids who played tennis, even if they weren't from his school. He also realized that Coach Parrish couldn't help me much because he didn't know much about tennis.

In the second set I decided to really focus on what Coach Hicks had whispered to me. I dug in and tried to hit every ball back to the middle of the court where the service lines met, commonly called "the T." I used all of my athletic ability to scramble and get to every ball that Watts hit. It started working, and the second set was really a battle. I ended up losing the match, 6-1, 9-7 (the tiebreaker in tennis hadn't been invented yet). I was so close to winning the second set, and there is absolutely no question in my mind that if I had won the second set I would have won the third, as the momentum would have been all on my side.

I ended my high school athletic career on Court number 10 at Oberlin College losing to Dale Watts one win away from qualifying for state. Jimmy Rakestraw defeated Joe Wendell to become the other state qualifier. For the season of 1970 I was undefeated at 23-0 in the regular season. When you combine my sectional tournament with the regular season, my complete record for the year was 26-1, one of the best records anyone in Lorain has ever achieved.

77

Senior Class Field Trip To B & M's

Many of my friends had started hanging out at a local bar called B & M's. The bar was located on Long Avenue in Lorain and was a gathering place because they basically never checked anybody's ID. They just served their wonderful draft beer for 21 cents a glass. How they set that price I will never know, but it was 21 cents for a glass of draft. Mackie MacGregor and JD Szollzy were almost regulars in the place during the school year. It's also important to remember that in Ohio in 1970 there were two levels of beer, 3.2% and 6%. If you were eighteen years of age you could buy and drink 3.2% or "low" beer. B & M's had both low and high beer on tap. Of course this didn't mean that Mackie MacGregor was old enough to drink even low beer, as he was one of the youngest kids in our class with a birthday in August.

One day late in the school year somebody decided that our class needed to get together one more time before we graduated. Mackie suggested that we go to B & M's after school. So, after school one day a whole bunch of us headed to the local bar. It was really a working man's bar, dark, relatively dingy, with a long bar and few tables. It also had a great, old bowling machine with the sliding disks. The senior class from Lorain Catholic pretty much took over the place, which wasn't real hard, since there were only about three people in the place when we arrived.

B & M's featured very little food, but they did have a Polish sausage sandwich that was delicious and a Poor Boy sub that was Mackie's favorite. We just hung around as a class for about an hour and a half and eventually went home for dinner.

Why was this little trip important? Well, it was a first and last for a lot of people, including me. For some people it was the first time they ever drank a beer. For others it was simply a chance to hang out together one last time before graduation. It was the kind of thing that was really a precursor to our future reunions. I can remember talking to some people to whom I had hardly ever spoken. I know that some of them commented that they were surprised that I would attend an event like that in a bar. My high school athletic career was over, and I was just hanging out with my friends and classmates. Again, it was just one of those times you remember about your senior year.

78

The Senior Follies

An exciting tradition had been started by my brother's class at St. Mary's two years before Lorain Catholic opened. The Class of '68 created a talent show in the spring called The Senior Follies. In order to get the administration to agree to allow the program during the school day, the students had to convince Sister Mary Neumann that it was, indeed, going to be a talent show. Since she thought talent meant musical talent and she had been the choir director, she thought it would be a great idea to allow some of her singers to showcase their singing abilities. There definitely was some singing involved, but it also became a showcase of comedic talent, including some scathing references and impersonations of faculty members, especially the nuns.

When we approached Sister Mary Neumann about keeping the tradition alive at Lorain Catholic, she was very skeptical. She wanted to make sure that we didn't criticize faculty members through the use of sarcasm, mocking, etc. We assured her, of course, that we wouldn't think of doing that. We did have to hand in our list of acts, and even some scripts that we were going to use for small skits about the school and the faculty.

Robbie Cavellini and I were chosen as the Masters of Ceremony. I guess "chosen" isn't really accurate, as we just decided that we would do it. We introduced the acts, read some poetry between the acts, and, generally, tried to keep the program moving. We were billed as "The Kings of Conceit." We were generally thought of as the two guys who thought they were the coolest guys in the school, even if we weren't (and I definitely wasn't). We came out on stage and introduced ourselves and read a revised version of the famous poem "How Do I Love Thee? Let me count the ways." Our version, of course, was "How Do I Love Me? Let me count the ways." We sang a couple of lines from the famous song "I Can't Stop Loving Me," and various other plays on words.

Mackie MacGregor and Will Fitzpatrick were stars of the show as they really could sing, and they were backed up by a band of guys which included JD Szollzy playing the accordion. Conor Flanary did some of his dead-on impersonations of political and performing stars, and we had numerous other acts. The program was during the school day and allowed the entire school to witness the seniors performing some really stupid acts. The program itself was sort of a take-off on a very popular program of the era, "Rowan and Martin's Laugh-In." The acts came fast and furious and we encouraged everybody in the senior class to participate, even though less than half of the kids chose to join in and perform. I guess some of the others were a little too cool to participate. Either that or they didn't have any talent.

79

Prom . . . . The Senior Farewell

I took Bridgett Mulroney to the Senior Farewell. The Prom was sponsored by the junior class, and was held both at Lorain Catholic High School and the Aquamarine Lodge in Avon Lake. The theme was "Splendor on a Carousel," and there was a beautifully decorated carousel in the Commons. The Prom was one of the few times when everybody actually danced, not just Bert Knouwer and the girls.

After the actual Prom at Lorain Catholic, the seniors headed to the Aquamarine Lodge in Avon Lake. Aquamarine had a dancing area, a motel, and a large, indoor pool. We rented a few rooms in the motel so people had a place to change clothes. Basically, we all sat around the pool deck, listened to music, and went swimming.

Later in the evening I was alone with Bridgett, and let's just say my hormones were racing. I had decided that it was time for our relationship to reach new heights (some people would say new depths). I was this horny high school guy trying to experience something I had never experienced before. She wouldn't let me. It never happened. Talk about disappointment. I broke up with Dominique Pavlak and Shelby Boca for this?

80

June 13, 1970
Lorain Catholic's Very First Graduation

June 13, 1970 marked the very first graduation from Lorain Catholic High School. The 80 graduates marched in to the theatre for the ceremony. There was a speaker from the Diocese, but no one remembered anything he said. Principal Sister Mary Neumann spoke, but no one remembered anything she said. School Director Father Thomas Boone spoke, but no one remembered anything he said. We just wanted to get out of there and head to our parties.

When our names were called we paraded across the stage and received our diplomas from Father Boone. Somewhat to my surprise I was awarded the very first Lorain Catholic Academic-Athlete Award. Early in my high school career my father had pointed to a similar award at St. Mary's and sort of challenged me to go for it. I was always a pretty good student, and I played three sports all the way through high school, so I thought I might be considered for the award, but it was still a surprise when they called my name. I was really happy, as were my parents, when I went on stage and received the beautiful plaque for the award.

After the graduation ceremony everyone went out in front of the school for pictures. My parents hosted a great graduation party/open house for me, and I received plenty of envelopes with monetary gifts. Around nine o'clock that evening my party was winding down and I asked if I could leave. My parents said it was okay to leave at that point. I first went to Grace Orsini's party which was only a short distance from my house. I had a few drinks there, and then I took some others across town to Will Fitzpatrick's party. I stayed there the rest of the evening and had a great time.

Before I left his party that night I had one final talk with my best friend. We both knew that things would never be the same. All of the great traditions and friendships that had been built through high school would all be changed when we left for college. Will was headed to St. Joseph's College in Indiana to play football, where he eventually had a great career. In fact, he later became the head football coach at St. Joe's.

Our last handshake was a firm one, which served as a congratulatory note as well as a promise to keep in touch. We looked into each other's eyes and knew that was it.

81

The Right Reverend Monsignor James J. Duffy

Monsignor Duffy retired as a pastor in 1971, shortly after St. Mary's Academy closed as a high school. He died September 25, 1973, leaving behind a legacy shared by anyone who had ever come into contact with him. He was scary, saintly, supportive. He loved his sports, but he loved St. Mary's as a parish and the school even more. His influence lives on in every student who ever went to St. Mary's Academy.